# Surviving Camp Inca

# Surviving Camp Inca

## A Life-Changing Prison Experience

Julienne Burleson

Copyright © 2015 Julienne Burleson
All rights reserved.

ISBN: 1511947381
ISBN 13: 9781511947381
Library of Congress Control Number: 2015906836
CreateSpace Independent Publishing Platform
North Charleston, SC

# Dedication

*This book is dedicated to my two fathers: Jesus my Lord, and my Dad, Bob Brewer. You were both there through the best and the worst.*
*I love you, Jesus, and I love you, Dad*
*I am very grateful.*

# Contents

| | | |
|---|---|---|
| Chapter 1 | Quito, Ecuador Airport Arrest | 1 |
| Chapter 2 | Interpol Barbed Wire & Concrete | 8 |
| Chapter 3 | Interpol Drug Trafficking | 14 |
| Chapter 4 | Interpol Law 108 | 21 |
| Chapter 5 | CDP - El Centro de Detención Provisional Rat Fights & Chicken Claw Soup | 26 |
| Chapter 6 | CDP Bucket Bath and Inmate Beating | 35 |
| Chapter 7 | CDP Drag Queens | 43 |
| Chapter 8 | Camp Inca Butch Up | 54 |
| Chapter 9 | Camp Inca Joan The God Woman | 63 |
| Chapter 10 | Camp Inca Hunger Strike – Lips Sewn Shut | 70 |
| Chapter 11 | Camp Inca Smells like Urine, Cigarettes and Alcohol | 76 |
| Chapter 12 | Camp Inca Kill the Rats Campaign | 83 |
| Chapter 13 | Camp Inca Ramie Escapes | 89 |
| Chapter 14 | Camp Inca Queen Contest | 98 |
| Chapter 15 | Camp Inca Molotov Cocktails | 106 |
| Chapter 16 | Camp Inca A Sudden Transfer | 110 |
| Chapter 17 | Latacunga Prison Migraines and a Seizure | 114 |
| Chapter 18 | Latacunga Prison Quito Investigation | 124 |
| Chapter 19 | Camp Inca 2nd Time Take My Baby! | 134 |
| Chapter 20 | Camp Inca Mama Lucha's Deadly Birthday Bash | 146 |
| Chapter 21 | Camp Inca Clandestine Night Out | 159 |
| Chapter 22 | Jail Four Country Club Jail | 167 |
| Chapter 23 | Camp Inca 3rd Time Sentenced! | 174 |
| Chapter 24 | Camp Inca Escape Plan | 181 |

| | | |
|---|---|---|
| Chapter 25 | Guayaquil Prison Attempted Escape – Inmate Shot | 189 |
| Chapter 26 | Guayaquil Slithering Snake and Dengue Fever | 198 |
| Chapter 27 | Guayaquil *60 Minutes* Interview | 211 |
| Chapter 28 | Guayaquil Torture, Murder, Suicide | 220 |
| Chapter 29 | Guayaquil Two for One Law | 228 |
| Chapter 30 | Camp Inca 4th Time Factory Fire Explosions | 232 |
| Chapter 31 | Camp Inca Life-changing Decision | 239 |
| Chapter 32 | Camp Inca Bakery Business | 244 |
| Chapter 33 | Camp Inca Volcano Eruption | 251 |
| Chapter 34 | Camp Inca Stabbing Attempt and Freedom | 265 |
| Chapter 35 | Joan's House – Ecuador Poor Decision – One Last Fling | 273 |
| Chapter 36 | Knoxville, Tennessee New Beginning | 282 |
| Chapter 37 | Knoxville, Tennessee Proposal – Fireworks - Marriage | 292 |
| | Epilogue | 292 |
| | Thank you! | 303 |

# CHAPTER 1

## Quito, Ecuador Airport Arrest

THE BUZZ OF the alarm clock echoed through the room. Julienne rolled over, forced her eyes open and shut off the alarm. Seven a.m. Today she was flying home.

She jumped in the shower. Her thoughts went back to Miami just a few days before. She and her friend, Ashley had spent the 4$^{th}$ of July weekend at Miami Beach enjoying the sunshine and hitting the clubs at night. Ashley's boyfriend, Evan had flown down from New York to join them.

"Julienne, why don't you come with us to South America?" Evan asked.

"What part of South America?"

"Ecuador — Quito. It's a beautiful place on the equator," he said.

"Sounds exotic," Julienne said, "but I doubt I can afford it and I've already booked my flight back to L.A. from here."

"Changing your flight to another day won't be a problem. I'll pay for your ticket and you can pay me back next month," Evan said. "You and Ashley can hang out while I take care of some business."

"It'll be fun," Ashley said. "Come on, Julienne. You always say you want to travel the world. And I saw that you have your passport with you."

Julienne laughed. "Yeah, my Dad says my favorite book is the World Atlas. I told him he was right. My goal is to travel all over its pages."

"Is that a yes?"

"It's a yes."

"We'll see you in the morning then. The flight leaves at noon." Evan held the door open for Julienne.

The next morning when Julienne went to their room, Ashley was frantically searching the hotel room, tossing things around.

"What are you looking for?" Julienne asked.

"My passport! I can't find it!"

Evan came in holding an envelope. "Here's your ticket. It's all arranged." He handed it to Julienne. "What's going on here?'

"I can't find my passport! I've searched everywhere several times. It's not here."

"Calm down, Ashley. We'll get you an emergency passport and change our flight to tomorrow." He turned to Julienne. "Right now we need to get you to the airport."

"Wait a minute. I'm not going by myself," she said.

"You won't be alone. Our friends, Juan and Pablo, will meet you. They'll entertain you until we arrive tomorrow. Come on, let's go. If you miss your flight, I'll have to pay an extra $100 to change your ticket." He called a taxi for her and ushered her in. "See you in Quito tomorrow."

Three days later, Ashley's replacement passport had still not come through and Julienne was going home. She couldn't take any more time off work.

Fresh from the shower, she pulled on a bright, flowered sundress and laced up her sandals. She brushed her long blonde hair and dabbed on some lipstick.

There was a loud knock on her hotel room door. "Julienne, are you ready to go?" It was Juan.

"Why so early?" she asked as she opened the door. "My flight doesn't leave for three hours."

"We just want to make sure you get there on time." Juan glanced around the room. "You haven't packed yet?"

"I don't have that much. Only one suitcase."

"That's fine, but we have three boxes of artwork in the trunk of the taxi waiting downstairs. It will take a little longer to check everything in at the airport."

Pablo appeared in the doorway, wearing a T-shirt and baggy jeans. His dark eyes peered out from under his shaggy hair. He and Juan said they were friends, but Juan seemed more educated, stylish, wore Ray-Bans and spoke English. They were Evan's friends who had showed her around Quito the last few days.

Pablo gave her a hostile glare. "¡Vamanos!"

Julienne looked at Juan. "What's wrong with him? It'll take a few minutes for me to pack."

Juan told Pablo to go downstairs and tell the taxi driver it would be a little while longer.

"By the way," Julienne said, "I'd like to see the artwork that Ashley and Evan asked me to bring back for them. I just want to be sure it's the same art I saw at the gift shop."

"I'm sorry, but it's all wrapped and packed in a box."

"I just want to be sure it's what we ordered," she said. "Evan is going to use it in his Ecuadorian-themed restaurant, so it's important that it's right."

"Of course it is," Juan said. A shadow of annoyance crossed his face. "I'll get the box." Juan left the room and Julienne finished packing.

He came back with eight small, white boxes in a larger box. He opened one of them, folded back the tissue paper, and handed her a 6" x 12" ceramic painted art piece.

Julienne took it and ran her hand over the rough texture. She admired the oval painted country landscape of rolling hills. Tiny ceramic natives and animals were glued to it as part of the scene. *Creative and unique.* She tapped on it.

"The pieces look like they'd be heavy, but they're light." She handed it back to him. "They're really nice. I think Evan will be pleased."

"Are you satisfied that they are the ones we saw at the store?"

"Yes, they're the same ones, but…"

"But what?" Juan asked.

"I still don't understand why you don't just ship them to the States. Wouldn't it be less expensive?"

"Not really," he said.

"There are twenty-four of them, right?"

"Yes. The scene on each picture is just a little different and there are eight in each box." He took the piece, wrapped it in tissue paper again and packed it back inside the box. "The taxi is waiting, we need to go."

"Ok, I'll be right down."

Juan left with the box and Julienne went to the bathroom to make sure she hadn't forgotten anything. She glanced at herself in the mirror. All of a sudden, she felt dizzy. She gasped at her reflection as her face blurred in the mirror. It appeared gaunt and dark circles had formed under her eyes.

*What's happening?* she wondered as she grabbed the counter. She squeezed her eyes shut for a few seconds until the feeling passed. When she opened her eyes, she looked normal.

Shaking, she said, "Am I hallucinating?" She had gone to a club the night before and had a few drinks, but she hadn't been drunk and didn't have a hangover. She stumbled over to the bed and sat down. Her body trembled. She heard a quiet whisper.

"Don't go."

Her eyes darted around the room. No one was there.

"Get a grip, girl," she told herself. "Your mind is playing tricks on you."

She jumped at the ringing of the phone.

"Let's go!" Juan called.

"Okay, okay. I'm coming." She tried not to think about what had just happened and hurried down the stairs.

Juan sat in the back seat with Julienne; Pablo climbed in front with the taxi driver.

"Are you sure you're okay?" Juan asked. "You don't look so good."

"I'm fine," she snapped. "What's the big rush?" *I can't wait to get back to Los Angeles.*

"Here," Juan said. He handed her two hundred dollars and her return airline ticket. "Evan took care of your ticket like he promised."

"What's the money for?"

"You'll be charged for the extra luggage, the boxes. This will cover it. If it's less, keep the difference."

She tucked the money in her purse and looked at the airline ticket. "What?" She checked it again. "This isn't right!"

"What's wrong?" Juan asked.

"This says I'm flying from Miami to New York. I'm not going to New York. I'm flying from Miami to Los Angeles."

"Ashley and Evan told me they're going to meet you in New York," Juan said.

"But I'm not going to New York. I'm going to Los Angeles."

"That's right. But you have to go to New York first. You can't send your luggage to New York and you go off to Los Angeles. It has to stay with you."

"This is not the way it was supposed to be."

"It'll be okay. When you arrive in New York, Evan will pick up your luggage. Ashley will hang out with you for a few hours until you catch your flight to Los Angeles."

They pulled up to the airline terminal and Pablo, Juan, and the taxi driver each carried a box inside. Juan told Julienne to put only the flight number and Evan's name on the box tag so he could get them without a problem in New York.

He pointed to the check-in area. "I can't go past this point because I'm not a passenger." He motioned for a baggage handler to come over and help with the boxes. Juan reached out and shook her hand. "It was nice meeting you, Julienne. I've enjoyed giving you a tour of Quito the last few days."

"You're leaving?" She looked around. Pablo was nowhere to be seen.

"I really have to go," he said. "Have a nice flight."

The baggage handler helped Julienne with the boxes, taking them to the ticket counter for her. She thanked him and gave him a tip.

"Passport and ticket," the attendant said. As she checked them and tagged her small suitcase, Julienne thought, *I'm so ready to go home. I'm glad I got to see Quito, but Juan and Pablo – there was just something about them that made me uneasy. When Juan tried to come on to me, I made it clear that nothing was going to come of that. How well did Evan and Ashley really know them?*

"Do you have anything else to check?"

"Yes, I have these three boxes."

The attendant weighed them and Julienne paid the extra charges.

"Where's the money exchange window?" Julienne asked. Juan had told her to exchange her Ecuador *sucres* for U.S. dollars before leaving in order to get a better rate.

The attendant pointed across the room and Julienne headed in that direction. She poked through the items for sale at a small kiosk and then bought some gum. *Soon I'll be on the plane on my way home.*

As she approached the exchange booth, she heard her name.

"Julienne Estrada, Julienne Estrada… Please report to customs."

She glanced around, not sure where to respond. A woman wearing an airline uniform stepped up to her. "Are you Julienne Estrada?"

"Yes, I am."

"We need you to come to the loading dock."

"Okay. Is everything all right?"

"It will only take a moment. Follow me, please."

Julienne followed the woman to the cargo area. Three men in military fatigues waited there, German Shepherds at their feet, machine guns strapped on their backs. Julienne spotted her suitcase next to the three boxes.

"We need you to open these boxes," one of the men ordered. He handed her a box cutter and she opened the first box. Each of the eight boxes inside looked like white gift boxes.

He pointed at one of the boxes. "Open that one."

She opened it and pulled the white tissue paper from around the art. The guard took it and examined it, turned it, tapped it, shook it hard and held it up to the bright lights. He even smelled it and then released the dogs to sniff the packages. They detected no abnormal scent. The men removed the other small boxes and spoke among themselves in Spanish.

The woman translated. "We have to put them through the X-ray machine."

"Okay," Julienne said.

They ran the boxes through three times.

"Is everything all right?" Julienne asked.

"We check all international packages going back to the States," she explained. They appeared satisfied and the Customs officer started wrapping the artwork up.

Just as he was closing the box, a door opened across the cargo area and a different military official marched over. He nodded at Julienne, but didn't speak. He took the art piece from the Customs officer and hurried back toward the office.

A few minutes later Julienne glanced at her watch. "My flight is leaving soon."

"Don't worry," the woman said. "We won't let it leave without you."

Suddenly, the door burst open and the official came rushing toward them shouting, "Las drugas! Cocaine!" He had poked a small hole in one of the raised portions of the piece with a screwdriver and white powder drifted from it as he walked.

*What is this?* Fear swept through her. *What's happening?*

He and the other men began tearing open the boxes. Cocaine powdered the area as they broke into each piece, cracking them over their knees. They shouted back and forth as they broke open one after another shaking them and smashing them on the ground. White powder littered the floor.

"What?" Julienne breathed in shallow, quick gasps. "It's in all of them?" Her head was spinning and her knees buckled. She dropped her purse and passport. She lost consciousness when she hit the floor.

CHAPTER 2

## Interpol
## Barbed wire & concrete

Julienne tried to lift her head as she fought her way back to consciousness, but she felt dizzy. Slumped forward, her head rested on her knees and a heavy canvas duffle bag had been placed on her head and back, weighing her down. Looking down at the floor, she saw the legs and boots of two men, one on each side of her, their fatigues tucked into army boots. Her head pounded and she felt disoriented. *I'm in the back seat of a pick-up truck. What's going on?* Two men talked in Spanish in the front seat. Dogs barked and cages rattled as they drove over rough terrain. "Where am I?" she mumbled as she slowly sat up and pushed the duffle bag off her.

One of the men shouted something in Spanish, forced her head back down and covered her again. Icy fear twisted her insides and tears filled her eyes. Breathing came in shallow breaths. She remembered what had happened at the airport. *But how did I get here?* The truck stopped and the men got out. As the men moved something off the back of the truck, she heard scraping sounds. The dogs barked for a few minutes, then stopped. A short time later silence enveloped her. The duffle bag was gone.

She sat up slowly and looked around. No men. No barking dogs. The truck sat on a mountain, piles of rocks scattered here and there. No road. No buildings. No signs of civilization. *Where are they? What are they going to do to me?* Frightening images built in her mind and her body began to shake. *This is a drug deal gone bad and I'm a witness. Are they going to shoot me and just leave my body in some deserted place, never to be found?*

She looked around again. *Where did they go?* Through the back window, she noticed the bed of the truck was empty. *They took everything and probably have the drugs. Now they need to get rid of me.* Sheer black terror swept through her. *Maybe they're going to blow up the truck with me in it. I have to get out of here fast!* She opened the door and tripped as she tumbled out. As she started to run, one of the men who had been resting on the ground next to the truck, jumped in front of her. He took the machine gun draped over his shoulder and aimed it at her.

"Pare! No te muevas!" He motioned for her to get back inside the truck.

Deep sobs racked her insides and her chest felt as if it would burst.

Unmoved by her hysterics, he poked at her with the gun until she backed into the seat of the truck.

"No!" she shouted at him, flailing her arms and kicking wildly.

He pointed the gun in her face and she stopped.

When she settled into the backseat, he slammed the door shut and walked around to the driver's seat. The world spun and closed in on her. She tried to focus her thoughts. *They must have drugged me. Oh my god. Who are these people?*

She lay down on the seat and the truck lurched forward. She felt herself fading out of reality. When she awoke, she felt something hard pressed against her side. As she forced herself upright, she reached for it—a Spanish/English dictionary.

The truck was parked in the courtyard of a concrete compound, closed off from the world by a huge, padlocked, iron gate. A three-story, cement building towered in front of her and to her right, a cluster of old dingy buildings. Bars covered all the windows. High concrete walls topped with barbed wire and crushed glass surrounded the place.

*This is a jail? The police brought me here?* Alone in the truck, she glanced around. She saw no one and slipped out of the truck. Clutching the dictionary, she made her way to the first building. A woman sat in the doorway and stared at Julienne. She didn't speak, but pointed toward a hallway.

Julienne walked cautiously down the hall and up a stairway. At the top of the stairs, an officer sat at a desk, smoking a cigarette. He motioned for her to sit down.

She pulled up an old chair and placed the dictionary in front of her on his desk.

He shouted, pounding his fist on the desk.

She had no idea what he was shouting about and just stared at him.

He pointed at the dictionary.

*What am I supposed to look up? He talks too fast and I don't understand. I need to tell him this whole thing has been a set up. A trap. That I'm innocent.* She looked up the word trap.

"Trampa!" she said. "Trampa." Then she looked up the word innocent.

"Inocente!"

He glared at her.

"American Embassy," she said. "Call the Embassy so I can have a translator. All this can be straightened out." She suddenly remembered that she had photos in her camera of Juan and Pablo. She flipped through the dictionary pages and looked up the word camera.

"Cámara, mi cámara?"

The officer stood and walked around the desk. He grabbed her by the arm and jerked her out of the chair. He pulled her over to the sliding glass doors and forced her through the doors onto a small terrace balcony, locked the doors and left her outside.

Shaken, Julienne glanced around. The narrow balcony faced a cement wall on the other side of the alley. No view. The smashed artwork lay on the floor. It looked as if they had swept it all up at the airport, including the cocaine, brought it here and dumped it out on the balcony.

*Why would they do that?*

She picked up a piece of the artwork to check it out. There were layers. Ceramic on the outside; a layer of some kind of hard goo that reminded her of chewed bubble gum; then under that, clear plastic bags with cocaine inside.

Julienne pounded on the sliding glass door. "Why did you put me out here?" Her voice raised an octave. "What do you think I'm going to do? Snort this cocaine?" She beat on the door again, rattling the door handle.

The officer walked over to the door and pulled the curtain across the window so she couldn't see inside.

She looked at the floor covered with white powder. *Not much room to walk without stepping in it.* She forced herself to settle down on a small stool in a corner. She glanced at her watch. Every thirty minutes, she knocked on the door, but they ignored her. After two hours outside with the sun slipping behind the mountains, Julienne felt chilled dressed only in her sundress and sandals.

*Did they contact the embassy? I'm cold. I'm hungry. I don't understand the language. The officers are convinced that I'm guilty.* Tears rolled down her face.

Trembling from the cold, she pummeled the door again.

"Let me back inside! I want to speak to the American Embassy."

She heard the lock twist and an officer slid the door open. He handed her the dictionary. Another officer came in who spoke some English.

"Your last name is Estrada?" he asked.

"Yes."

"Then you must speak Spanish."

"No, I don't."

"But if your last name is Estrada, you must speak Spanish."

"No, that's my mother's name and she's from California. I didn't grow up speaking Spanish. Neither did she."

"You're lying!" His voice was cold and lashing.

Her eyes blazed. "I'm not lying."

"Where did you get the drugs?" he demanded.

"I didn't get the drugs from anywhere. Two guys named Juan and Pablo brought the artwork to my hotel. I never knew there was cocaine inside it until customs showed me. Where's my camera? I took pictures of them. I can show you. They're the ones you need to find. I'm innocent. I was set up."

In Spanish he ordered another officer to get her camera from security and have the photos developed.

"I need to make a phone call to the American Embassy," she insisted.

"Mañana." He stood and told her to follow him.

"But I'm entitled to a phone call," she demanded. "I need a lawyer."

"Mañana."

Her temper flared. "I'm an American! I have rights."

He stopped and looked at her, a faint glint of humor in his eyes. "Blonde hair and green eyes. Yes, I see that you are an Americano. Now follow me."

They walked down to the first floor and outside. The officer turned her over to a guard. A machine gun hung across his back and he had a handgun strapped to his side.

"Ven conmigo," he said. He marched her down an alley, through narrow passageways and a maze of damp and dingy concrete buildings.

She shivered. *This is like walking through a dungeon.*

After a long walk with many twists and turns, they came to a dead end with a square courtyard. The guard stopped in front of a holding cell and unlocked the gate.

"Entra!" he ordered, pushing her forward.

Julienne stretched out her arms and held onto each side of the doorframe. She poked her head in just far enough to see inside. Seven male prisoners stood to her right and stared at her. Filthy and wet, they looked drunk.

She tightened her grip on the doorframe.

To the left she saw individual tiny rooms with open doors and in one corner of the open courtyard some stairs led down to what looked like a torture chair with wires attached to it.

"Are you crazy?" she shouted at the guard. "I'm not going in there!"

The guard jabbed his gun into her back.

No!" she screamed. "No! I won't go in there!" She slid to the floor. "You can kill me now! I'm not moving."

He reached down to pull her up, but she scrambled out of his grip and backed into the hallway. He waved his gun at her, his face glowering in anger.

She spotted a motorcycle leaning against the opposite wall and backed over to it.

"I'd rather die right here from a bullet than get raped or tortured in that cell." She climbed onto the seat, crossed her arms in defiance and told the guard "Go away. I'm not moving."

Angry tears streamed down her face. Terror filled her heart.

# CHAPTER 3

## Interpol Drug Trafficking

SHAKEN, JULIENNE SAT on the motorcycle and rocked back and forth. She stared at the ground, not wanting to meet the angry glare of the officer wielding a gun. He stood close to her and cracked his knuckles with a loud popping sound. Julienne braced herself. *Is he going to hurt me?*

He used his walkie-talkie and called for another guard. Tempers flared as they argued and shouted back and forth for several minutes.

*I know they're arguing about what to do with me.* Her chest felt as if it would burst.

The first officer stomped off and Julienne dared a glance up at the one still standing there. He holstered his gun.

"Just stay there," he said, waving his hand as a dismissal of the matter. His tone held a spark of anger. He walked away and entered a small guard station at the end of the passageway.

Julienne trembled as she sat there on the motorcycle up against the wall. *What kind of a crazy place is this?* She looked over the motorcycle and noticed the rust and dirt. *It's obvious it's been here a while. But why? If it doesn't work, why would they just leave it here?* She sat for hours, not daring to move or get off to stretch her aching back. *How long are they going to leave me here and what happens next?* Tears rolled down her face.

At dusk, a guard brought in a woman with two little girls and a baby. When he opened the gate to the holding cell area, the woman and children started to cry and wail.

## Surviving Camp Inca

*Are they going to put her in there with the men? What will happen to her? I can't believe they allow children in a place like this.*

The woman clutched her children and plopped herself down on the cement floor not far from Julienne. Her children clung to her, everyone crying. The guard rubbed the back of his neck, then shrugged his shoulders and left them there. Later, he brought two blankets and a thin mattress, tossed them on the cold floor and left. The mother and her children scrambled onto it.

Julienne didn't dare move for fear of being forced into that holding cell. She hugged her knees to her, leaned her back against the cold cement wall and closed her eyes. Her body ached and she felt utterly alone. Sleep escaped her other than the few brief times she dozed off.

In the morning, she felt someone touch her hair. Instantly awake, she almost tumbled off the motorcycle. The two little girls giggled. Their mother yelled at them and they immediately sat down with her on the mattress. Relieved it wasn't a guard touching her, Julienne forced a smile and the girls giggled again. They had dark hair and skin. *Maybe they haven't seen someone with long blonde hair and blue eyes before.*

A guard came over to them with a small container of rice and offered some to Julienne. She shook her head no. *This place is so dirty, who knows what germs might be in the food.* He didn't seem to care if she ate or not and simply walked away.

"What's your name?" Julienne asked the woman.

The mother gave her a questioning look.

"My name is Julienne," she said, placing her hand on her chest. "And you?"

The woman smiled, revealing the space of her missing front tooth. "Marty," she said.

They didn't get beyond that. They were taken to use the outdoor toilet. It was disgusting, swarming with flies and spiders, and she refused. The odor turned her stomach. *I haven't had anything to eat or drink, I can wait. I'm sure someone from the Embassy will come today and I can get out of this horrible place.*

That afternoon one of the guards came and told her to follow him.

"Where are we going?" she asked.

"Officina."

*Office? The delegate from the Embassy must be here!*

At the office, someone handed her an English/Spanish dictionary and motioned for her to sit down.

"We have the photos developed from your camera." The officer spoke some English with a heavy Spanish accent. He spread the pictures out on the desk in front of him. "Explain these to me."

Elated, Julienne sorted through the photos. *Finally, I'll be able to show them who the real drug dealers are.* She went picture by picture, showing all the locations she had visited and people she had met.

"Who are these people?" the officer asked, pointing to one photo.

"Just some tourists I met. They said they were from Europe and Italy."

She spotted the photo of Juan and Pablo and pushed it across the desk toward the officer. "That's them! Juan and Pablo, the men who packed the artwork. You need to find them and you'll see that I'm innocent." She leaned back in her chair with a sense of relief.

"Where are they from?"

"Ecuador."

"No!" He pounded his fist on the desk. "They're Columbians. You're lying!"

"They told me they were from Ecuador," she said. "That's all I know. They're the men you need to find."

"Okay, so now we're getting somewhere," he said, looking at the photo.

"I'd like to make a phone call to the Embassy now," Julienne said.

"Tomorrow," he said and motioned the guard at the door to take her back. This time she did take him up the offer to use the toilet. He handed her a bucket and pointed to a large barrel of water, then pointed at the dirty, cracked toilet. *Oh my god. Everything is so filthy and I have to flush it with a bucket of water?* She took a determined breath and scooped some freezing cold water out of the barrel into the bucket. She squatted over the cracked and dirty bowl without a toilet seat and tried not to gag. Then she flushed it with the bucket of water.

That night the guards brought in a young teenage girl who screamed and yelled non-stop. The officers handled her rough and tossed her into the holding cell that Julienne had refused to enter. The girl wrapped her arms around the bars of the gate and sobbed, staring at Julienne with pleading eyes.

*She looks so scared. I wish I could help her. What if the men rape her?* She was relieved to see the guards putting the male prisoners in the small cells around the perimeter of the courtyard, locking them in for the night. The girl stayed on the floor next to the gate all night and talked and cried. Her name was Theresa. She was seventeen. That was all Julienne understood.

In the morning when the guards let the men out of their cells, they allowed Theresa out to sit with Marty and her kids in the hallway. More female prisoners were brought in and because they didn't seem to have a place to put them, they were allowed to line up on mattresses in the passageway.

*I'm not giving up my spot on the motorcycle,* she said to herself, realizing that the motorcycle didn't represent any security. *It's not like it will start and I can ride it out of here. This is all so unreal. I'm so glad I'm from America where you're innocent until proven guilty. Not here. Everyone is guilty until proven innocent.*

She looked around at the crowded passageway. *If they bring in any more women, where will they put them?* She was surprised that anyone would be held there for more than a day or two before being transferred to a real jail, or released on bail.

Later that day, an Italian man had been arrested and brought in. He noticed Julienne and said hello to her in English as he passed through.

"You speak English!" she said.

"I speak five languages," he answered. "My name is Armando."

"Julienne," she said. "Maybe we can talk?" She was surprised to find someone so educated in this horrid place.

"I'll arrange it," Armando said.

The guard put him in the courtyard area and locked the gate.

That afternoon the military police came to talk with Julienne and called for Armando to translate. At first they stood by the cell and tried to communicate through the bars, but there were too many distractions from the other prisoners. Men yelled and banged their fists against the bars of their cell.

*They're like wild animals,* Julienne thought. *Caged, wild animals.*

Marty's girls tugged at the officer's shirt, begging him to give them some gum.

*This place is insane,* Julienne thought. *When will this nightmare be over?*

The military officer ordered the guard to take Armando out of the cell and bring him and Julienne to an office where they could talk with the head of Interpol for Quito.

"This document states the basic information of your case and explains how it will be investigated." Armando translated as the officer spoke. "Sign this statement and you will be released." He placed it on the desk in front of Julienne, tapped the signature line and handed her a pen.

She picked up the document.

"It's in Spanish," she said. "I don't understand it."

"I just told you what it said." The officer's voice revealed his irritation.

*I may be gullible, but this is ridiculous,* she thought.

"I'm sorry," Julienne said, "but I cannot say a word or sign anything without my Embassy representative or a lawyer present."

"Are you sure?" Armando asked her.

"Yes, I'm sure," she said. She swallowed hard, lifted her chin and boldly met the officer's eyes.

Armando translated her response and the officer exploded in anger. He called the guard and ordered him to take them back down to their cells.

"Back to the dungeon," Julienne mumbled to Armando.

"Signing that document may have been your way out," he said. "You could have made a deal."

Julienne didn't respond. *A deal? What kind of a deal? I'm innocent!*

"The Embassy probably doesn't know you're in here yet," he said.

Julienne wondered if Armando might be working with Interpol, not her. *There's no way I'm signing anything. It might have been a confession of guilt. And then they're going to release me? Right.*

Armando went to the men's holding cell and Julienne back to the motorcycle.

A few hours later, one of the military guards told Armando to give another message to Julienne.

"They're going to take you to wash and clean up because you're going to see someone from the American Embassy and be released to them. They will be able to help you."

"Do you think this is true?" she asked Armando with a cry of relief.

He hesitated. "Well, what do you have to lose?"

Julienne hadn't cleaned up since her arrest at the airport. *My body odor is pretty strong by now.* The guard handed her a dress and toothbrush taken from her suitcase. In a cement basin next to the toilet, she washed her face, brushed her teeth and wet down her hair.

The guard came back, grasped her by the arm and rushed her over to a large iron gate on the other side of the cell area. He unlocked it, pushed her through it and locked it behind them. On the ground in the middle of the large, open courtyard, sat her open suitcase. Twelve one-kilo blocks of cocaine surrounded it, along with decorative ceramic pieces similar to the ones confiscated at the airport. But still intact!

"Where is the representative from the Embassy?" *What's all this? What's going on?* She stared at it in bewilderment.

The guard didn't answer. He forced her closer to her suitcase and the display of cocaine. She looked up and saw media gathering with cameras and microphones. It was the Ecuadorian press.

Shutters clicked, bulbs flashed as the reporters crowded around Julienne, bombarding her with questions in Spanish and thrusting microphones in her face.

She didn't understand or answer until one reporter asked her something in English about the lining of her suitcase.

"What? What are you talking about?" Julienne asked.

"Did you hide the cocaine in the lining of your suitcase?"

She stiffened at the question. "Look how small it is. How can you even think that?"

"Are you the drug dealer? Or are you a mule?"

"I understand you were arrested with 24 kilos of cocaine."

"Do you know you can get a ten-year sentence here for drug trafficking?"

Assaulted by the thrust and jabs of the reporters' questions, Julienne felt defenseless. She couldn't understand the questions, much less give articulate answers.

"Have you talked with your Embassy?"

"Embassy?" She understood that word. "I've been here for three days and nobody has come to help me." She glanced around. "I thought they were here now."

The Quito Interpol officials made a statement in Spanish.

She wondered what they said.

"Please let them know at the American Embassy that I'm here," she said.

A television camera zoomed in for a close-up of her face.

"That's enough!" She held up her hands and shook her head from side to side. "That's enough," she choked out again as the tears began to flow. She turned her back on them.

The guard stepped over, took her by the arm and walked her back through the iron gate, cameras clicking behind them.

Inside, Julienne tried to keep her fragile control. *It was a set up—my suitcase, the cocaine, all of it.* Fear and anger knotted inside her. She crawled up on the motorcycle. *Dad thinks I'm on vacation and look where I am.* She felt desperate and alone. Her stomach wrenched as she thought of the worst possible scenario. *Will the drug trafficking charge stick and I'll spend the next ten years in this hell?*

# CHAPTER 4

## Interpol Law 108

"This is the worst day of my life," Julienne said to herself. She dropped her head in her hands and wept in silence.

*Nobody cares. My friends betrayed me and got me into this mess. The Embassy hasn't come to help. I'm afraid to eat. My family doesn't even know I'm here in this hell hole. Even God seems to have forgotten about me.*

"Come with me," a guard said, intruding on her thoughts.

"Where are we going?" She stepped off the motorcycle and felt dizzy as she stood. She hadn't eaten for several days and had only drunk a little water.

"The representative from the Embassy is coming."

"The Embassy?" *Another lie,* she was sure.

She followed him to an office that smelled of cigarette smoke and stale coffee and was told to wait.

She sat alone for a long time. A pain squeezed her heart as she wondered if anyone was coming. *Any minute they'll take me back to my cell area.*

"Julienne?" A pleasant male voice greeted her as he entered the office. "I'm Alfred Rodriquez from the American Embassy," he said, extending his hand. He showed her his I.D. card. An attractive and well-groomed man in his forties, he projected an air of confidence.

"You're here!" A flood of relief flowed through her.

"I'm sorry I wasn't notified sooner," he said. "Have they read you your rights?"

"I'm not sure. I can't understand most of what they say."

The officer said something to Mr. Rodriquez and he interpreted for Julienne. "They asked me to translate the statement they want you to sign."

"Oh, good," she said.

"But I can't."

"You can't?"

"I don't have authorization to do that. I'm not a lawyer, so I'm limited as to what I can officially do. What I can do is answer your questions and translate some of the things you don't understand. But you will have to get a lawyer to do the rest."

"How do I find a lawyer?"

"Interpol hasn't given you a list of available lawyers?"

"No. They haven't done anything to help me. Nothing."

"I'll have them get that to you. I'll help in any way I can, but you need to know that I can't be part of any court case. No one in the Embassy is allowed to do that." He hesitated. "You have to be careful when hiring an attorney to represent you. There are some unscrupulous lawyers who ask for money to conduct an investigation and then they disappear."

"I'm innocent," Julienne blurted out. "What happened to innocent until proven guilty?"

"I'm afraid things are very different here." He leaned back in his chair. "Tell me what happened."

"My so-called friends tricked me! That's what happened! They lied to me. Ashley claimed that she lost her passport when we were in Miami and asked me to fly here ahead of them. They promised to join me in a day or two. Then they called here and said the passport situation couldn't be straightened out right away. They asked if I would I pick up some artwork they had ordered and bring it back with me. I cannot believe I fell for it!"

Rodriguez waited patiently as she tried to control her irritation and frustration.

"When I arrived at the Quito airport, they checked my luggage and found cocaine inside the artwork. I was shocked. The next thing I know,

## Surviving Camp Inca

I'm in the back seat of a pick-up truck with armed men. I didn't know what was happening or who they were. At first, I thought they were drug dealers and they were going to shoot me or blow the truck up with me in it. Get rid of me as a witness against them. Instead, I ended up here, in this hell hole, arrested for drug trafficking." Breathless, she struggled not to cry.

Rodriguez nodded as she spoke and jotted a few notes. "We'll do what we can to help you. Is there someone back home you want me to contact? I can do that from the Embassy and they can call me anytime, as well. We'll keep the communication lines open. We can arrange for family or friends to send money, food, clothing, medical care or other supplies through us."

She gave him her father's phone number in Tennessee. "Please call my Dad." Her eyes brimmed with tears. "He thinks I'm still on vacation."

"I'll call him right away."

"When can I leave here?"

"They can't hold you at Interpol for more than a few days," he said. "They have to charge you with a crime and process you to another location, or let you go."

"It's already been three days!"

The officer stepped back inside and told Rodriguez that his time was up.

"I have to go now," he said to Julienne. "Don't worry. We'll continue to monitor your case. I'll make some calls and will be in touch."

The guard escorted him out and Julienne went back to her spot on the motorcycle.

It started to rain and the temperature dropped thirty degrees. She wrapped herself in a blanket on the corridor floor next to the motorcycle and let the tears flow.

The next day she went with the other females to the courtyard area. Marty and her girls handed her some popcorn and sat with her. *This should be safe to eat. I'm so hungry.*

Armando made his way over to them and told Julienne that he heard one of the guards saying they were going to be moved to C.D.P.

"What's C.D.P.?" she asked.

"El Centro de Detención Provisional," he said. "It's a provisional detention center."

"Anything's better than this. What about bail? Can't I post bail and get out until I have a court hearing or a trial?"

"Not here. Not when narcotics are involved. The U.S. government has a narcotics rewards program with Ecuador and other countries where money is available for the capture of drug dealers and traffickers. So, it's in the interest of the National Police to prosecute and sentence someone. At least that's what I've been told."

"Well, I'm innocent, so they won't make any money off me." She fought to control her swirling emotions. "Do you have any other good news?"

"Do you know about Law 108?"

"What's that?"

"It doesn't distinguish between small scale offenders and large scale traffickers. A few grams of marijuana can get someone a twelve year sentence, same as someone accused of smuggling a much larger amount of cocaine."

"So much for justice." She walked away from him, thinking *I can't wait to talk to my dad. He'll be able to help me.*

That afternoon the guards rounded up a small group of prisoners, including Julienne. Outside the gate, they were crammed into two small cars that looked like they had been in a demolition derby. A few men, women and children all piled in on top of each other. The children cried and the men and women chatted in Spanish. No one in Julienne's car spoke English. Armando rode in the other car.

As they drove off, she wondered if the C.D.P. was really any better than Interpol. She also thought about something else. *There are enough of us in these two cars to overtake the drivers and escape.* But she had no idea where she could go if she did escape. As an American, she would stand out in a crowd of Ecuadorians. She settled in for the ride, unable to move with everyone jammed in so close together.

She felt overwhelmed by the insanity of the last few days. *What's next? Will the Embassy reach my dad today?* The pungent odor of sweaty bodies in the car became oppressive and she took shallow breaths. *Will the detention facility be a safer place?* She looked out the window. A foreboding dusk was fast approaching.

# CHAPTER 5

## CDP - El Centro de Detención Provisional
## Rat Fights & Chicken Claw Soup

A GUARD SWUNG open the entrance gate and Julienne walked into the jail with a small group of prisoners. Men were herded to the left, women to the right. Julienne looked around at the chipped and crumbling cement walls and felt as though she had stepped back in time into a small dilapidated village from another century. Women walked around as if at home doing their daily chores. Children roamed about. Clothes hung on lines made from old broomsticks and wire stretched from one end of the courtyard to the other.

There were three large cells, one called 'the cage' to which Julienne was assigned. It had a roof over it, but two of the four sides were barred gates, two were solid walls. Two other cells were enclosed rooms with one gated entrance.

As she was escorted to her cell, she saw thin mattresses piled up against one of the walls. In another area of the courtyard stood three cubicles with toilets and two shower stalls. Several cement basins that looked like feeding troughs for cattle sat next to them. Someone washed clothes in one and a woman bathed her child in another. A wooden table near the basins held an efficiency stove with a large propane gas tank attached to it. A prisoner appeared to be selling to the others whatever she was cooking.

*I feel like I'm in an old movie. Where am I supposed to go? What am I supposed to do?* She felt light-headed and queasy. *I must be coming down with something.*

One of the women sensed she wasn't feeling well and approached Julienne. She took her to the cell room and laid a mattress on the floor.

"Necesito dormir bien," she said, motioning for her to lie down. Exhausted, she fell asleep and when she woke up it was almost dark.

An older lady placed her hand on Julienne's forehead. "Fiebre," she said. She called out to one of the other women in Spanish and within minutes the woman offered Julienne a drink of cola with lemon and put a cool damp cloth on her forehead.

She forced herself to sit up and sip the cola. "Thank you," she whispered. The dizziness increased and she had trouble sitting up. More women crowded into the cell and each laid a mattress on the floor. Wall-to-wall, twenty women took their place for the night. Julienne stayed curled up in her corner.

Just before the guard locked the cell for the night, she placed two large buckets inside in case someone had to go to the bathroom.

*I sure hope I don't need to use one of them.* She dozed off, but woke up to loud Latin music blaring and echoing through the walls. She glanced around. *The noise doesn't seem to be bothering anyone else.* Her whole body ached but she managed to fall asleep again.

Then a burst of gunfire exploded. Instantly awake, Julienne sat up. Each crack followed another, like a shootout in a western movie. *Gunfire? Here in the jail?* She froze. A rapid-fire succession of sharp, shrill explosions followed, as if someone had set off a string of firecrackers. Fear gripped her.

Some of the women began yelling, but they didn't appear to be afraid.

*Maybe it's my imagination. Maybe it is firecrackers and not gunfire.* Once more the shooting began, this time accompanied by Latin music and loud singing.

Marty, the woman next to her with an infant in her arms, explained in Spanish that it was some kind of celebration going on outside in the streets. Julienne understood the word celebration and laid back down, her heart still pounding. *What is it with these people?* The baby cried for a short time, but Marty rocked her back to sleep.

After a while, Julienne fell into a fretful sleep, but woke again to catlike screeching and what sounded like a metal pipe pounding on the cement pavement. The women shouted obscenities, then went back to sleep. *Are there rats roaming around in here?* She dozed off and on, her fever spiking. In her delirious state, she thought she saw giant rats the size of cats scurrying around in the dark. *It must be my fever. There's no way.*

In the morning, the women drug the mattresses outside the cell into the common open area and beat them with brooms. Julienne forced herself up and stepped outside. Several other women filled buckets with water and scrubbed the floors with lye soap and brushes that barely had any bristles left on them. They used more buckets of water to rinse the floor. *Am I supposed to help?* She tried to lift a full bucket of water, but she didn't have the strength to carry it. Her body shook and she felt faint. She watched them complete the process. Wheezing and feeling too sick to help, she simply tried to stay out of their way.

A guard announced roll call and inspection. She listened for her name to be called out, but it didn't happen. *Don't they even have me on their list? Have I been forgotten in this godforsaken place?*

Marty came over and offered her a tiny piece of bread. Julienne hesitated, but took it, hoping it would make her feel better. Then she recognized her. She was the inmate at Interpol with the two little girls and a baby. She forced a smile and nodded her thanks.

Once the floors dried, the mattresses were stacked back inside the cell room against the far wall. Julienne went back inside, placed a mattress on the floor and fell asleep. She roused to someone calling her name.

"Julienne Estrada! Telephone!"

It took her a few moments to clear her head. *Telephone?*

The guard stood at the entrance of the cell and motioned for her to follow her to one of the phones on the wall in the courtyard area.

*Who's calling me? The Embassy? Someone from the court?*

She picked up the receiver. "Hello?"

"Julie?"

"Dad?" Her voice shook and the tears flowed. "It's really you."

"Yes, it's me. I've been so worried about you." His voice quivered. "It's so good to hear your voice.

"Someone from the Embassy called you?"

"They asked if I had a daughter named Julienne. I said yes. It all sounded so official it scared me. I thought maybe there had been an accident."

"Oh, Dad, I'm so sorry."

"They told me you were in Ecuador. I said, 'Yes, I know she's there. She's on vacation.' That's when they dropped the bomb. They told me, 'You need to know that she's been arrested for drug trafficking.'"

"I can't believe this is happening," Julienne said. "I would never…" She choked on her sobs.

Are you all right?"

"I'm trying to hold it together, but I'm so sick."

"You're sick?" A twinge of alarm flashed in his voice.

"I have a fever and I need a doctor, but there's no doctor here. I'm so scared. This is a hellhole, Dad. You can't even imagine how bad it is. And I don't understand the language. It's all so frustrating."

"Hang in there, Julie. I've made some calls and I've got a couple coming to see you. They're with the Peace Corps and she's a nurse. She and her husband will be able to help you."

"Okay." A flood of tears washed down her face. "I just feel so alone."

"Please don't cry, honey. I'm sorry I didn't call sooner, but it took the Embassy a few days to find me. I was out of town on business. When they told me you had been arrested for drug trafficking, I couldn't believe what I was hearing."

"I still can't believe it," she said. "I keep hoping I'll wake up from this nightmare."

"I don't know how much time we have on the phone, so tell me exactly what happened."

She relayed the details of the events over the past week.

"I was such a fool," she said.

"Has anyone from the Embassy been out to see you? To help you?"

"Only once while I was in the holding jail at Interpol. Apparently, they can't do anything to assist with my case. They can only help with communications with family. They can't even translate stuff for me." She burst into tears. "Dad, I feel so helpless. I don't understand the language, I'm sick…Dad, you have to get me out of here!"

"You'll get through this," he said, his voice choked with tears. "I promise."

"I'm so sorry for putting you through all this and worrying you. It's my naiveté that caused all this. I was so gullible. And now I've caused you all this worry."

"It's okay. Things happen. We'll get through this together."

After the phone call, Julienne went back to the cell and managed to sleep again for a short while. She woke up to the aroma of something cooking.

She wandered over to where a woman stirred a pot of broth on the stove. It smelled like chicken soup. *Chicken soup would be good for me right now.* She glanced at the pot. *Not very clean, but I do need to eat something.*

The woman stirring the pot glanced up at Julienne.

"Copa," she said, motioning for Julienne to get a cup.

The jail didn't supply dishes or utensils. The inmates had to get these on their own from family or friends. Julienne stood there, not knowing what to do.

Another inmate came over and handed Julienne her cup and spoon to use.

"Gracias." Julienne nodded her thanks, inhaled the aroma of the soup and sat on a bench to sip on the broth. After a few sips, she used the spoon to scoop out a bite of chicken. She bit into it and screamed.

She gagged. "It's a chicken claw! Oh, my god! No! Gracias, but no!" She shuddered and handed the soup to one of the other inmates.

They laughed and pointed at her, slapping their sides. "Americano!"

"Delicacy!" One of them said.

*Delicacy? I don't care. I'm not eating it.* She wanted to throw up. *Oh my god, I bit into a chicken foot!*

That night she awoke to shrieking noises that increased in intensity. A guard came out with a flashlight and a metal bar in her hand and started banging on the pavement as she came closer. *Oh my god, what's happening?* When the flashlight shone over an area close to the cell, Julienne saw four or five huge rats fighting over a morsel of food on the floor. *Rats! They're as big as cats!* The women got up and gathered to watch them through the cell bars. Everyone started shouting as though they were encouraging the fight.

*Cheerleaders for rats!* The guard kept banging the cement floor with her metal rod until the rats scattered. The women settled back down on their mattresses.

*This is insane! We're in the cage and the rats are free. Something's wrong with this picture.* She realized the dream she'd had about cat-sized rats a few nights before hadn't been a dream. They were real.

Later that night Julienne's stomach cramped in agony. *I can't go in that bucket!*

She poked Marty and woke her up. "Please," she said. "I'm so sick." She held her stomach and rocked back and forth in pain.

Marty yelled for the guard to open the gate to let Julienne out to use the toilet. She came, hammering her metal rod on the floor as she walked. Julienne could hear the rats squealing and scurrying around close by. The guard unlocked the cell and let Julienne out. She handed her a metal rod to use as they made their way to the toilet area and she gave her some toilet paper.

*I can barely stand up and I have to ward off rats too?* She made it to the toilet just in time for her stomach to explode. She turned quickly and sat on the dirty, cracked toilet bowl to finish the job. Her tears fell freely.

"Chica! Chica!" the guard called. "Rapido! De ratas!"

Fear replaced her tears. *What if the rats run into the stall that I'm in?* She heard the guard banging the metal rod just outside. She stood up, grabbed a bucket and scooped water from a giant barrel. She flushed down the waste, picked up the metal rod and banged on the pavement as she went over to the cement basin to wash her hands and rinse her mouth.

"Rapido!" the guard shouted again.

She hurried back to the cell and the guard locked it behind her. The women began chattering and though Julienne didn't understand what they were saying, she sensed that the rats had become the topic of the night.

*I can't take much more of this,* she thought as she crawled onto her mattress and tried to control the sobs that surfaced. *I never would have believed a place like this existed. I'm living like an animal.* She didn't sleep much the rest of the night.

The next morning she was surprised to see Armando in the courtyard.

"Armando!" She walked over to him, relieved to speak English with someone. "What are you doing over here on the women's side?"

"During the day we can come here to the common area with permission to use the phone." He looked at her flushed face. "You don't look so good. Are you sick?"

"Yes, I have a fever," she said, her voice weak. "Do they have a doctor here?"

"I think you have to go outside the jail for one. And you have to get permission, get an appointment, and pay a guard to bring you."

"You're serious?"

"Afraid so."

She sighed and looked down at her dress, the same one she'd been wearing for days. "I'm filthy," she said. "How can I get a change of clothes?"

"Wait here. I'll talk to a guard," he offered. He returned with one of the guards and said, "He's going to walk you over to the men's prison."

"The men's prison?" She backed away from him. *No way am I going there.*

"It's okay," Armando said. "Your suitcase is being held in an office over there. You can get some of your things and bring them back here."

She followed the guard and did her best to keep up with him, but had to slow her pace. She felt weak and didn't want to cause a scene by fainting. They walked around the outside of the building, past some administrative offices and down a dank passageway that led to the guard's quarters. The entrance gate with rusted iron bars stood open. Beyond that, another wooden door opened to a room that held a bunk bed, a single cot and a small table and chair. The officer motioned for her to step inside

Her suitcase and purse sat on the cot. She looked through her suitcase. Everything was there except for some small souvenirs she had bought to take home. She checked her purse, but all the money was gone except for two dollars in her wallet. Her passport had been confiscated during the arrest.

She glanced toward the doorway. A different guard, a short man wearing a red beret, stood there watching her.

He smiled at her. "My name is Sandoval and I will take care of you. Is everything in your suitcase?"

"Yes, except for my money. There's only two dollars. The rest of my American dollars and the Ecuadorian money I had are gone."

"Impossible!"

"Look," she said, holding open her purse. "Someone took it. I would not be in a foreign country with only two dollars."

"Just change your clothes," he ordered. He stood there, watching.

"Can you please leave the room and shut the door?" she said, getting nervous.

He got a wicked smirk on his face and closed the door, but stayed inside. "I need to keep an eye on you. You can trust me."

Frightened, Julienne didn't move. *Oh my god, is this where I get raped?*

"Hurry up," he barked, glaring at her.

Trembling, she turned her back toward him and started to change, slipping her dirty dress over her head. He stepped closer and reached out his hand to caress her hair. "You are beautiful," he said. "Lovely blonde hair."

"Stop it!" she screamed. "Get Out! Stay away from me!" She clung to the dress, holding it in front of her.

A loud rap on the door made Sandoval back off. He opened it.

"What's going on?" another guard asked.

"Everything is okay," Sandoval said. "She's getting her clothes." He stepped outside and closed the door behind him.

Heart pounding, she quickly put on clean underwear and a dress. She slipped on a different pair of sandals. She had only packed beach clothes, sundresses and sandals thinking she would just be in Miami for the weekend. She wished she had taken more clothes on the trip.

"Are you ready?" Sandoval called through the door.

"Yes," she said, picking up her suitcase. She opened the door and held it between him and her.

"No, you must leave that here," Sandoval said.

"Why?"

"Someone will steal it over there. Just take out the few things you need."

She opened the suitcase and grabbed her toothbrush, toothpaste and shampoo.

"When you need something else, you can come get it." He raked his eyes over her and reached out and touched her hair. "You can come anytime. It will be safe here."

She shuddered. *Yeah, but will I be safe?*

# CHAPTER 6

## CDP
## Bucket Bath and Inmate Beating

JULIENNE PLUNKED DOWN on a mattress. Marty came to check on her and brought her a little water to drink. She took a few sips and lay down, worn out and shivering, even though it was hot and muggy. She fluctuated between feeling chilled and burning up with fever.

A short time later, she heard a guard calling her name.

"Julienne! Visita!"

Surprised, she stood and walked over to the guard. A man and a woman stood beside him.

"Julienne, your father called us and told us you were here. We're with the Peace Corps in Quito." The woman reached out her hand. "I'm Helen Brown and this is my husband, Gene."

Tears streamed down Julienne's face. "You already talked to my dad?"

"Yes, we did and also with the Embassy." She reached out and felt Julienne's forehead. "You are burning up." She motioned for her to sit on a bench. "Come, sit down. I'm a nurse," she explained as she pulled some medication from a large canvas bag she carried. "I have some antibiotics for you." She took Julienne's temperature. "102.5 degrees," she said as she prepared an injection. After she gave Julienne the shot, she held up a bottle of pills. "You need to take these antibiotics every four hours."

"Thank you," Julienne said. "I've been feeling so sick."

Helen pulled out her stethoscope and listened to Julienne's breathing.

"You may have pneumonia, but the injection and these meds should take care of it." She glanced around. "Keep them in your pocket at all times, or someone will steal them."

"Can you get me out of here?" Julienne pleaded.

"I wish we could," Gene said. "The justice system functions very differently in Ecuador." He patted her on the back. "But we'll keep close tabs on you and do everything we can to help."

"We brought you some bottled water and juice to drink and some fresh fruit," Helen said as she handed Julienne the large plastic bag. "You need to get some liquids into your system and eat what you can. Some of the basics you'll need for the moment are in here as well.

Julienne looked through the large bag. Plastic bowl, cup and silverware, toilet paper, washcloth and towel, soap, shampoo and a sheet and a blanket.

"This is all so bizarre," Julienne said. "The jail doesn't even provide the basics. Nothing." Tears glistened in her eyes. "Just a bare mattress."

"We'll see that you get what you need," Helen said." She reached out and took Julienne's hand. "Now, tell us a little about your case."

Julienne explained again what happened before, during and after the arrest.

"Have you talked to a lawyer yet?" Gene asked.

"No. It's so hard for me to communicate because of the language barrier. I need a lawyer who speaks English."

"We know a Human Rights lawyer who may be able to help. We'll contact him," Gene said.

"His name is Alejandro Ponce," Helen added.

They visited a short while, then told Julienne to lie down and sleep as much as possible.

"How can I ever thank you for all this?" Julienne said. "It's so nice of you."

"We're happy to help. Now, go rest and we'll see you again soon."

The meds helped her sleep and when she got up it was dinnertime. Julienne got her bowl and silverware as women and children lined up for whatever food there might be. *I don't think I can eat a thing. I'll just have some juice.* She started to put her bowl away when one of the women pointed at it, then at herself and her child.

"You want my bowl?" The woman kept pointing at Julienne, her bowl, the food line and then back at herself. "Oh, you want my share of the food?"

"Si!" She nodded.

Julienne stayed in line for food and then handed it to the woman so she'd have more for herself and her child. The woman smiled. "Gracious!" She hurried off to eat. When she finished, she washed the bowl and brought it back. *She washed it in the same cement basin as she washes her child. Probably with the same soap. Great!* She put it in her canvas bag and decided she'd wash it again herself when she felt ready to eat.

Lying on her mattress that night, Julienne realized how grateful she was for the things Helen and Gene brought. *I never thought I'd be so grateful for something as basic as a sheet to cover a mattress. So far, no bed bugs. Must be the lye soap.*

The next day Julienne's father called again.

"How are you doing? I've been so worried about you. Are you feeling any better?"

"A little," she said. "Gene and Helen Brown came to see me and brought antibiotics."

"That's great."

"How did you find them?"

"I was at a business meeting and a friend noticed that I wasn't my usual cheerful self. When he asked what was wrong, I told him about your situation." He paused to control his voice. "They knew someone who is a friend of Gene and Helen and gave me their number. When I found out they were right there in Quito…" His voice waivered. "I told them what happened to you and that you were sick with no one to turn to. They promised to visit you right away."

"They did," she said. "They brought meds, some bottled water and juice, some fresh fruit and a sheet for my mattress."

"You didn't have anything to cover the mattress?"

"No, Dad. You can't imagine how horrible it is here unless you see it for yourself. I would never have believed it. You have to buy anything you need, silverware, bowl, cup, even toilet paper."

"What if someone is really poor or doesn't have family to help them?"

"Then they have to negotiate or trade. Like maybe do some work or something for another inmate."

"Wow. Well, I'm glad you're feeling a little better at least."

"It's so good to hear your voice." She swallowed hard and bit back the tears. "I feel so isolated and alone."

"I'm sorry, Julie. Things should start moving along as we get more people involved. I talked to someone from DEA and he said you should be coming home within a month or two because you're an American and our government will take care of you."

"A month or two?"

"Yes. We hope he knows what he's talking about and isn't just playing politics. I've made so many phone calls. We'll keep at it."

"Thanks, Dad. I was hoping to be out sooner, but at least a month gives me a light at the end of the tunnel. I want this nightmare to be over."

"I wired money for you through the Embassy, so you should get that soon."

"Thank you, Dad. I love you."

Julienne needed a shower. She'd just been washing her face, hands and feet at one of the basins. One of the women showed her how to get warm water, instead of taking an icy cold shower. She got a large bucket and filled it with water. Then she used a *culuentedor*—an electric warmer. One end of the small unit was placed into the bucket of water while the two loose wires on the other end of it were stuck into the electric socket on the wall.

*Oh my god, I was taught never to do something like this. Sticking bare wires into a socket?*

"Veinte minutos," the woman said. "Se tarda veinte minutos."

*I think veinte means twenty.* While the woman waited for the water to heat up, she got her soap and shampoo and a large cup to scoop water out of the bucket to use for pouring. Before she stepped into the shower enclosure with the warm water, the woman pulled the wires out of the electric socket and then took the heater out of the bucket. She stepped into the shower stall and when she finished, she nodded to Julienne that it was her turn.

*This is not a shower. It's a bucket bath.*

Julienne went through the procedure, but when it was time to poke the wires into the socket, her hands shook so badly that it took her five minutes to get up the courage to do it. *How ironic if I get electrocuted trying to bathe.* When the water was ready, she reached into the bucket to pull out the warmer. When she did, the wires in the socket sparked and caught on fire. She quickly tossed the bucket of warm water on the fire to put it out.

"Loco Americano!" one woman shouted.

Several others came over yelling and swearing and calling Julienne names. She was supposed to pull the wires out of the socket *before* taking the heating unit out of the bucket. She had done it backwards. One inmate looked at the ruined heater with its burned wires and seethed with mounting rage. She got in Julienne's face, screaming at her. Julienne froze. *The water heater is ruined and now they have to take cold showers and they're probably going to beat me for it.* She didn't move or say a word and avoided eye contact.

The commotion brought the guard over and the women slowly scattered, muttering and complaining.

Julienne trembled as she filled the bucket again and stepped into a stall to take her cold bath.

When she finished, it was time for lunch. Julienne doubted she would eat whatever it was. That morning they had served bread with watered-down coffee for those who had a cup to pour it into. Even the children drank coffee. Some mothers boiled oats in water and poured the liquid into a cup or baby bottle for their children. The paste of oats left in the bottom of the pot was given to pig farmers.

"But the nutrition is in the oats," Julienne said to Marty, knowing she probably didn't understand.

"No, es bueno," Marty said. "Aquí, saborearlo." She poured a little into Julienne's cup.

To be polite, Julienne took a small sip. *It tastes like dirty water. How do these babies survive?* She nodded and managed a slight smile. *No need to insult them. Besides, what choice do they have?* She realized that the children were 'sentenced' along with their mothers.

"Where are your girls?" she asked Marty.

One of the inmates translated for Marty and said the girls were sent out to be with her family.

For lunch they served white, oily, crunchy, burned rice with a tiny piece of meat about two inches in size on it.

*Mystery meat. I can do without that.*

Again one of the mothers noticed Julienne wasn't in the food line and came over to her. Julienne told the guard to give her share to the mother. Julienne drank some orange juice and ate a piece of fruit, a mango that Helen had brought.

Julienne carried her bag of personal items and drinks with her at all times. With all the rain, it was a good thing the bag was plastic. It rained almost every day. The inmates had to huddle under the limited covered areas against the walls until the rain stopped.

*The inmates in the other two cells have it better than the rest of us,* Julienne thought. They could go inside their room when it rained.

Julienne struck up a bit of a relationship with Elizabeth, one of the guards. She spoke some English and liked practicing it with Julienne. One day she told Julienne she could go to the other cells and visit with the women there if she wanted to. Julienne went and mingled with some of the women to relieve the boredom. The next day she went back.

"No, no" a different guard said to her. "You can't go in there. It's not allowed. You have to stay in your own area."

"I was in there yesterday."

"No, you can't do that. It's breaking the rules."

Julienne walked back to the courtyard. *Does this mean I can only go when Elizabeth is on duty?* She didn't want to get Elizabeth in trouble with the other guards. They each appeared to have their own rules.

A few days later, when it was raining, another guard saw Julienne huddled under the roof against the wall. "Come, you can go to the other cells."

"No, no," Julienne said. "I don't want to get into trouble."

She learned that when certain guards, like Elizabeth, were on duty, she had more freedom. Some guards didn't even bother with roll call. It was hard to keep track of where she could go and when.

One time she heard two of the guards fighting and yelling at each other. Julienne couldn't understand their Spanish, but she heard her name mentioned and knew they were fighting about her. Where she could and couldn't go. No special privileges just because she was an American.

Hearing the conflict made her nervous. *I don't want to get anyone in trouble,* she thought. *And I don't want to be in the middle of their drama, or have a guard mad at me.* She kept to herself after that and didn't socialize much with other inmates. She was glad that many of the women in her cell were older. They didn't argue and fight as much as the younger ones.

One day Julienne watched a young male prisoner brought over to the women's side to clean the walls and repair some wiring. When he finished, the guard handed him a broom and ordered him to get up on the ledge of the roof and sweep off anything that was up there. He scaled the wall and hopped onto the roof without a ladder or a rope. *He climbs like a monkey,* she thought. He swept as he had been told.

At three o'clock the guards changed. The new guard spotted the inmate on the roof, pulled out his weapon and fired his gun into the air. He yelled at the inmate to come down off the roof at once.

The young man obeyed and scrambled down the wall. The guard shoved him face down on the ground, kicking him and yelling obscenities. Then he grabbed a metal rod, the same kind used to keep rats away and began striking the inmate on his back. Over and over the guard pounded the prisoner until the young man's shirt was soaked with blood.

Horrified, Julienne looked around. The women watched, but stayed back. *How can they just ignore something like this?*

"No!" Julienne shouted and headed toward the guard. "He was just doing what he was told by the other guard!"

Two inmates grabbed Julienne and pulled her back.

"Silencio!" one said.

"There's nothing you can do about it," the other added.

Julienne tried to squirm loose from their grip, but realized she could be next.

The guard stopped and glanced up at all the women standing around staring at him. He shouted at the young inmate, "Levántate!" When he didn't move, the guard stormed off and left him lying there.

The women rushed over and dragged his limp, bloody body over to the wash basins. They peeled off his shirt and washed the blood from his back. The original guard came back, helped him up and took him back over to the men's side.

*How can people do such mindless and horrible things? The poor guy was only doing what he was told.* She sat on the ground and hugged her knees, rocking back and forth, fighting a rising wave of panic. *Could something like that happen to me if a guard was having a bad day?*

CHAPTER 7

# CDP
# Drag Queens

ON THE NEXT scheduled visit day, Marty came to Julienne to ask a favor, going through motions and holding out her baby. Still not understanding many Spanish words, Julienne had no idea what she wanted. Marty went and got one of the guards who spoke some English to translate for her.

"She wants you to watch her baby while she goes to visit her husband," the guard said.

"She's going home to visit her husband? She's allowed to do that?"

"No, no. He's over in the men's prison."

"Your husband is there?" Julienne asked, pointing toward the men's side.

Marty nodded.

"And they allow inmates to visit each other?" *This is crazy. They have conjugal visits between prisoners? Imagine if they did that in the States.*

Before Julienne could respond, Marty handed the baby over. "Gracias," she said and hurried off.

Julienne looked down at the baby boy in her arms. *I don't know anything about babies.* The little one smiled at her. *He sure is cute.* She found a spot to sit and sang nursery rhymes to him. He started fussing a little so she walked around the courtyard with him.

One of the inmates came over to her.

"He's hungry," the woman said.

*What can I feed him? He's so little.*

The baby cried.

*Why did Marty put me in this position? She didn't say anything about feeding him. How long will she be gone?*

"What should I give him?" Julienne asked.

She snatched the baby from Julienne's arms and called another inmate over.

The woman came over and took the baby, lifted her shirt, and began nursing him.

"No!" Julienne said. "What are you doing?" She reached for the baby.

The other women nearby started snickering.

"It's not funny!" Julienne shouted, trying to pull the baby away from the nursing woman. "He could get a disease!"

The woman turned her back to Julienne and continued to nurse the baby. Just then Marty came back and Julienne ran over to her.

"She took your baby," she said, pointing at the woman.

"Está bien," Marty said.

"Don't worry," a female guard said, walking over to them. "She's a mother too and has enough milk to nurse her own child and another if she needs to." She grinned at Julienne's worried face. "The mothers help each other."

Trembling, Julienne shook her head. *People are so backwards here. Don't they realize they can pass germs to the baby?*

"Julienne Estrada!" a guard announced

Helen and Gene Brown had arrived for a visit.

"Are you feeling better?" Helen asked as she pulled out her thermometer to take Julienne's temperature.

"Yes, I'm doing much better."

"Normal," Helen said as she checked the thermometer. "Continue to take the rest of the antibiotics. You have enough for a few more days. Finish them up."

"I will. Thank you so much for all you're doing for me. I don't know what I'd do…"

"You're welcome," Helen said. "We brought you a little money, Ecuadorian sucres, until you get the funds your dad sent through the Embassy. Right now the exchange rate is 3,000 sucres to one U.S. dollar. It's not safe to keep too much on you. If you pay one of the guards, he will get some things for you from the outside."

"They'll actually do that? I can trust them?"

"Yes, if they know you will continue to use them and pay them for errands, they will get what you need. Food, personal items."

"I guess money talks." Julienne said.

"It's the way it is here." Helen reached into her bag and pulled out a small plastic bag of coins. "These are fetches to use for the pay phones. For local calls, you have to put fetches in every three minutes. Usually, you only get about six minutes at a time if someone else is waiting to use the phone. When it rains, often the phones don't work. You can call us, or the Embassy, or your family. For international calls it would be better if your dad got you a phone card to use."

"Thank you. Dad called me twice this week," she said.

"That's great. It's usually hard to get through directly to the jail. If the one answering the phone doesn't understand English, they may just hang up on the caller. Often the phones are so busy it can take hours to get through. I'm glad he got through to you."

"I'm so grateful for all you're doing for me," she said. "It's so confusing and crazy in here."

"It's definitely a far cry from America's justice system." She handed Julienne a bag. "Carrot juice," she said.

She smiled. "I love carrot juice."

"We called Sandra Edwards from Human Rights and she'll be stopping by to see you. We've also contacted Alejandro Ponce, the attorney we told you about. So you should be hearing from them soon."

They visited a while longer and before they left asked, "Is there anything else we can do for you right now?"

"Help me escape?" She tried to force a smile, but a look of tired sadness passed over her.

"That's not in our job description in the Peace Corps," she said smiling. "But we'll do everything else that we can." She took Julienne's hand in hers. "We'll be praying for you."

Julienne didn't respond. *Yeah, I'll be praying too. For a way to escape.*

After the Browns left, a commotion broke out over by the phones. Fifteen new female prisoners had been brought in and told to stay in that area. Marty and some of the other inmates walked over to see who they were.

"Drag queens!" someone shouted. Many started jesting and mocking, circling around them, making comments about their body parts.

"You got what it takes to be a woman?"

"Maybe you got what it takes to be a man," another quipped.

"So what is it? Are you a man or a woman?"

The bantering and noise escalated.

Julienne stayed in the background, keeping her distance. *Is this going to end up in a brawl? Where are the guards? They must know this could be a problem.*

"Drag queen prostitutes," an inmate explained.

"You mean they had a sex change? They sure look like women," Julienne said.

"Some have a sex change because it's illegal to be gay in Ecuador."

*So these men become female prostitutes to have sex with men. Wow.*

When the clamor reached a high pitch, several guards came back and herded the drag queens back to the men's side of the prison.

"They don't know where to put them. Are they women or are they men?"

Everyone started laughing, but not Julienne. *I'm staying out of this.* She listened to the hooting and hollering over the wall as the new prisoners reached the other side.

That night loud and violent sounds emanated from the men's jail. Julienne heard screams that sounded as if someone was beaten. She tried to block it out, but the uproar increased throughout the night and kept her awake for much of it.

The next day Armando came over to the women's side to use the phone and Julienne went over to talk with him.

"What went on over there last night?" she asked.

"You don't really want to know," he said.

"That bad?"

"Many of the men took turns raping them."

"But what about the guards? Why didn't they stop it?"

Armando glanced around to be sure no one was within hearing distance. "They took their turns too."

Fear and outrage surged through her. *How can they get away with this? Hurting them like that?* She walked away. *Oh, my god. I better not screw up and make someone mad. No telling what could happen to me in this insane asylum.*

That day Alfred Rodriguez came from the Embassy.

"I heard you were sick," he said. "I spoke with Helen Brown."

"I'm better now," Julienne said. "She brought me antibiotics and my fever is gone. My energy is slowly returning."

"Good. Glad to hear it. If that happens again, just call the Embassy and we'll make sure you get the medical attention you need. "

"I didn't know how to contact you," she said. "And the guards around here…" She hesitated. "I don't want to irritate them or get on their bad side. Besides, most don't speak English."

"That's why I brought you this," he said. He reached into his briefcase and pulled out an English/Spanish dictionary. "This should help."

"I had one at Interpol, but don't know what happened to it when they brought me here." She sighed. "How can I defend myself when I can't even speak the language?"

"I know it's difficult right now, but you'll pick it up."

"Why should I have to learn their language? They should provide me with an interpreter."

"As you're finding out, they do things quite differently here than in the States."

"My Dad called me and said he wired money for me to the Embassy."

"Yes, I have most of it right here." He handed her an envelope. "Be careful with it."

"I've been told I can pay a guard to go outside into town and get me food. Is that right?"

"Yes, that's one of the many unusual things here."

"What's unusual is that I don't seem to have any rights. What happened to innocent until proven guilty? Why can't I get out on bail?"

"Again, it's very different here. We're subject to Ecuadorian law and to the local judges. I did send a list of attorneys to your father. It's one the prison provides, so I doubt it's up to date."

"Sandra Edwards is supposed to come see me," Julienne said.

"She's from Human Rights. She's very good. She'll be able to help you in ways that I can't."

They talked about the prison and the Ecuadorian culture for a while. Before he left he handed her a business card.

"This is my personal line at the Embassy. Please feel free to call me when you have questions or a problem of any kind."

*I wonder how many times I can call him. I have a lot of questions. He seems like a nice guy, but what can he really do?*

"Julienne Estrada!" a guard announced soon after Mr. Rodriguez left. This time is was Sandra Edwards.

She shook Julienne's hand and got right down to business.

"Helen Brown has filled me in on your case, but I'd like to hear from you what has happened from your time of arrest until now."

Julienne went through her whole story again, leaving nothing out. Sandra took notes as she listened.

"Obviously there have been some conflicts here," she said. "Interpol is supposed to notify the American Embassy of an arrest within twenty-four hours. That didn't happen." She circled something in her notes. "When they sent you here to C.D.P., they didn't forward your paperwork right away. That's why your name wouldn't have come up for roll call the first day or two."

"I wondered about that," Julienne said. "Nothing surprises me anymore. This is third world mentality."

"I'm going to file a writ of *habeas corpus* on your behalf in Quito."

"What does that mean?"

"No one can be held incommunicado without formal charges or presentation to a judge for more than a month. C.D.P. cannot arbitrarily hold anyone in an unlawful manner or deprive him or her of his or her freedom without a formal decision by the judge ordering imprisonment. Once *habeas corpus* is filed, the judge must have a hearing concerning this and within twenty-four hours, you must be moved out of here to El Inca Penitentiary for Women in Quito. If he doesn't, he has to set you free."

"There's a chance I could go free?" For the first time, she blinked tears of hope.

"Julienne, listen. It's not likely they will let you go free. But they will scramble to file all the proper paperwork, do what they have to do and get you moved to El Inca. The writ of *habeas corpus* will force their hand."

Sandra told her that Alejandro Ponce Jr., another Human Rights lawyer, would also be working on her case. They reviewed some paperwork and Sandra promised to call Julienne's father to fill him in on what she was doing.

*Something's finally happening. I can't wait to get out of here.*

Later that night tempers flared over an inmate claiming another prisoner stole shampoo from her. The two of them got into a fistfight and someone tossed a knife to one of them. The one with the knife poked and jabbed and screamed at her opponent. Blood spurted from a gash on one of her arms. Another thrust cut her cheek. Inmates gathered around, goading them on, shouting and jeering.

Terrified, Julienne dashed to the opposite side of the courtyard and crouched in a corner to stay away from the ruckus. *Oh god, I hope no one gets killed. I couldn't handle that. Where are the guards?*

Finally, several guards came running into the area and managed to separate the women, dragging out the one who had started the fight.

*Where are they taking her?* Overwhelmed with fear, Julienne's stomach knotted and she covered her face with trembling hands.

"Are you okay?"

Julienne looked up into the face of a male guard she hadn't seen before.

"You speak English?"

"Not very well, but yes, I do," he said. "My name is Jose." He smiled at her. "Come on, get up. Things are calm now."

As she stood, Julienne asked, "Where did they take her?"

"The one who started the fight? To solitary confinement. She needs to be isolated."

"And the other one?"

"She's getting her cuts medicated and bandaged. She'll be all right. At least as long as she doesn't go for revenge."

"Thank you for talking with me," Julienne said. "It's difficult not knowing the language."

"Well, maybe while I'm assigned here, I can teach you a little Spanish and you can help improve my English."

*I don't know. Can I trust this guy?*

"But right now everyone has to go to their cell and settle in for the night. I'll talk to you tomorrow."

<hr />

After the morning routine of cleaning and roll call, Julienne sat with her dictionary. *I don't really want to do this. Why should I have to learn the language when I may be going free soon?* As she flipped through the pages, the aroma of something cooking attracted her attention. *It smells good. Now that I have a little money, I could buy a bowl of it, depending on what it is.* The experience of the chicken claw stayed fresh in her mind.

She looked up the words for I - *Yo*, and for hungry. – *hambre*. She repeated the phrase out loud a few times and walked over to the kitchen area to try out her Spanish.

"Yo hombre," she said to the cook.

"Que?" The woman stared at her.

"Yo hombre," Julienne repeated, pointing to her stomach.

The woman burst out laughing and a few others gathered around.

*What is so funny about being hungry?*

"Que?" the cook managed to repeat, trying not to snicker.

"Yo humbre!"

The women hooted and pointed at Julienne's stomach.

Marty came over and explained, "You just told them you have a man in your stomach." She grinned at Julienne. "Hombre means man, hambre means hungry."

"It sounds the same to me," Julienne said, embarrassed.

The women waited to see what she might say next. She pointed to the pot on the stove and asked in English what was cooking.

"Cuy," the cook said. "Delicioso!"

Julienne nodded and went back to her dictionary to look up the word. She tried looking it up the way it sounded, kooey. *Nothing.* She flipped to the letter c. *This is frustrating. You have to know how to spell a word before you can look it up!* Finally she found it. She stared at the definition.

"Guinea pig! A guinea pig is supposed to be a pet, not food." She held her stomach. *I would never. How horrible. They thought I said I had a man in my stomach and I was about to put a guinea pig in my stomach?* She shuddered at the thought.

"I see you're working on your Spanish."

Julienne looked up. It was Jose, the guard.

"My first attempt didn't turn out so well," she said.

"You'll learn. Be patient."

She closed the book. "I have a question for you. I've been told that I can ask a guard to bring me some food from the outside if I can pay for it. Is that true?"

"Yes, it is. If you like, I can do that for you after my shift and bring you something tomorrow. What would you like?"

"Something healthy."

"I'm a vegetarian myself," he said. "That won't be a problem."

They chatted a while and she gave him some money when he had to get back to his shift.

*This will be a test to see if I can trust him. If not, at least it isn't much money.*

Over the next weeks, it was a break from all the negatives around her and he brought her the healthy food she asked for. Her trust in him began to build and she enjoyed her talks with him, but soon that stopped as well.

"Sandoval found out that we are becoming friends, so he's transferring me to the men's prison," Jose said. "Guards are not supposed to communicate as friends with prisoners."

"Sandoval did this?" *Figures. Probably jealous because I rejected him.* She wondered if he came on to most of the women he dealt with. *Maybe having an American woman is on his bragging list. I won't be on it, that's for sure.*

In the next few days Alejandro Ponce visited and he filled her in on the legal proceedings. She should be transferred to El Inca in Quito any time now.

*Or set free*, she told herself.

"You are considered a high risk at this point," Alejandro said. "They see that you've been friendly with a few of the guards. "

"That makes me a high risk?"

"Some inmates, if they have the resources to bribe a guard, would plan an escape."

*I wonder how much money it would take. If I had the money and the connections, I'd walk out of this rat-infested place.*

"Julienne Estrada!" A female guard called out her name. "There's a taxi waiting for you."

*A taxi?*

"Good! They're moving you to El Inca," Alejandro said. "I'll get your suitcase and meet you there."

He left while a guard looked through the bag Julienne carried and let her take it with her. She followed the guard through the gates to the outside. Three other prisoners and two guards crowded into the small vehicle.

As the taxi drove off, Julienne felt claustrophobic. Her nerves tensed and she wondered what the immediate future held for her. *Would El Inca be a better place? Would the attorneys be able to prove her innocence? Would she be set free? How long would it take?*

Her mind became a crazy mixture of hope and fear.

# CHAPTER 8

## Camp Inca
## Butch Up

THE TAXI DROVE through an old residential neighborhood in Quito and arrived in front of a large iron gate. A group of people, who appeared poor and possibly homeless, stood blocking the gate.

*Surely they're not trying to get inside?*

Across the street Julienne noticed a small convenience store. *I wonder if they let you send guards out to buy things there.*

"Avanzar!" the taxi driver shouted at the people as he blasted his horn.

The small crowd parted as the heavy, iron gate opened.

The driver pulled inside and stopped. The guards escorted the prisoners out of the car and the taxi turned and left.

Led into an office, Julienne saw that Alejandro was already there ahead of them. He held her suitcase.

"You need to go through a few procedures before going inside," he said as he handed her the suitcase. "They need to fingerprint you and then you can go through the things in your suitcase to be sure everything is there. After that a guard will take you inside."

*My new home.* She took a deep breath and tried to calm the pounding in her chest.

The attorney left after the initial procedure was complete and papers signed. Julienne sat, waiting for someone to lead her where she had to go. One by one the others who had transferred with her, left with guards. They seemed to know the guards and were familiar with the whole process and what was next. Julienne couldn't understand their Spanish and sat there alone for quite a while.

*Did they forget about me?* She glanced at a clock on the wall. Another hour passed before a female guard came over and motioned for her to follow.

She picked up her suitcase and followed to another heavy iron gate, which the guard unlocked, then locked again after they passed through. They walked past what looked like a greenhouse, but appeared to be a souvenir shop with flowered baskets, bird feeders and other items on display.

*How strange to see something like this in here. Is it a retail shop? For who? Visitors?*

The prison was surrounded by gray and white chipped cement and clay walls, topped with barbed wire. The inner wall was cemented with shards of green and clear glass.

*It would be painful to try to escape over one of these walls!*

Just beyond the greenhouse were two more iron gates. The one directly in front of them led to Maximum Security. Through the bars, Julienne saw a young woman gardening and watching her children.

*Wow! This must be the country club of maximum security.*

The gate to the left led into the general prison, El Inca. The guard stopped and peered through a small, open, barred window in the solid gate and gave orders to someone. A guard on the other side opened the gate and Julienne stepped into a long, outdoor corridor with cement benches along the wall. She looked up at the old buildings with clothes hanging everywhere, draped out barred windows. Some openings were boarded up with scraps of wood. She noticed a booth in the distance with a Coca Cola logo on it. *What is that?* Inmates roamed, some with young children. Chickens wandered freely and pecked at the ground. Julienne stood there, holding her suitcase and bag.

"I've been waiting for you!" A girl who looked like a punk rocker got up from a bench and came over to Julienne. "Hi, I'm Peggy, dude."

Julienne stared at her. *Dude?* She had several piercings on each ear, a nose ring, multi-colored hair in red, green and pink and wore army cut-off shorts with a tee shirt.

*Is she a prisoner? How did she know I was coming? And why was she waiting for me?*

Peggy snatched up Julienne's suitcase. "Follow me," she ordered, as she started down the alleyway.

Julienne followed, looking around. *This is like an antiquated village.* She looked at Peggy and wondered, *Should I be following her? Not that I have a choice. She has my suitcase.*

"I heard you were coming," Peggy said, "and I've been trying to get permission to have you stay in my room." She talked as she hurried along. "They usually put new inmates in the Red Zone and that's very dangerous. You don't want to go there."

Fear and dread gripped Julienne. *Red Zone? This is like moving into the slums.* Her trembling legs had trouble keeping up and she stopped for a minute.

Peggy turned around. "Come on, let's go," she said.

Julienne stood there, very shaken.

"Girl, you got to butch up if you're going to survive in here!" She looked Julienne up and down. "That girly sundress and sandals with your blonde hair will get you a 'Barbie Doll' reputation." She walked around her in a circle. "Don't you have a pair of jeans?"

"No."

"Where are you from?"

"California."

"Aahh, a California girl. Well, you're in an Ecuadorian prison now. You'll need to make some changes." She continued walking and this time Julienne kept up with her.

"I'll give you a tour later, but right now we're going to Mida Flores, the pavilion where I live."

They climbed a wide cement stairwell to the second floor and Peggy pulled out a key to unlock the gate that read Mida Flores. After they entered, Peggy handed Julienne the key and said, "Lock the padlock behind us."

*She has her own key to this whole floor?*

"We keep the gate locked so women from other pavilions won't steal from us," she explained.

Inmates poked their heads out of their doors to see who was entering their territory. Another key unlocked the padlock on Peggy's door. Her room was small, about six by eight feet, with blue painted walls, chipped and covered with graffiti, punk slogans, torn-out magazine photos that ranged from Frankenstein to Einstein glued to the walls and penciled song lyrics.

*Wow. There's so much clutter, I'm surprised the prison allows it.* She looked around at the tiny space. *How are two people going to fit in here?*

"Okay, let's get your bed set up," Peggy said. "I moved things around so we can attach a bedframe on top of mine and have a bunk bed. I slid the end of the bed into the closet space to give us a few more feet in the room."

She dragged an old, rusty metal frame leaning against one wall over to the bed. "I need your help to get this up."

They struggled to lift it up and attach it properly to the bottom one.

"Damn!" Peggy said, looking at her hand. "I cut it on that jagged edge."

"Are you bleeding?" Julienne asked. "Are you okay?"

"I'll be fine," she said as she dabbed at the blood from the cut. "I'll probably have a scar though." She grinned at Julienne. "It will remind you of what I had to go through to get you to live in my room."

"Why did you want me in your room?"

"You speak English. I speak English. We're both Americans."

"Where are you from?" Julienne asked.

"Originally, Chicago, but I lived in California for a few years before I came here."

"Where in California?"

"Los Angeles. But I'd like to move to San Diego when I get out."

"Is that where your family is?"

"No, they're in Chicago." Changing the subject, she said, "Okay, now let's go find some plywood for the frame and a mattress. You might have to pay for the plywood if we can't find some scrap."

"The prison doesn't supply the bed?"

"There's a storage area that sometimes has bed frames like this one that somebody didn't need or want. Sometimes there's plywood, sometimes a mattress. It changes from day to day, depending on who takes what."

"What if there isn't anything available?"

"Then you buy what you need from another inmate. Or get someone from outside to get it for you." She looked at Julienne. "You got money?"

Julienne hesitated. "A little." *Can I trust this girl?*

"Don't worry, I'm not after your money," Peggy said. "I can take care of myself. I have an ice cream shop and hair salon downstairs. That's how I make money to eat and pay the fees."

"What fees?"

"To live here."

"You have to pay fees to be in this prison?" *You've got to be kidding me!*

"Only if you want to live where it's semi-safe. You pay dues for the pavilion you're in. The money is mainly used to buy propane for cooking. This pavilion has a President, Vice President and a Treasurer to run things. If you're a thief or a regular drug user, you live on the lower pavilions. They're not organized or honest enough to do what we do here."

*Am I hearing this right? This is crazy.*

"Wait a minute," Julienne said. "Did you say you have a hair salon here?

"Uh-huh, and the ice cream shop."

Julienne looked at her in surprise. "I take it there are not many rules here."

"Rules? This is South America, not California, dude"

"So what do you do all day?" Julienne asked.

"Whatever you feel like doing. Did you think there was rehabilitation here, like with classes or something? There's no rehabilitation here." Peggy smirked. "Don't worry, you'll figure it out. There's a certain amount of freedom within these rat-infested walls. Like my shop, you can make money by offering services or selling things. Some like to cook and sell their food. It's better than the rice and sardine meals that the prison serves. Others will do your laundry or sew for you."

"I guess I've got a lot to learn," Julienne said. "This is surreal." She shook her head. "What really gets to me is seeing young mothers with their children. I never would have imagined such a thing. Children in prison?

"When a mother gets sentenced, in a way, so do her children."

"That's so sad," Julienne said. "How can they be safe here?"

"Some do get used and abused," Peggy said. "Some older girls sleep with the guards for favors; some simply get raped."

"Oh my god," Julienne said." She blinked back tears.

"Sorry... I guess it's more than you wanted to know. But you need to brace yourself to deal with these things."

*That's so wrong. How can this kind of stuff go on? How can they get away with it? Doesn't anyone care?*

"By the way," Peggy said, "if the lead guard tries to have you moved somewhere else, just ignore him."

"Ignore him?" *Sounds like a way to get into trouble.*

"Yeah, just play the dumb blonde, like you don't understand Spanish. Just say, 'I'm an American. I don't understand what you're saying.' If you keep saying that, he'll get tired of trying to communicate with you and just wave you on and let you stay here. You have to learn ways to take control of the situation."

"I won't have to fake it. I really don't understand Spanish," Julienne said.

"Then it's not a problem. Come on, time for the tour."

Peggy locked the cell door behind them, and then unlocked the pavilion gate to pass through. Julienne followed her down a flight of steps to the open courtyard. She pointed to one of the buildings that had two floors.

"That's the Red Zone, the oldest building," Peggy said. "That's where they put the drug addicts, the worst of the worst. There's four to six women in each room and the rooms are the same size as mine. If it's full, they have to sleep two per cot on the bunk bed, each facing the opposite direction in order to fit, and two more sleep on the floor if they have kids. The place is dirty and infested with roaches." She looked at Julienne and said, "Aren't you glad I asked for you to be placed in my room?"

"Definitely."

Peggy pointed to another building. "That one holds prisoners with confirmed sentences, or foreigners."

"Is that where they might have put me? I'm a foreigner."

"Not likely," Peggy said. "Because you haven't been sentenced yet."

"I won't get sentenced," Julienne said, "because I'm innocent."

Peggy didn't comment.

"You already know which building is ours," Peggy said. "We're on the second floor and El Condado is on the third floor. That's where a lot of the foreigners are and it costs more to live there. If they approve it."

"The guards?"

"No, the inmates. You have to meet their requirements and rules."

*So there's politics and a pecking order even in prison. Great.*

"Let's get over to the storage area," Peggy said. "It's getting late and we have to be in our room for roll call by seven."

They found a piece of plywood to fit the bed frame and got a mattress that was not being used. Peggy dragged and carried the plywood, Julienne brought the thin mattress.

When they got to their building, Peggy stopped. On the bottom floor at the base of the stairwell, there was a small room with a telephone where people could call in, but inmates couldn't call out. Right next to it was another little room.

"That's my space," Peggy said.

"Your salon and ice cream shop?"

"Yeah, I'll show it to you tomorrow."

When they got back to their room, they put the bed together and Julienne put on the sheet from Helen Brown. *At least the mattress is covered. I'm afraid to think about who might have slept on it. I wonder if they have bed bugs here.*

"There's so much to absorb, Julienne said. "It's so different from C.D.P."

She opened her small suitcase. She had three sundresses, a pair of black dress pants, a ruffled summer blouse, two bathing suits, one sarong, a pair of sling-back high heels and two pairs of sandals.

Peggy watched her and shook her head.

"Not much to 'butch up' in, huh?" Julienne said.

"You need to get someone to bring you clothes," Peggy said.

*Maybe Helen would do that for me.*

"By the size of that bag you carry around, I assume you don't have anything to cook with either."

"No, I don't. I didn't think I'd be doing things like that in prison."

"We can share," Peggy said. "I have all the basics."

"Thank you. Hopefully, I won't be here too long."

"Good luck with that."

"But I'm innocent; I was set up."

"Doesn't matter. It takes forever to get your case heard in court before a judge. Unless…"

"Unless what?"

"Unless you have a chunk of money to bribe him and others."

"I don't think my attorney, Alejandro, is the type of man who would attempt bribery."

"Too bad," Peggy said. "Money talks. Big money talks louder."

Julienne listened in bewilderment. *Is everyone corrupt here? Even the innocent have to bribe their way out?*

At seven o'clock at night, prisoners had to be in their rooms in each pavilion for roll call. Peggy explained that following roll call, they were allowed in their pavilion's common area. It had a kitchen, bathroom, and a table for playing cards or doing crafts. Most stayed in their rooms. Julienne saw no reason to socialize or build relationships because she expected to get out soon.

*Who knows what crime some of these women committed to be imprisoned here. Until I get out, I need to be careful who I associate with.*

At ten o'clock, the guards came back through and locked the individual rooms by pulling a sliding lock bar across the outside of each door. The only way anyone got permission to get out during the night was if they had medical issues or had to use the toilet.

Julienne lay in bed that night, thinking about all the things Peggy had told her. Especially about women and children getting raped. *Could that happen to me?* The thought tore at her insides. *I've got to get my own set of keys so I can lock myself in the room when Peggy isn't around.*

CHAPTER 9

## Camp Inca
## Joan-The God Woman

THE NEXT MORNING Peggy told Julienne about visitor procedure. "When visitors come, the guards ask which pavilion they're going to. Then the Passadora will go to that pavilion and announce who has a visitor."

"Passadora?"

"It's whoever gets paid to announce a visit. Could be a prisoner or a guard."

"They get paid for doing that?"

"It's expected," Peggy said. "It's not much, but it gets you favors."

*I've got so much to learn!*

A short time later, someone yelled from the ground floor below their pavilion.

"Julienne Estrada! Visit!"

She went to their pavilion gate and unlocked it with the key Peggy loaned her. Julienne gave a few sucres to the inmate, and followed her to the entrance gate.

Gene and Helen Brown stood there.

"I didn't think I'd get a visit today," Julienne said. "I was told visitors came on Wednesday, Saturday and Sunday. "

"Because we're with the Peace Corps, they allow us to come when we can."

"I thought that was just for C.D.P. All the rules, or lack of them, have me confused."

Helen smiled. "Show us your cell," she said. "Let me see what you need so we can pass on a list to our friends at church."

"Visitors can go to the inmate's rooms?"

"Rules are so different here; I know you have a lot to absorb. But as a warning, don't allow some of this so-called freedom, to let your guard down. It's a tough prison and you must be careful who you trust."

"That's what Peggy, my roommate, told me," Julienne said. "She has a hair salon and ice cream shop near the stairwell. I just have trouble believing some of this stuff."

They talked a while, gave her more food, juice and toiletries, and some money from her Dad. Julienne showed them the only clothes she had. "Not appropriate for prison, I don't think."

"What size do you wear?" Helen asked.

"I'm not sure," Julienne said. "By the way my clothes hang on me, I've lost some weight."

"We'll get you some clothes," she said, looking at the size on the dress tags. "The members of our church will be happy to help. Some of them may even come to visit you. Would you like that?"

"It would be nice to talk with English-speaking visitors," Julienne said.

The Browns stayed for about thirty minutes. Before they left, Gene handed her a Bible. "I hope you'll read this," he said. "It will encourage you."

"Thank you for coming and for bringing me food," Julienne said.

"You're welcome. Just remember, you also need food for your soul," he said, tapping the Bible.

She walked out to the gate with them.

Back in her cell, she tossed the Bible on her bed. *I'm not ready for this. God seems to have forgotten about me. Why should I read his book?*

When Peggy came in, she noticed the Bible. "Are you one of those Bible believers?"

Julienne shrugged and didn't answer.

"I did the God thing my first year here," she said. "I learned it was an easy way to get food from the outside delivered here. I showed interest in a Bible study that some missionaries provided. It got me food and other supplies and visits from church people."

"Do you still get those visits?"

"No. I pleaded innocent on my case and I thought I could get all these people to back me up and it would help me to get a reduced sentence or even go free."

"What happened?"

"I was convicted and sentenced to eight years. I figured the God thing just wasn't working for me. So I dropped out."

"Dropped out of the Bible study?"

"Yes, and, for a while, they would visit me occasionally, but I made it clear to them that this religious thing was just not for me."

Julienne didn't respond.

"Listen, everyone finds their niche after a while and that usually decides what kind of stay you'll have here. For me, it was starting my business. The hair salon and ice cream shop."

*I wonder if she was really innocent,* Julienne thought. *Or what she was convicted of. I'm sure she'll tell me eventually. It's best that I don't ask.*

"The Browns brought me some food today," Julienne said. "I'm happy to share it with you. After all, you're sharing your room with me and teaching me what to expect."

"Thanks," Peggy said. "Hey, you should meet Joan, the God woman. I think you'd like her."

"The God woman?"

"Yes. Let me tell you. Joan has been coming here for some time, teaching a Bible study and visiting with some of the inmates. The women who practiced witchcraft hated her coming. I think they felt threatened by her. So they planned some kind of a trap. The witch was going to cast a spell or hurt Joan the next time she came to visit or to do a Bible study.

"The next time Joan came, the witch looked out from her cell window and saw her walking into the entrance way from the gate. Walking next to Joan, was an old man with long, white hair and a full beard, dressed in a white robe.

"She was so scared, she didn't carry out her plan. She came to me after Joan left and asked me who the man was that stayed by Joan's side. I asked her, 'What man?' She said, 'The man with white hair, dressed in a white robe.'

"I said, 'There wasn't a man. What are you talking about?'

"'The one walking next to Joan, the one in white,' she insisted. I told her there was no man, that Joan came alone. That really agitated her. When she realized no one else saw the man, she was even more terrified. From that day on, Joan has been known as the 'God woman.'"

"Wow," Julienne said. "That's quite a story."

"It's true," Peggy said. "One of the women refers to Joan as a bright light that shines in this dark place. Right now she's on furlough and won't be back for a month."

*Just as well*, Julienne thought. *I'm not going to play that God game.*

Julienne told Peggy she was going to do her laundry. She carried her few clothes over to the wash area, put them into one of the cement basins with some soap, and started to swish them around and rub them together. Two Indian women stood near the other basin, watching her. After a few minutes, one of them came over to Julienne and reached for her wet clothes.

"Hey!" Julienne shouted. "What are you doing? Give me my clothes back!"

A tug of war ensued and caused a commotion.

"Why are you stealing my clothes?"

Peggy came over. "Let the woman take your clothes."

"What? Why?"

"She just wants to help, to earn some money."

Julienne released the clothes and watched as the woman used a bar of lye soap to scrub them, then beat them with a mallet.

"She's going to ruin them," Julienne complained.

"If you don't let these women do your laundry, you'll get a reputation as a selfish American. It's the only way they can get money for food and support their children."

Julienne cringed as she watched.

"They're hard workers," Peggy said. "If you let them work for you, it will help keep theft down."

"If I don't, they will steal from me?"

"They do what they feel they have to do. They see you as a rich American."

"Okay," she relented. "I'll do it for the children."

"And for yourself." Peggy grinned at her." Whether you realize it or not."

"Hey, we need to get some water buckets for you today. When water and power rations kick in, you'll want to be ready with your own supply. You can pay one of the women to carry the water up to the cell for you. They'll become your friends, willing to help whenever you need them. When the water gets shut off, it's miserable. And it happens quite often, not just in jail but all over the country. You need to have enough water to carry you over until the fire trucks come with water or until the rationing is over."

Julienne hired one of them to bring her two buckets of water, and then found two boards to place over the top of them to keep bugs and spiders out. The water was clear, so it seemed okay. She used the covered buckets as a small table to place some of her things on.

After a few weeks, she took the boards off to check the water.

"No!" Microorganisms floated in the water. *And I'm drinking this prison water!* She experimented with putting some water in a clear glass and after a few days, sure enough, it also had things growing in it.

Peggy said, "Get someone to bring you bottled water from outside."

Julienne did ask and pay a guard to get her a gallon of drinking water. The guard at the gate who inspected everything that came in, opened the gallon jug and drank out of it. He laughed and joked with the other guard.

*Really? You're drinking out of my jug of water? Gross. Now I have to worry about his germs.*

She learned that fresh drinking water was a treat for the guards too, so the next time she bought an extra gallon and gave one to the guard to keep. The water inspection and drinking out of her jug stopped as long as they got theirs. Or, if she gave them money. It made the water expensive, but it was worth it.

"You might as well learn to drink the prison water," Peggy said. "Because if you don't keep paying the guards or giving them free water, they have the authority to stop your visits with anyone who brings you things. It's their call."

Since she couldn't always get enough drinking water from the outside, Julienne asked her visitors from Helen's church group to bring her bleach or iodine pills to put in the prison water. She boiled it first, but had to pay for the propane to do that. *The bleach won't do any more damage than the water would do without it.*

Flies were another problem in the cells. To help keep them away, Julienne and Peggy filled plastic bags with water, tied them like a balloon, and hung them in two corners of the room. It seemed to help a little, although Julienne didn't understand why. After a few weeks, Julienne looked to see what was growing in the bags. She didn't want to waste bleach on the flies, so she changed the water in the bags every few weeks. Of course, she had to pay for the plastic bags too.

Day after day, Peggy told Julienne prison stories—who was who, and who to stay away from. She told of prison guards beating people caught trying to escape, inmate fights that ended with women getting badly cut, riots, searches and lockdowns.

"Then there's the government," she said. "When the current governor is overthrown, they replace the judges and the heads of the police and other agencies with their own people. That causes all kinds of chaos. Like, if you have a pending case, a new judge starts the process all over, which means major delays."

"How often does that happen?" Julienne asked, fearful.

"More often than you'd think. And then there are the strikes—taxi drivers, government employees, bus service, trash removal, all kinds of strikes." She went into details with some of the stories and horrified Julienne.

"Then you have the lawyers taking your money and making promises about what they're going to do and you never hear from them again. Even the judges are corrupt."

*Oh, great.*

She told one horrible story after another and Julienne would lie in bed at night, struggling between feeling terrified, to thinking that Peggy must be delusional and had exaggerated all those stories. Even the ones about rats. But then she'd wake up to the sound of creatures scurrying inside the dried clay walls, borrowing and searching for food scraps. She made a point of keeping their room as clean as possible.

Every day she observed new dramas. Pregnancies were common. Female inmates getting paid by outside visitors for sexual favors, weekend conjugal visits between prisoners, and female prisoners getting pregnant by the guards.

Fights would break out between lovers, male and female or two females.

Theft occurred on a regular basis, usually for drugs, which were prevalent in the jail. Women stole clothes off the clotheslines and sold them to support their drug habits. If someone was accused of stealing, they became indignant.

"I'm not here for stealing; I'm here for drugs! I'm not a thief!"

Prison culture considered a thief lower than a drug user.

Her mind was reeling with the insanity of it all. *I don't belong here.*

What she had seen up to this point would pale in comparison to what she was about to experience.

# CHAPTER 10

## Camp Inca
## Hunger Strike-Lips Sewn Shut

"Stay away from Lucia," Peggy warned Julienne on one of the visitor days.

"Why?" *She dresses nice and seems to have some class,* Julienne thought. "Her little girl is adorable with her blonde hair and green eyes."

"She's trouble. Haven't you noticed that a lot of the inmates strut around, hoping to pick a fight with her?"

"Maybe they're just jealous. She's pretty. She can't be that bad."

Ecuadorian, Lucia had long, dark hair which hung to her waist. She had brown eyes, light tanned skin and a shapely figure. She dressed stylishly compared to most.

"Rumors are that she's an informant for Interpol," Peggy cautioned. "If you associate with her, others will hate you for it. Be careful."

That night Peggy talked about a strike that was being planned and the rumblings through the prison about the "Two for One" law. "If it passes, the prisoners can be released when half their sentence is served. That means I could serve four years instead of eight."

In the morning, Julienne got up, dressed, made her bed and headed downstairs with a list of food items to buy from a small store one of the prisoner's ran. Downstairs, she noticed a crowd of people gathered in a room next to the little store.

*What's going on?* she wondered as she approached. Small groups of prisoners huddled around something on the floor. She moved closer and gasped at what she saw. On the ground, a prisoner was bound hand and foot to a life-size cross. Like Jesus, she had a crown on her head, this one a wreath made out of leaves instead of thorns. Her lips had been sewn shut with a fishhook and thread and the blood from her lips smeared across her forehead.

*Oh, my god! What are they doing? A crucifixion?*

Julienne stared at the woman on the cross. Her face was contorted in pain, but oddly she appeared to be cooperating. She looked around the room. Two other groups were doing the same thing. She felt her knees go weak and she could hardly stand. Trembling, she made her way back to the door and went looking for Peggy.

*This is an insane asylum! Where are the guards?*

She found Peggy in her shop listening to music like it was any normal day.

*There is nothing normal in here!* "Did you see what's going on over there?" Julienne asked, pointing.

"It's a hunger strike. It happens every year."

"A hunger strike? Are you kidding? They sewed their lips shut! Those women will have permanent scars!" She caught her breath. "And they're tying them to a cross like it's a crucifixion!" Her features contorted with shock and anger.

"They don't care about the scars. They just want to make a point, get some attention and be on television."

"Television?"

"The news crew will be coming. I'm sure someone got the word out."

"Where am I? I thought it was hell before, but this is off the charts!"

"Yeah, well, they get pretty dramatic and over the top here."

"There has to be a better way to carry out a hunger strike."

"They're doing it as a demonstration for the camera crew."

The prisoners in charge of the event rounded everybody up. An inmate from the Red Zone approached Julienne and Peggy. Her lips, face and arms were covered with scars.

"The TV reporters and crew are on the way. Come on." She motioned for them to follow her.

Julienne gave her a "you've got to be kidding" look.

Peggy whispered to Julienne. "Keep your mouth shut and follow her. It's mandatory."

*This is a freaking nightmare,* Julienne thought.

"If you don't cooperate, she'll hit you with a belt or a metal pipe."

Shock and anger lit up Julienne's eyes.

They joined the others in the breezeway area where visitors come in through the gate. Julienne and Peggy lined up on the cement benches against the walls with the other inmates. A few of the women came by with rolls of tape and began taping everyone's mouth shut.

Julienne flashed a fearful look at Peggy.

"Just go with it," Peggy said. "Be glad you're not having your lips sewn shut."

"Or that we're not being tied to a cross?"

"That, too."

The women on the crosses were dragged out to the breezeway and leaned against the wall. Blood still dripped from their lips. They were able to sit on the small platform nailed to each cross.

"It's amazing how there wasn't a guard in sight during all that," Julienne said.

"They know when to stay away. If the guards had interfered during the strike there would have been a riot. This hunger strike is a tradition here."

"So who's in charge? The prisoners? This is all so outrageous." *Dear god, get me out of this hellhole.*

"Right now, the prisoners have control, at least of the gate. They broke the original lock off the gate and put their own padlock on the inside and no one can come in until they take it off. They'll only do that when the news crew arrives."

The director of the prison came to the entrance gate, waving a letter in the air.

"This is from the director of National. The Two for One law is passed!" he shouted.

The news rippled through the crowd and the inmates cheered.

"Open the gate," one of the inmates called out.

They took the padlock off and the director walked inside. Lucia ran over and snatched the paper out of the director's hands.

"Wait a minute!" she shouted. "It's missing the notarized stamps from the Congress." She held it up for others to see. "And it's typed on El Inca letterhead." Lucia waved it back and forth in the air yelling, "It's a fake!" She glared at the director. "You think we are stupid and believe that lie! You just want to use this to end the strike and take back control of the jail!"

The inmates went crazy, shouting and pumping fists in the air.

"Let's show them we're serious," Lucia shouted. A few inmates ran with her to the offices just outside the gate and pulled the psychologist, the doctor and a paralegal inside the gate, along with the director of the jail.

"Lock the gate! Now they must pay for trying to trick us!" Lucia said.

*Oh, my god. Now what are they going to do?* Julienne backed up to the outer edge of the crowd. *This mob's completely out of control.*

Lucia pushed the director to the head guard's office, but it was too small for all of them to fit inside. "Move the filing cabinet out," she ordered the inmates. They dragged it out of the office into the breezeway area. Then they forced all of their captives inside the office.

*Now they've taken hostages?* Her heart was hammering, her breathing ragged.

The news crew arrived at the gate and the Red Zone girls unlocked it to allow them inside to film what was happening.

"Open the cabinet," Lucia said. "Our files are in there."

They broke the lock and began pulling out folders, one by one and reading them. "Esperanza!" Lucia shouted as she read the name on the folder.

Everyone grew silent. She pulled out the papers and held them up.

"Estos son papeles por mala conducta," she said. She tore up the papers and tossed them into the air.

Everyone clapped and screamed. "Destroy the Parts!"

"What are Parts?" Julienne asked Peggy.

"Bad conduct papers," she said. "They can extend the time you serve."

One by one they pulled the files, read the name on it, and silence fell for a brief moment. The papers were ripped and tossed into the wind. The roar of the crowd echoed throughout the prison and torn papers littered the floor.

The news media recorded it all. The hostage situation, the inmates on crosses with lips sewn shut, and the ruined files.

"They tried to fake us out with the letter about the Two for One law," one of the inmates said to a reporter. "Now the world will see that we're not stupid and we mean business."

When they had destroyed all the files, the inmates unlocked the gate again and escorted the news crew out, locking the gate behind them.

As soon as the reporters left, tear gas canisters lobbed in over the gate and over the cement walls of the prison. Everyone dispersed, coughing and sputtering, running to their cells.

Julienne and Peggy dashed up the stairwell to their room and locked their door.

"My eyes are burning and my head is pounding," Julienne said.

"Mine too," Peggy muttered.

Julienne looked out the barred window through her watering eyes. "Look!"

She and Peggy watched as military police scaled the prison walls with ropes, tossing more tear gas. They wore full black tactical gear, including face and head masks.

"It's like a swat team!" Julienne said.

The prisoners went into an uproar. They backed away from the window and crouched on their beds, covering their mouth and nose with a towel. Julienne saw one of the military scaling the wall outside their window. Her fear went into overdrive. A moment later, he pounded on their door. "Open up!"

Julienne slipped off the bed.

"Don't open the door!" Peggy said in a hoarse voice.

Julienne unlocked it and opened the door slowly. The military officer stood there in full tactical gear with tear gas in his hand, ready to toss it into their cell.

"American!" Julienne shouted. "I'm an American!"

He stood there for a moment, lowered the hand holding the tear gas, and held his index finger to his lips. "Shhhh!" he whispered, and pulled the door shut.

Julienne couldn't control the spasmodic trembling within her. She listened to the screaming and smelled the tear gas thrown into other rooms.

"Help me," Peggy said, trying not to choke on the gas filtering into the room from other cells.

Together, they stuffed towels under their door and hung a blanket over their open barred window to keep out as much of the tear gas odor as they could. The sound of coughing and cursing echoed through the prison.

"I'm so glad to be an American," Julienne said to Peggy.

"I think that's what saved us," Peggy agreed.

Her head was buzzing and her eyes stinging as she tossed and turned the rest of the night.

*I've got to get out of here! I'll call the Embassy and my Dad tomorrow. What's going on with the lawyer? I need to get out of this insane asylum before I lose my mind.*

CHAPTER 11

## Camp Inca
## Smells Like Urine, Cigarettes and Alcohol

THE NEXT MORNING the rumors flew.

"Lucia was placed in solitary confinement and is being transferred today," Peggy said.

"Where to?"

"No one knows for sure. Probably Guayaquil."

"Where's that?"

"It's south of here, the worst prison in Ecuador."

"Worse than this?" *What can be worse than this?*

"They're calling her a revolutionary."

Because of the chaos of the strike, the Ecuadorian courier from the Embassy stopped by to check on Julienne. They called her down to the office for a short meeting.

"I saw the news coverage of the strike and the chaos that followed," he said. "Are you okay?"

"I guess so. It was such insanity."

"It really is," he said. "And it really doesn't accomplish much, except, they get media coverage."

"I need to get out of here before I lose my mind," Julienne said. "Can you please call my dad and let him know I'm okay? In case he heard about the strike. I don't think they're allowing us to use the phones today."

"Of course. I'll call as soon as I get back to the Embassy." He reached for an envelope in his pocket. "I have some money for you from your dad."

"Thank you."

"And I brought you three canisters of Sustagin nutritional powder in vanilla and chocolate. The embassy provides this for all the American prisoners. I can bring them to you every three months. That way I can check on you to see how you're doing." He smiled at her.

"Well, that's really nice of you. I'll look forward to your visits."

Back in her room, Julienne looked around to find a place to keep the money. *Maybe I can hollow out some pages in a book and put it in there.*

"What are you looking for?" Peggy asked.

"My dad sent me some money through the Embassy and I'm looking for a safe place to keep it. Like maybe rip out some pages of a book and put it in there."

"You can. I've done that. But if they have a rakeesa they might find it."

"What's a rakeesa?"

"A raid by the police, looking for drugs, alcohol or other contraband. They tear the place apart when they come."

"Great."

"Climb up on your bunk and I'll show you what to do."

Julienne climbed up. Her bunk was very close to the ceiling.

"Unscrew the light fixture," she said, handing her a screwdriver. "There's enough room inside and no one thinks of looking there."

Julienne counted the money, put most of it in a small bag, and stuffed it in the space around the fixture. *This should be enough to pay my fee for the pavilion, and buy some food and supplies.*

Peggy left to check on her hair salon, but Julienne decided to stay in their room for the day with the door locked. She wasn't quite over the trauma from the day before and didn't want to be in the middle of any controversy in the aftermath. She lay on her bunk and felt a panic attack coming on.

*Get a grip,* she told herself. She took a deep breath and let it out. *Dad used to tell me that you can't always control what happens to you, but you can control how you respond to it. Don't dwell on it. Focus on something else.*

Her thoughts went back to her childhood in California. Her parents bought a home that needed repairs and they lived there while they remodeled it. Her dad did the repairs; her mom, an interior decorator, made it charming. Then they would sell the house and buy another to remodel and decorate. She attended twenty-one schools in the thirteen years her parents bought and sold houses.

She loved to ice skate and her mother took her to the ice rinks every spare moment they had. Her dad often took her to amusement parks or they spent a day at the beach.

*I always felt loved and secure.* All their moves taught her to reach out and make friends quickly, like her dad did. He was outgoing and no one was a stranger to him for long. *I can still hear him telling me, 'Julienne, there's nothing you can't accomplish if you put your mind to it.'*

"Julienne!" Peggy's voice pulled her out of her thoughts. "I just heard that Joan is back."

"Joan?"

"The God-woman. Joan."

"Oh."

"She's downstairs in the classroom. I guess she just got back from the States."

"You want me to meet her?"

"Yeah, I think you two might hit it off, like mother and daughter."

*I don't know about that, but at least it's a diversion.*

Julienne went down to the classroom where Joan was meeting with some of the other inmates. She watched from the doorway while Joan handed out clothes and other items. *That's nice of her.* As they left, Julienne stepped inside.

"Hello," Joan said in a cheerful voice. "We haven't met before." She reached out to shake hands. "The girls told me there was a new American here."

"I'm Julienne."

"It's nice to meet you, Julienne. Come sit and tell me a little about yourself."

Julienne told her about her vacation in Miami and how she ended up in Ecuador with a drug trafficking charge. "I'm innocent," she said. "Definitely naive and too trusting, but definitely innocent."

"I imagine this is a difficult time for you."

"Difficult? It's a nightmare."

"Maybe I can be of some help. We have a church service here on Sundays. Sometimes Helen Brouch teaches and sometimes I teach. We share the Bible and faith in Jesus."

"I really don't have any interest in that."

"Do you believe in God?"

"I believe there is something out there— matter, energy, something that controls the universe, but I don't put a name or a face to it. It's a mass of something that no one can explain."

"I hope at some point you will come to know that God loves you," Joan said.

"I really don't want to talk about God," Julienne responded.

"That's fine," Joan said, her tone still pleasant. "I won't bother you about it again." She stood. "It was great meeting you, Julienne. I'll come and visit from time to time, along with the other English-speaking girls. We can talk about whatever you like." She shook hands again and asked, "Is that okay?"

"Yes, of course. I'd like that," Julienne said.

. Joan left and Julienne went back to her room. *I'm so glad she didn't try to pressure me into believing what she believes. Besides, if God loves me, why am I here in this hellhole?*

She lay on her bed again, looking out the barred window at another prison pavilion across the way. *A far cry from the sun and surf of California beaches.* Her thoughts wandered to her life there. Her parents had separated and Julienne stayed with her mother, while her dad moved east to Tennessee. Her mother searched for something spiritual to fill the void in her life. She'd found Calvary Chapel Church and Julienne had enjoyed attending with her. She met other young teens there and got involved with their church and social activities.

At age thirteen, she went to a youth retreat at Twin Peaks by Arrowhead, California. That week had been a turning point in her life. *I felt so peaceful there,* she remembered. At the end of the retreat, she'd dedicated her life to God and later baptized in Corona Del Mar. A scenic hill overlooking Newport Harbor Bay led down to the cove. She remembered climbing over the rocky bluffs down to the ocean where the baptisms were held. Hundreds of people from all walks of life came to be baptized, while thousands watched.

As Julienne's turn came and she walked waist deep into the bay water, Pastor Chuck Smith asked her if she understood the meaning of what she was doing, dedicating her life to Jesus.

"Yes, I do," she'd said. He prayed with her and submerged her beneath the cool ocean water. When she came up, she felt a new life was ahead of her. Pastor Chuck gave her a hug, then welcomed her mother to be next.

Bonfires lit up the beach for as far as she could see. People roasted hotdogs and marshmallows. Others strummed guitars, singing some of the songs Julienne had learned at teen camp. She thought the joy she felt that day would last forever.

She looked around her. *No joy here.*

On Sunday, the next visit day, Julienne watched from a bench as many of the women came downstairs all dressed up with makeup on. Visitors lined up an hour before the gate was scheduled to open. The guards allowed ten people at a time through. One by one, the guards confiscated each visitor's ID and checked through any personal items or gifts they had with them. The individual guards had the authority to decide what would come in and what wouldn't. Some visitors paid a bribe to get items in, but if you attempted to bribe a guard who didn't accept bribes, you risked losing your visit, your money and anything else you had on you.

The local visits consisted mainly of friends or family members coming in, or single men looking to score with one of the inmates. Some brought in a bag of fresh fruit and there were always some inmates who would go for it, inviting them to their rooms. Julienne heard that it wasn't just fruit in those bags; drugs were hidden in the fruit. The men would strut around afterwards because they'd gotten what they came for. Some of the women got pregnant though free birth control was offered in the prison doctor's office. Many inmates simply didn't want to wait in a long line to get it.

*So, okay, get pregnant instead. No waiting in line. Brilliant. Or risk getting a sexual transmitted disease. Awesome. Don't they even think about it before they get involved?*

Other visitors came to be with their lesbian girlfriends who also had lesbian relationships with other inmates.

Julienne always dressed up on visitor days, just in case someone came to see her. Some visitors came in from different church groups. If they asked about any English-speaking prisoners, the guards usually directed them to Julienne. There were a few others, but Julienne stood out as the blonde American who didn't speak Spanish, the California girl. They brought her food and toiletries. If they asked her what she would like them to bring the next time, she asked for books or magazines. There was a small library at the jail, but most books were in Spanish, some in English.

Julienne preferred reading in her room, rather than socializing with the other inmates. Most of them smoked and the pavilions and rooms reeked of smoke. Julienne despised the smell. She was relieved that Peggy rarely smoked. When she did, it was because she was stressed. Whenever anyone lit up a cigarette around her, Julienne walked away. There were no rules about lights out or smoking, so the odor was there night and day. Other than the smell, there were no remnants of cigarettes because the women had to sweep and wash down the cement floors every night. Inmates were assigned to do this, but they could pay someone to take their place. Julienne didn't mind paying someone to do it because the place was nasty by the end of each day. The prison smelled like urine, cigarettes and alcohol. *Everything is backwards here. I would think they would call me a selfish American if I didn't help scrub the place down. But I'm only considered selfish when I do help and I don't pay someone to take my place.*

What bothered Julienne as much as the stench, were the rats. She was about to discover that most inmates were not ready or willing to take on the rat problem.

## CHAPTER 12

# Camp Inca
# Kill the Rats Campaign

ON ONE VISIT day, Julienne noticed a little boy trying to catch and play with one of the many rats that came into the prison through cracks in the cement. Horrified, she ran over to him.

"No! No! Ratas! Dangerous!" She pulled him away.

A guard came over when she noticed the tug of war.

"Don't worry about it. He's fine."

"But he might get bit!"

The guard shook her head and dismissed it, motioning for Julienne to move on.

*Don't they realize that rats carry disease?*

Another time she saw a visitor sitting on a bench, visiting an inmate, when the visitor let out a scream.

"Rato!" Blood ran down her leg from the bite.

"A rat just bit her!" Julienne yelled. "She needs help!"

The guard came over to see what the problem was.

"Ratta!" she shouted.

The guard shrugged it off like it was no big deal.

"She needs to see a doctor!"

The prisoner took her visitor to her room and put some ointment on the bite and covered it with tape.

*Don't they realize how dangerous this is? That woman needs a tetanus shot.* She looked around and realized she was the only one freaking out.

Later, she talked to Peggy about it.

"I've seen little kids, about 3 years old, with wounds from rat bites," she said. "The children don't seem to be afraid of them. It's almost like they're pets."

"They've been around and invading this place for so long that it's become a normal part of prison life," Peggy said.

"It's not normal!"

"To some it is. Have you heard about the inmate who walks around with a rat on one shoulder and a pigeon on the other? She keeps them in her room."

"How could those two different animals co-exist?"

"She has a little bracelet around a leg on each one. I asked her where she got the pigeon and she said it flew into her window, so she kept it."

"That's just weird," Julienne said.

"Some of the inmates threaten to eat her pigeon and she gets into big fights with them over comments like that."

"That's mean," Julienne said. "Back to the rat problem. Has anyone ever died from a rat bite in here?"

"Not as far as I know. Some have gotten really sick though."

"I saw a lot of rats today," Julienne said.

"It's because it's visit day and there's more food around to attract them."

"Is there any way to get rid of them?"

"Well, I've tried going to the director, but he keeps putting me off and does nothing," Peggy said.

"My dad always taught me that you can either complain about it, or you can do something about it. What can we do about it? How do they come in?"

"They eat through the cement from the outside and make holes in the walls and the floor. They come from underground sewage I think."

Julienne shuddered. "Gross! How about if I go to the director and tell him that people are being bitten more and more. It's worth a try."

Julienne did meet with him the next day and reported back to Peggy.

"He said he wouldn't allow the use of poison, but if we could figure something else out, to go ahead and do it."

Over the next few days, they discussed a variety of ideas.

"Well, we can't shoot them because they don't allow us to have guns," Peggy said.

"And they won't let us poison them," Julienne added.

They sat and thought about it for a while.

"What if we took broken glass and mixed it with cement, then used that to fill in all the rat holes? When they eat through the cement, the crushed glass will get into their bodies and they'll die," Peggy suggested.

"That's a great idea," Julienne said. "I think we're on to something." Then her smile changed to a frown.

"What?"

"Where are we going to get glass? And cement?"

"We already have glass," Peggy said. "There are coke bottles and all kinds of glass bottles in the trash. We'll start a glass pile and instead of tossing glass into the trash, we'll ask the women to smash it and throw it into the pile."

"Let's do it! But what about the cement?"

"We'll ask visitors to bring it in for us."

"We can do that? "

"Why not? We've been given permission to try to do something about the rats. If the visitors or the guards question it, we'll just tell them the director gave us permission."

"I'll ask the Browns, the missionaries, church people and whoever else comes to visit to help us."

They got approval for a designated area to use for the glass pile and created a sign for it.

"Break your glass items and toss them into this pile." The word spread through the prison about what they were doing. The inmates loved smashing glass bottles for the pile and it grew quickly.

Julienne started her requests to visitors.

"Can you bring me a bag of cement?"

"What?" one church lady said. "Cement?"

"Yes, it's to help get rid of the rats." She explained what they planned to do and the lady was happy to oblige. The rat problem was no secret.

"You have someone waiting for you outside the gate," the guard said.

Calls to the front gate were becoming frequent.

The director heard rumors and asked Julienne, "What's going on? What are all these things waiting for you outside?"

"Outside? Oh, probably cement."

"Cement? For what?"

"When I talked to you about the rat problem, you told us to figure it out ourselves. So we did."

"And?" The director waited to hear more.

*Maybe we should have asked permission for all this*, Julienne thought. *But he probably would have turned us down. Sometimes it's just better to do it.*

Julienne explained to him what they were doing, mixing cement with broken glass.

"We already have a big pile of it."

"Glass? You have broken glass?"

"Yes, come see it," Julienne said.

The director looked at the three-foot-high pile of smashed shards of glass and read the sign next to it.

"Don't worry, we'll clean it up when we're done. We're calling it 'Save the jail from rats campaign.' Everyone's excited about it. More people are being bitten so we have to do something. We think this will work and we're not using poison." *I hope he's convinced.*

He walked away, shaking his head.

*I think that means we have his approval.*

The inmates started to have fun with it. They would gather up as much glass as they could find, would stand around the pile, and smashed the glass to pieces, laughing and whooping as they did it.

"They've made a game out of it," Julienne said to Peggy. "I think it's helping them to get rid of some of their frustrations."

"And the more they do it, the less work we'll have to do ourselves."

## Surviving Camp Inca

Fifty bags of cement ultimately came in from the outside. Julienne went to every cell in their pavilion and told the inmates of their plan. Peggy went along to translate. Everyone was excited about it.

"We need ten volunteers to help us," Julienne said. "Peggy and I can't do it alone. We need to mix the glass and the cement and then fill the holes with it."

Ten women volunteered. Julienne and Peggy made up a schedule with a time for each volunteer to work. They used wooden cooking mallets to smash the glass into tiny shards and water from the washbasins and, bucket by bucket, they mixed the cement.

"This is hard work," Peggy said as she stirred the mixture and carried it over to fill a hole. It's heavy."

"The holes are bigger than I realized," Julienne said. "I thought it would be like spackling cracks in a wall."

They packed four cups of the cement mixture at a time into a hole and then had to wait overnight for it to dry and harden before putting more on top of that.

"What happened to all our volunteers?" Julienne asked.

"A few said they would help tomorrow, but don't count on it," Peggy said.

"So much for making up a schedule for them to follow."

As she crawled into bed that night, Peggy said "I sure hope this works. My back is aching and my arms are sore."

"Well, you'll just have to butch up!" Julienne chuckled.

They spent the next few weeks mixing and stirring and filling. Only a few volunteers showed up to help.

"Look!" Peggy said a few days after they finished. "A dead rat! It's working!"

Dead rats showed up everywhere. Inmates picked them up and tossed them into big barrels used for garbage disposal.

Julienne and Peggy congratulated themselves on a successful project.

"How many dead rats did you pick up?" Peggy asked her.

"Are you kidding? I'm not touching them. I just wanted to kill them. My job is done."

"Did you see where they were tossing the rats?"

"Yeah, some in the dumpster and some in the garbage barrels."

"Do you realize those are special barrels for farmers who come from the outside and use the garbage in them to feed their pigs and livestock?"

"Oh my god," Julienne said. "You mean those glass-filled rats will be eaten by other animals?" She made a horrified face. "What have we done!"

"I don't know," Peggy said, "but we better not say anything about it."

They remained silent for a few minutes.

"Make sure you don't eat any pork," Peggy said. "You might be spitting out glass." She broke into a big grin.

"Gross!"

# CHAPTER 13

## Camp Inca
## Ramie Escapes

"De Lista!" A guard shouted standing just outside Julienne's doorway one morning.

Startled from a deep sleep, Julienne sprang off of her top bunk and tumbled to the floor. Her ankle snapped and she crouched in pain in a fetal position. Within seconds her ankle swelled to the size of an orange.

"Owww!" she yelled. Doubled over in pain, she groaned.

The guard looked down at her ankle and motioned for her to stand.

"I can't stand!" she yelled at her. "I need a doctor! Now!" She moaned and rocked back and forth.

One of the male guards came and carried Julienne to the doctor's office located outside the first gate. Her ankle continued to throb and she wondered if she had broken it.

"I need an x-ray to see if it's broken," she said to the doctor. "How am I going to get that done?" She knew the prison had no major medical equipment, only the basics.

He checked her foot and ankle and agreed that she needed an x-ray. He issued a permission slip for her to go to the emergency room at the hospital.

"Do you have money to pay for this?" he asked.

"Yes, I do."

"Okay, I'll make arrangements."

"Thank you."

He busied himself with other work and was in and out of the office. Julienne sat and waited and waited. The throbbing pain increased. She tried to control her tears. Hours passed and still the paperwork had not been processed. *How difficult can it be to get this handled? What is wrong with these people? If I do have a broken bone, shouldn't it be set right away?*

At four o'clock, the doctor came in. "Nothing ever gets done after four o'clock, so I'll have a guard help you back up to your room so you can rest."

*So I can rest? Why didn't they let me do that hours ago instead of making me sit here?*

Back in her room, the pain increased and kept her from sleeping. The signed orders came through the next day at ten in the morning and a different guard came for her.

"Let's go." He helped her down the stairs, through the gates and out to the curbside where he hailed a taxi.

As they settled in, Julienne realized she hadn't been in a cab or outside of the prison for quite a while. It felt strange. *The guard looks like he's seventy years old, and it's just the two of us. If I wasn't in so much pain and I could walk, I bet I could escape.*

When they arrived at the hospital, most of the staff were on strike and picketing outside.

*Being on strike is like an Ecuadorian pastime.*

The guard helped Julienne out of the taxi, but didn't attempt to help her walk into the hospital. She hopped on one foot from the curb toward the hospital entrance, trying to keep her balance. Some of the picketing staff stared at her.

She wore jeans with a patchwork of the American flag down the side of one pant leg. *I guess it's obvious that I'm an American prisoner, with the guard walking alongside me.*

She managed to hop through the entrance and plop into a chair. When she looked down at her swollen ankle, she realized she only had on one tennis shoe. *I doubt I'll be able to fit into a shoe for at least a few days, so it doesn't really matter.* The throbbing continued while she waited another hour before a male nurse came.

He helped her into a wheelchair. "We're going to take some x-rays." He told the guard to wait there.

"But I can't do that," he said. "She's a prisoner and I'm responsible for her."

"Okay, you can come, but you'll have to wait outside the room."

Once in the room, Julienne glanced around, looking for a way out. *Not even a window and only one entrance—the way I came in. What am I thinking? I can't even walk.*

After the x-rays, the nurse wheeled her down the hallway into another room.

"The doctor will see you in a few minutes."

Julienne looked around and realized she was in an operating room. *Do they think I need surgery?* Three other patients lay on gurneys in each corner of the large white room. No partitions or curtains provided any privacy. Everything was out in the open.

One patient was getting a dislocated arm reset. Another was in labor. Across the room, a young boy who had been in a car accident lay motionless. The limited staff worked frantically on him. Blood and soaked through his clothes and splattered on the floor. *I hope he makes it. I almost feel guilty taking up space next to people in life and death situations.*

A doctor who appeared to be from India made his way over to Julienne.

"You are very lucky," he said.

"You speak English!"

"Yes, I do. You're lucky you only have four hairline fractures. No broken bones." He examined her foot, checked the x-rays again, and gave her a shot for pain. He scribbled on a pad and handed the paper to her. "Here's a prescription for antibiotics." He smiled and said, "You're good to go."

"Thank you."

They stopped at the hospital's financial office and Julienne paid her bill. Her guard wheeled her outside and helped her out of the wheelchair. She leaned against a street lamp. With the crowd picketing, it was difficult for the taxi to pull up right in front of the hospital.

While the guard returned the wheelchair, Julienne began daydreaming as to how she could possibly hop across the street, catch a taxi and be gone before the guard returned. *I doubt he has any money on him, so he wouldn't be able to chase me in another cab. I bet I could make it to Columbia before he could walk back to the jail.*

The guard returned and she giggled.

"Are you okay?" he asked.

She grinned and nodded. *It must be the painkiller taking effect. What was I thinking?*

Back at the prison, Julienne paid the guard for taking her to the hospital and Peggy helped her back to their room.

"No more acrobatics off that top bunk," Peggy said with a grin.

"At least I got out of here for a little while."

She settled on her bed with her foot propped up. "The sad thing is the lack of medical care for those who can't afford it. It seems to be difficult to even get a proper diagnosis in here."

"That reminds me," Peggy said. "I have something for you. I've had it for a while, but haven't used it." She rummaged around and pulled out a thick medical book, *Where There Are No Doctors.*

"A Village Healthcare Handbook," Julienne read and started flipping through the pages. "This is great; it gives a diagnosis according to the detailed symptoms you have."

"Hey, maybe you can become our resident diagnostician."

"You know, I used to watch this medical show on cable TV in California. They filmed all kinds of surgeries that you could watch and learn from. It was a bit bloody at times, but I loved it."

"Well, there you go. Enjoy. You should stay off that foot for a few days anyway."

Julienne grinned at her. "Yes, doctor."

## Surviving Camp Inca

Over the next month, inmates in their pavilion started to come to Julienne and ask her to look up various symptoms they had. If it seemed remotely serious, they would go see the doctor and try to get a prescription. *I hope they're not using me to get drugs!*

Julienne's dad called every week, updating her on calls he was making to government officials in the States, asking for help. A few attorneys he contacted in Ecuador took his money, but did nothing.

"Corruption seems to be the norm there," he said. "All kinds of promises to investigate or a court date, but once you pay them, the whole process stops, or slows to a crawl." He blew out a deep breath. "We'll just keep at it. Listen, I got you a calling card number for the phone. I don't dare send the card or even get it to you through the Browns because other inmates may steal it. You need to memorize the number. That way, you won't need to keep dropping cash in the phone when we talk."

"Thanks, Dad, for all you're doing for me." She choked back a cry. "It's so scary and depressing here. Your phone calls keep me sane."

"I love you, Julie. Like I've said before, we'll get through this." A short silence fell between them as they regained their composure. "Oh, by the way, your friend Joanna called me. She was worried about you. I told her what happened."

"Can I use the card to call her?"

"Of course." He gave her the card number. "Use it however you want, for local or international calls."

"Thanks for the money you've been sending me, Dad. I couldn't have gone to the hospital for x-rays without money."

"You just ask when you need something, Julie. Hang in there. We're doing our best to get you out."

Julienne used the card right away to call Joanna in California. They had met right out of high school and remained good friends. Julienne filled her in on all that was going on and the horrible condition of the prison with the rats and spiders and the disgusting food and water and inmates fighting and some being raped.

"It's third world country mentality. No real freedom or rights like we're used to. Bribery and corruption are rampant."

"That's terrible!" Joanna said.

"Are Dexter and Sidney okay? Are they being fed?"

"I fed them for a week, but then I thought you came home on the 10th as planned. When I hadn't heard from you by the 15th, I went over to your apartment and discovered you weren't home yet. I was really worried and called your dad."

"And the cats?"

"The apartment was a mess. The cats ran out of food and tore the place up. Their hair was all matted and they were freaking out."

"Oh no! My poor cats! Where are they now?"

"I found a good home for them once I heard from your dad what happened to you. Don't worry about them. They're fine."

They talked for about ten minutes and then Joanna asked, "What can I do for you? Can I send you something? Can you get mail and packages there?"

"Yes, I can. Everything is opened and inspected, of course. You know what I would love to have? Some music and a Walkman. I really miss listening to music. You know the songs I like."

"I'll do that," she said.

"Send it through the Embassy; I think that would be safer."

"Okay, I'll get the address and send you some things."

"Thanks, Joanna. I miss you. I feel so alone and isolated here."

"I'm sorry you have to go through this. It's so unbelievable and crazy."

Julienne started to mingle with inmates a little more on her own. She really didn't want to build many social relationships because she still felt she would be released as soon as she managed to see a judge. She also knew that it was important for her to try to fit in, so she tried.

One night at dinner time, Julienne walked over to the Red Zone pavilion. She'd heard about an inmate there who made and sold delicious potato, eggs and spinach pie. She cooked it in a heavy skillet like a giant pie and sold it by the slice. Julienne planned to buy five slices and bring them back to share with Peggy and a few others in their pavilion.

As she left with the pie, Julienne saw Ramie sitting on the floor of the Red Zone. She had seen her a few times before and spoke briefly with her. Ramie knew how to speak a tiny bit of English.

As Julienne approached her, she said, "Hi, Ramie. How are you doing?"

Ramie got up on her knees and put her hands up near her face, like a dog with paws. She panted like a dog and started swinging her head back and forth.

A bit nervous, Julienne played along and patted her head like she would a puppy's.

"What pretty hair you have."

Ramie continued to swing her head back and forth, panting.

"Are you okay?"

She barked and nodded, and continued panting like a dog.

"Okay... I have to go now."

Ramie growled at her and snapped her teeth a few times.

Julienne hurried past her. *She is losing it.* She left Red Zone and walked to her Mida Flores pavilion just before the guards closed and locked the gate for the night.

*That was so weird.* She told Peggy about it.

"Maybe she was begging for a piece of this pie," Peggy said. "It sure tastes good."

"I don't think that was it. Maybe she's having a mental breakdown," she said as she brushed flies away from her slice of pie.

The next morning after roll call, the women sensed that something was going on. Guards were scurrying around the prison and a rumor was circulating that someone had escaped.

At nine o'clock, the guards ordered everyone back to their cells. They walked around the prison with a bullhorn, calling for Ramie. "You have a phone call," they said.

"Ramie escaped!" someone shouted.

*Ramie escaped?*

"One of the other inmates told me this morning that Ramie has been acting strange for the last couple of days," Peggy said.

"I certainly got a taste of that," Julienne said. "She acted like an animal. She really was losing it."

"Or it was all an act, a cover up for a planned escape?"

By noon, the inmates were restless from being cooped up all morning and the guards looked frazzled. They unlocked the cell doors and went around interviewing anyone who knew Ramie and lived in the Red Zone pavilion with her.

All kinds of stories about Ramie acting strange surfaced as the inmates gathered in small groups to talk about it. They offered their theories back and forth.

"When the guards went to her cell, a bar was missing from her window. Sawed off. She must have squeezed through and escaped."

"Was she skinny enough to crawl though that narrow space?" Julienne asked.

"And then she would have had to get past the pavilion gate, climb up on the roof, then somehow slide down the outside wall," another said. "And have someone out front waiting for her."

"And she'd have to get past the guards at each spot," one of the inmates said.

"Unless she waited for the shift change and maybe wasn't noticed," another offered.

"She wasn't the Rambo type," Julienne said to Peggy. She also wasn't in great physical shape."

"Maybe she sawed the bar to make it look like she got out that way," Peggy said. "To keep the focus of the investigation off of the guards. Someone said if you could come up with $20,000, you could bribe a guard to sneak you out in the middle of the night."

"We'll probably never know the truth. We just know she's gone," Julienne said. "Lucky girl."

Over the next weeks security tightened and guards questioned the women in the Red Zone and some of the other inmates. They asked if they'd heard anything about the escape. Everyone said "no."

Julienne thought about it a lot. *I guess she wanted it badly enough that she didn't let fear stand in her way. If I can't get my day in court, and prove my innocence, escape might be my only option.*

# CHAPTER 14

## Camp Inca Queen Contest

"I FINALLY HAVE some good news!" Julienne said to Peggy.

"About your case?"

"No. Nothing on that yet. But my Dad and stepmom are coming for a visit in a few weeks. I can't wait to see them."

"That's great. How long can they stay?"

"A week. The Browns arranged for them to stay at a missionary house about thirty minutes from here. There's a vacancy that week. It's used for visiting missionaries or Americans who come to visit a family member in prison. They'll even have a driver for their protection so they won't have to use local taxis.

"And the Browns arranged through the Embassy that they can visit every day while they're here, not just on regular visit days." She exhaled a long sigh of excitement. "My dad asked me what he could bring me."

"Let me guess. You asked for a one-way ticket home?"

"That would be perfect," Julienne said. "I hope they can make some progress on my case while here. Maybe even get me out."

"Don't count on it," Peggy said. "Justice moves slowly here. Sometimes it doesn't move at all."

"But I'm innocent!"

"Okay, I believe you," Peggy said. "I'm just sayin' don't get your hopes up." She changed the subject. "So you asked for…"

"A massage therapy book and oils."

"You know how to do massage therapy?"

"I took a course in California and at one point planned to become a massage therapist."

"And did you?"

"I'm not licensed. The school offered free massages so we could practice and a lot of old men used to come in. A creepy old Middle-Eastern man came in one day smelling like he'd showered in cheap cologne and hit on me. It was disgusting. I decided if that's what I would have to deal with, I didn't want to do it."

"So why do you want the book?"

"Just in case justice moves slowly," she said sarcastically, "maybe I can do something with it here. I see you with your hair salon and other inmates doing business. I don't know, maybe I could do some massage therapy to pass the time and make a little money."

"Okay, you go for it, girl."

"Oh yeah, and my Dad is bringing me a VCR so we can watch some movies." She heaved a sigh. "Anything to get our mind off all this," she said, waving her arm around their room.

The prison was abuzz about the upcoming Queen Contest. The Day of the Recluse, Day of the Prisoner, was a fiesta that El Inca celebrated every year, rain or shine. National police, guards, politicians, the media and other visitors all came to the jail for the event.

"The inmates in charge of the Queen Contest want to talk to you," Peggy said. "Come with me. They're having a meeting."

"I don't get it," Julienne said. What's the purpose? Just so the men can gawk at the female prisoners? I don't want to be part of it."

"They're making plans, lining up the contestants and want you to represent the States."

She sighed in frustration. "It's like playing into the hands of the officials and the media, giving the impression that this place isn't the hellhole it is."

"I understand all that," Peggy said, but this is a tradition. You have to do this. If you don't, the women and the officials will label you defiant and rebellious."

"It's crazy. I don't want to do it," Julienne said stubbornly.

"You'll have a really tough time here if you go against the grain," Peggy warned.

"So I've got to play their game, their way. Is that what you're telling me?"

"Pretty much. Didn't you tell me you did some modeling back in the day?"

"Yes, so now I'm going to further my career by being a model in jail?"

"Come on, just have fun with it."

Once Julienne realized she had no choice, she agreed.

Downstairs, the seamstress inmate took Julienne's measurements. "I'm going to make two dresses for you."

Over the next few weeks the other models were chosen, the seamstress made or altered dresses; a stage and catwalk were built a few feet off the ground.

"Julienne!" an inmate shouted from downstairs.

Julienne came out of her room. "What?"

"You need to come and try on your clothes."

"Already? It's only been two weeks." She felt just a twinge of excitement looking forward to what the seamstress had come up with. *It will be nice to wear something stylish for a change. Even if it's just for a few hours.*

The first was a red, two-piece with a short, straight skirt and a double-breasted scalloped jacket with gold buttons. The second was a black and white taffeta party dress. They fit perfectly. *I'm impressed.*

"You did a great job," she complimented the seamstress.

"You look beautiful!" Peggy said. "With your long blonde, curly hair, you could be a winner."

"What's the prize? A get-out-of-jail-free card?"

The prison buzzed with excitement anticipating the big day. The inmate contestants experimented with makeup and Peggy was busy creating hairstyles at her shop. The morning of the pageant, Julienne was in her room, putting on her makeup. She glanced out her cell window and saw all the activity out in the gauncha. A disk jockey was setting up sound equipment on the stage, the catwalk was covered in green carpet and white paper flowers were glued along the sides. A white tent had been erected with chairs for the VIP section.

*If it rains, the diplomats and officials will stay dry, but not the rest of us. Figures.*

"Julienne! Julienne!" An inmate called from below.

Julienne went downstairs and the woman started pulling her by the arm. "Sígueme."

"Okay, what's going on?"

The inmate pulled her toward the entrance gate. "Visitantes," she said.

"Today? With all this going on, I have visitors?"

She looked ahead and saw her father and stepmom standing there, waiting.

"Dad!" She ran to him and leapt into his arms, crying. "I can't believe you're really here!" She clung to him, not wanting to let go.

The inmate poked at her arm.

"What?" Julienne managed to ask.

She held out her hand to be paid and pointed to Julienne's father.

The guard standing there with them said, "Pay the girl."

"Oh, dad, I'm sorry. The runners who announce visitors get paid."

"I'll take care of it," Kate, her stepmom said. "How much?"

"Do you have sucres?" Julienne asked.

"Yes."

"Just give her a few coins. It's crazy in here today," Julienne said, still clinging to her Dad's arm. "They're having a Queen Contest. It's an annual tradition."

"A queen contest?" In jail?"

"Yes, it's crazy. And I'm one of the contestants."

"Is that why you have all that makeup on?"

"Yes, and I have to dress in a few minutes." She glanced around. A lot of people were arriving and sitting in the VIP section. They even had food and liquor set out on a special table for them.

"I'll explain the details later. Let's find a place for you to sit."

As they walked over to the chairs, several children gathered around her parents. "Chicklets!" they called, holding out small boxes of them in their hands.

"Pulseras!" another one shouted, showing a series of homemade bracelets on her arm.

"They're like little walking stores," Kate said. She bought one of the bracelets and the children moved on to another visitor.

"I'll take pictures of the contest," Kate said.

"The guards let you take a camera in?" Julienne was surprised. "Usually they confiscate things like that and hold them in the office until you leave." She glanced around.

"They didn't search us," Kate said. "Maybe because Helen and Gene Brown walked us in?"

Julienne looked around. "I don't see them. Where are they?"

"They were off talking to someone. I don't think they realized all this was going on today."

"They have a lot of freedom to come and go here, because of their work with the Peace Corp. The officials respect them."

"There they are," Julienne's father said, motioning for them to join them.

Once they said their hellos, they sat together while Julienne went to dress for the pageant.

The competition began and the audience clapped and cheered as each contestant was introduced, their outfit described, and they walked down the runway.

Julienne forced a smile when her turn came. *I'm so glad my parents came, but did it have to be during this? Even they might not realize what things are really like in here. This is all so phony. I have to smile and act as if everything is fine.*

The Director of National and his entourage clapped as she passed by. Some whistled. The female inmates had their own favorites and cheered for them. One Ecuadorian inmate flirted with the judges as she swished and swayed past them. Her lips pouted, her eye lashes fluttered and she swung her hips. When it was over, the five government officials who served as judges chose her as the winner.

*Surprise, surprise. It's all a big game. One I don't want to play.*

"You look so pretty," Julienne's father said when the contest was over. He gave her a hug.

"I managed to sneak a few pictures," Kate said, tapping her pocket.

Because of the length of the pageant, there wasn't much time for visiting afterwards. Everyone was asked to leave so that everything could be torn down and put away.

"We have permission to come every day this week," her father said. "We'll be back tomorrow and will bring you some food and other things."

"In the morning we're going to visit the Embassy about your case," Kate said. "We'll come here right after that."

"I'm still hoping maybe I can go home with you this week," Julienne said. "Even though Peggy told me not to count on it."

"Peggy?"

"My roommate. You'll meet her tomorrow. She was busy fixing hair for the women today." Julienne thanked Helen and Gene for taking care of her parents and then she said a tearful good-bye.

When they came back the next day, Julienne invited them up to see her room.

"We can go to your cell?" Kate asked.

"Yes, the director of the jail said it was okay. Maybe because you're Americans. Or just because you're family and traveled so far to visit."

They followed her up to her room and met Peggy. After brief introductions, Peggy said, "I'll leave you to visit. I have an appointment at the hair salon."

"She's going to a hair salon?" Kate asked in surprise.

"It's her little business," Julienne said. "That's how she makes money to pay for food and things she needs." Seeing the amazement on Kate's face, Julienne explained. "Trust me, it's nothing fancy. She uses a spray bottle to wet down hair and give haircuts. If someone wants a shampoo or color, she has them go to the cement sink in the kitchen area of their pavilion. No frills here."

"I see that," Kate said as she glanced around the small crowded, cluttered room.

"We noticed all the little kiosks down there," her dad said. "Those are all businesses owned by inmates?"

"Yes and some operate right out of their rooms. Some will do your laundry; some cook food and sell it, all kinds of things."

"It's like a third world village," her father said.

"Yes, but don't let it fool you. It's still prison. There are fights and beatings and theft. And let me tell you about the rats." She told them about the rat campaign she and Peggy had waged.

Horrified, Kate held her hands up. "I don't think I want to hear any more of that story."

She looked around the room. "Let's make a list of the things you need." The list included utensils, non-refrigerated food, a mattress and toiletries. "We'll work at buying them this week and bring some to you each day." She took a few photos of the room. "It's so small," she said. "Hardly room for one, never mind two. It's a good thing you're not claustrophobic."

Julienne gave them a tour of the pavilion where she and Peggy lived, including the showers and toilets and the laundry and cooking area.

"Everything is so filthy," Kate said. "I'm not going to drink water while I'm here and I refuse to use these toilets." She shivered at the thought.

They told Julienne about their visit with the Ambassador at the Embassy and how frustrated it made them.

"When we walked into the waiting room at the American Embassy, the chairs were full of Ecuadorians," Kate said. "I guess they are trying to find a way to the United States. I don't know. But we had to wait quite a while and when we finally got to talk with him, I got so angry to find out how little the Embassy can actually do for American citizens." Her voice rose in anger when she thought about it. "I started to lose it."

Julienne's father chuckled. "She reached for him across the desk. I had to hold her back."

"I yelled at him, 'All you can do is bring her some powdered vitamins? That's it?'"

"And the list of attorneys we were given is useless," her father said. "Most don't speak any English; some on the list are even dead! That's how old the list is." He sighed. "We've been told that it can take a long time to even obtain an appearance in court. Meanwhile, they keep you locked up, guilty until proven innocent."

"There's no chance at all that I can get out and go home with you this week?" She struggled not to cry, but the tears were close.

"I'm afraid not, Jules. I've been on the phone constantly with politicians and lawyers who make promises to help. I paid one attorney $3,000 and he's disappeared. But, I'm not giving up. I'll continue to make calls and contacts. Somehow we'll get through this and get you home."

They brought Julienne clothes, bedding, a VCR, essential oils to use for massage and more toiletries.

"Some inmates call me the rich American," Julienne said. "With all the things you brought me this week, that reputation will spread." She tried to smile, but tears bordered her eyes. "I'm so grateful for you two."

Watching her parents walk through the gate on the last visit put Julienne into a downward spiral of depression. She stayed in her room, refusing to socialize or take part in anything. Her package from her friend, Joanna, arrived that week and she lay in bed listening to music with the Walkman she sent; familiar songs, like "Cruel Summer" by Bananarama.

She related to the lyrics. *Trying to smile, But the air is so heavy and dry… It's a cruel, cruel summer. Leaving me here on my own. It's a cruel, cruel summer. Now you're gone…My friends are away and I'm on my own…*

Her depression increased.

CHAPTER 15

## Camp Inca Molotov Cocktails

JULIENNE SPENT DAY after day locked in her room. She cried and thought of happier times at Newport Beach— swimming, surfing and building bonfires. As she sat on her bed, listening to music on her Walkman by Gwen Stefani and *No Doubt,* Julienne remembered meeting Gwen as a young teenager when the band was just starting out, playing in a garage, roller rinks and house parties. She enjoyed talking with her and thought she was very talented. Years later, *No Doubt* played at a fundraiser at the Palladium and Julienne spoke with Gwen again, telling her she was sure Gwen would make it big one day. They connected briefly again when Gwen and *No Doubt* were the opening act for Dave Wakeling and *General Public.*

The more Julienne thought about the past, the worse she felt. Even Peggy couldn't break her out of her funk, until the day the Red Zone girls threatened Peggy.

Peggy dashed into the room, her eyes filled with rage. She tore off the clothes she had on and rummaged through her things, tossing them around until she found an old worn pair of jeans and a tattered T-shirt. She yanked her combat boots from under the bed, pulled them on and laced them up.

Julienne snapped off the Walkman and watched Peggy pull her hair into a ponytail and remove her earrings.

"What's going on?" she asked.

"They want me to pay them to protect my store."

"Who? The guards?"

"No, the Red Zone girls." She reached for the metal pipe she kept in the room to fight off rats. "They've threatened all the businesses. If I don't pay them, they'll destroy everything and ruin my shop."

"You're going to fight them off by yourself?"

"I don't have a choice. That shop is my livelihood and I just put my last seventy dollars into it." Her voice reflected the rage and desperation she felt. "I don't have anyone sending me money like you do."

Julienne slipped off the bunk and grabbed her tennis shoes.

"Where do you think you're going?"

"With you," Julienne said. "You can't be down there by yourself."

"Are you sure?"

"No...but I can't let you go alone."

"Okay, then." She rattled off a list. "Grab the hairspray, nail polish remover, rubbing alcohol, coke bottles, ashtrays, pillowcase, and matches."

*What are we going to do with this stuff?* Julienne wondered. The mood Peggy was in, she didn't stop to ask.

They gathered all the items and stuffed them into the pillowcase.

Peggy reached under her bed. "And here's a metal pipe for you."

*What am I getting myself into? One-on-one combat?* Fear gripped her, but Julienne grasped the pipe, hands trembling.

They hurried down to Peggy's shop and glanced around. Everyone who normally hung out in that area had scattered.

"They must know what's about to go down," Peggy said as she unlocked her shop door and hurried inside. She locked the door behind them and dumped the contents of the pillowcase on the floor.

"Put the ashtrays back in the pillowcase," she ordered.

Julienne did as she was told. Peggy took a hammer she kept in her shop and smashed the pillowcase with it, crushing the glass. Then she unlocked the door and dumped some of the shards on the ground just outside the door.

"What's that for?" Julienne asked.

"So we can hear the glass crunch if anyone comes."

"Oh! Smart!"

"Now take the rest of the glass and divide it up into the five coke bottles."

Julienne filled the bottles, careful not to cut herself in the process.

Together, they dragged the large ice cream freezer in front of the locked door as a barricade. Then Peggy mixed up a concoction with the other ingredients they'd brought. When she was finished, she poured the mixture into each coke bottle.

"Help me tear the pillowcase into strips," she ordered.

She took these and forced the cloth strips into the top of the bottles leaving the end hanging out.

"What are those for?"

"Molotov cocktails," Peggy said.

"Molotov cocktails? Are you crazy?!"

"Look," she said, "thanks for helping me, but if you want to go back to the room, you'd better go now. It's getting dark and things could get crazy real fast."

Julienne didn't answer. *We are so going to get into trouble for this. And what if someone gets badly hurt?*

"If you want to stay, I'll teach you how to throw one of these so it doesn't come rolling back at you and explode."

"Oh my gosh, where did you learn all this?"

"In the military. I was a bomb specialist."

"A bomb specialist? Are you serious?"

"Really." She dropped her voice to a whisper. "Hold up, girl."

Julienne froze. Her heart raced and her stomach rumbled. She heard someone step on the broken glass outside the door.

Peggy reached for one of the Molotov cocktails.

Someone pounded on the door.

Panic swept through Julienne. Her hands shook as she reached for metal pipe.

"Chica!"

"It sounds like the heffe, the head guard," Julienne whispered.

"Chica! It's okay. Come out."

"Who is it?" Peggy called. She motioned for Julienne to hide the bombs. Then she asked the guard several questions to be sure it wasn't one of the Red Zone girls faking it. When she was satisfied, they moved the ice cream freezer out of the way and unlocked the door.

"Listen," the guard said. "We know about the threats, but it's over now."

Two other guards stood there, backing up the head guard.

"We locked up the Red Zone girls who made the threats, so it's safe to go back to your room."

The guards waited while Peggy swept up the glass and Julienne straightened out the shop. They followed the head guard back to their room.

"You know what I'm going to do with those Molotov cocktails?" Peggy said. "Tomorrow morning I'm putting them on display on the window ledge in my shop. It will send a message to the Red Zone girls."

"What message?"

"Don't mess with us."

"Just another normal day at Camp Inca," Julienne said as they crawled into bed.

"Camp Inca?"

She chuckled. "Yeah, that's what I call it when I write to my dad."

"Is that a smile I hear?" Peggy asked.

"You expect a smile from me after we made Molotov cocktails and I almost blew myself and others up?"

"You need to learn some guerilla warfare to survive in here."

"Yeah, I know. You always tell me to butch up."

As they started to doze off, Peggy said, "Hey Jules."

"Yeah?"

"Thanks."

"Sure."

CHAPTER 16

# Camp Inca
# A Sudden Transfer

JULIENNE'S FATHER AGREED with her to work with more than one lawyer at a time, hoping to make some progress with at least one of them. Julienne began calling her first lawyer, Alejandro, pushing for information and an update on her case. Her father paid him a retainer and she was determined to stay on top of the situation.

"Tomorrow, I will know something," he would say. But each time she called back, he would tell her the same thing. "Tomorrow. I should have some news tomorrow."

"I'm so tired of 'tomorrow'! Everything is tomorrow!"

For weeks she pestered him with her calls until one day he finally gave her some good news.

"The court has agreed to order an investigation. Detectives will go with you to where you stayed in Quito, and you can show them the places you visited. They have the photos from your camera and you can show them where each picture was taken. Maybe someone will remember seeing Juan or Pablo."

"Finally! Does this mean I'll be getting out of here?"

"Only for the investigation, yes. I'm arranging for permission papers to be signed by the Director of the Jail and we will need to schedule a guard to bring you out."

"When is this going to happen?"

"In a few days," he said. "I'll need another $300 to arrange for all this and to pay the court and document fees."

"I'll call my dad right away. He'll take care of it."

She called her father immediately.

"I'll wire the money to him today."

"Maybe this nightmare is finally going to come to an end," Julienne said.

"I hope so," he said. "This is the first actual progress I've seen."

"Thank you for all you're doing for me, Dad. I know it's costing you a lot of money."

"You're worth it," he said. "We love you."

---

Two days later, after the guards did roll call and locked the pavilion for the night, Julienne and Peggy settled in their room and prepared to have something to eat.

"I can't stop thinking about finally getting things moving and getting out of here," Julienne said. "I'm so excited."

"I hope it all works out for you, but I know how the system works. It takes a year or more to actually get a court date."

"Señoríta Julienne!"

Julienne stepped outside the door and saw two guards standing at the pavilion entrance gate. As she walked toward them, one of them unlocked and opened it.

"What's going on?" Julienne asked.

The other guard motioned for her to step outside the gate.

Peggy came to see what was happening.

"Where are we going?" Julienne asked the guard.

"Your lawyer is here."

"I don't believe them," Peggy said in a cautious tone.

"What should I do?"

"Don't go outside the prison with them," Peggy warned.

"Why? They said my lawyer is outside."

"Your lawyer wouldn't come this time of day."

The guards started pulling Julienne with them down the stairs.

"Your lawyer is waiting outside. He has your freedom papers," said one of the guards.

"They're lying!" Peggy yelled.

Other inmates came out of their rooms to see what was going on. They shouted along with Peggy and their voices rose to a loud din.

Julienne stopped at the bottom of the stairs and glanced around.

"I don't see my lawyer," she said to the guards. "Where is he?"

"Outside the gate." They motioned for her to keep walking.

"Don't go!" Peggy shouted.

Julienne couldn't hear what Peggy was saying over the noise from the inmates. She turned and ran back to a spot below where Peggy stood on the $2^{nd}$ floor.

"They're going to transfer you!" she shouted down to her.

"But I didn't do anything!" Julienne said.

"Just sit down!" Peggy shouted. "Cross your legs and sit down right there!"

The guards came over and Julienne plunked herself down on the ground. "If I'm getting transferred I need to get some things from my room," she said.

"No. You need to get up and come with us," one guard ordered.

"Don't move!" Peggy shouted. She dashed into their room and put some money and Julienne's asthma and allergy meds into a zip lock plastic bag. She snagged a blanket as well. Out on the barred balcony walkway, she tossed the bag through the bars and then squeezed the blanket through the bars. It landed close to where Julienne sat on the ground below.

Julienne scrambled over and grabbed the small plastic bag, stuffing it in her bra. The women started to bang on the bars and shouted at the guards.

"Get up!" the guards ordered Julienne.

"No, Julienne, don't do it!"

She stayed on the ground, clutching the blanket. She remained cross-legged and refused to move.

"Stubborn American!" one guard yelled and motioned for the other to help him.

One on each side of her, they lifted her by her arms and carried her through the gate with her legs still crossed Indian style. They put her down and left her there while they locked the first gate behind them. She looked around and saw no one. No lawyer. She stood and the guards came back and brought her to the big main gate, which was now open. Other guards came and brought five more inmates, handcuffed. All six of them were marched out to a large waiting van.

A female guard came up to Julienne and said, "Let me see." She took the blanket and shook it out. "No drugs?" she asked.

"No, no. Only my asthma medication." Julienne reached under her shirt and pulled out the small plastic bag to show her. "And some money."

"Okay, okay." She motioned for Julienne to get inside the vehicle. While the guards searched the other inmates, Julienne rolled down a window and tried to scramble out on the other side of the van. A guard snatched her and forced her back inside.

"Where are you taking me?" Julienne screamed. "Where am I going?"

"Vas Libre," one guard said.

"You're going free," another translated.

"What? You're taking me to the airport?" Sarcasm filled her voice.

He laughed and shut the door. Her nerves tensed. *They could be taking me anywhere. I have no control.*

The female guard climbed into the front of the van and leaned over the back seat. "Stay calm. I'll be with you on your trip," she said in a quiet voice. "You'll be okay."

Julienne sank back into the seat. Her hands trembled as she clutched the blanket to her chest. *Where are they taking me? Who will know where I am? What if I get lost in the system with no communication to the outside?* Waves of fear swept through her.

Another guard climbed into the front seat and started the engine. The massive gates opened to the street and they drove off into the night.

CHAPTER 17

## Latacunga Prison Migraines and a Seizure

*Is this an airport?* Julienne wondered. She squinted out the window and tried to clear her groggy mind. They had been driving for some time and she had dozed off. *I might really be going home?* She stretched and watched through the window as they pulled into a terminal. *It's a bus station. What now?*

"What's happening?" Julienne asked. No one answered.

The other prisoners were ordered outside to be taken to different buses.

"Where am I going?"

"Tranquillo, be calm," the female guard said.

Julienne sat quietly while the others got out of the van, and then she followed the female guard to another bus. A second guard got on their bus and sat in the back. The female guard sat in the middle next to Julienne as the driver pulled out of the terminal.

"Where are we going?" Julienne whispered.

She didn't answer, but handed Julienne her bus ticket.

*Latacunga*, she read. *Where's Latacunga?*

"Sleep," the guard said in a soft voice.

*Just when I thought there was a breakthrough! Now this.* Her heart raced and her stomach churned.

"I'm getting carsick," Julienne said.

The guard reached into a bag she had with her and pulled out some crackers. She handed a few to Julienne to nibble on.

## Surviving Camp Inca

The bus made several stops so everyone could get off and stretch.

*I wonder if I could escape at one of our stops. But I don't know where I am or where to go. And if I got captured, they would keep me in prison even longer, with a new charge of attempted escape. At least I still have a chance of getting to court to prove my innocence. Who am I kidding? I was supposed to go out on an investigation and now I don't even know where we're heading. Or, why.*

At the next stop she forced herself to stretch and walk around. She gazed up at the night sky. It seemed like a million stars shone above them. It reminded her of Las Vegas with all of its sparkling lights. *Wish I was there.* All she could see in the distance were silhouettes of mountains. She took a deep breath and stepped back on the bus.

They finally arrived at a small building used as a bus station. From there, they took a taxi to another location. *It looks like an old motel from a scary movie.* Cracked walls with chipped and peeling paint added to the image. Darkness shrouded the place.

The guard rang a bell and after a few minutes, a woman opened the wrought iron door and motioned them inside. The guard and the woman greeted each other as friends.

*Maybe this really is a motel and we're just spending the rest of the night here.*

After several minutes, the guard said good-bye to the woman and to Julienne.

"No! No! Where are you going?" Julienne couldn't stop the tears. "Don't leave me here."

The woman directed Julienne to an outside courtyard and pointed to an outdoor toilet stall with a small overhead light bulb hanging over it.

*Oh my god, this is just like C.D.P.!*

She looked around the courtyard in the dim light and saw two stone laundry basins. Large square columns went from one end of the two-story building to the other and clothes lines hung between them. Wooden, shed-like doors each had large padlocks on them.

A male guard came over unlocked one of the cells on the bottom floor. Inside, a young, pregnant girl stood up when Julienne entered.

## Julienne Burleson

The walls were pink and little blocks of wood in the shape of a duck were stuck on the middle of the wall. The floor consisted of uneven wooden planks placed on the dirt. Without a solid foundation, they creaked and lifted with every step she took. A few wires with light bulbs attached to the ends of them were tacked to the wall. The wires came in through the crack in the door.

*This makes C.D.P. look civilized!*

A second guard came with a thin mattress. They left and locked the door behind them. Julienne noticed that the door didn't fit properly, leaving about a four-inch open space. *I can see out, but it also means there's room for critters to wander in when we're sleeping. Creepy!*

The next day Julienne tried to communicate with her roommate. She had trouble understanding her, except that her name was Norma. She spoke Quechuan, an Ecuadorian Indian dialect. She had long, black hair down to her waist, weighed about 90 pounds, and was very pregnant. Over the next few days Julienne found out from others that Norma was serving time for writing bad checks. Her family and boyfriend had abandoned her. She was a sad, shy, soft-spoken, scared girl. She sat and stared at Julienne. Sometimes she'd reach out and touch her blonde hair and say, "Bonita."

There wasn't much to do except sit around and read or play card games. It was a small co-ed prison with eight rooms for sixteen women. One section of the roof had collapsed, so the rooms in that section couldn't be used. A concrete wall with fist-sized holes here and there separated the men and women. The prisoners passed things to each other—drugs, food, liquor, whatever fit through the holes. All the prisoners were indigenous Ecuadorians, except for Julienne. Most women were in for fraud, some for drugs, and a few had children with them.

Julienne watched a Columbian inmate one visit day. During visiting hours, several men came at different times and when each one left her room, she had a little more food and drugs. Over the next few days, the woman barricaded herself in her room and used the drugs. On the next visit day, the whole routine repeated itself.

## Surviving Camp Inca

*She just exists in her own little world. How sad. I guess the drugs make her forget where she is. I'd like to forget, but I couldn't do drugs.*

Food provided by the jail was almost nonexistent. Depending on what size bowl you had, you got some of that crunchy rice. Once in a while, you might get half of a boiled potato. Julienne watched the women peel them one day and saw that they were infested with worms. *I may never eat a potato again!*

Gene & Helen Brown came to visit and brought some of Julienne's things from El Inca.

"I'm so glad to see you!" Julienne said. "This isn't like El Inca where I could buy some of the things I needed right there in the prison."

"We brought you some food and clothes and bedding," they said. "And some of your personal things from Peggy, including this medical reference book. She said you were able to help inmates by looking up their symptoms and giving them some basic advice."

"That's true; this is a great book. And thank you for the other things. All I've had is a thin mattress, a blanket and the clothes I came in. It gets cold at night."

She used one of the blankets to hang as a divider between her bed and Norma's for some privacy. It also kept out some of the cold night air blowing through the crack in the door.

She was so grateful when someone from the Embassy came a few weeks later and brought her some money that her father had sent. With the money, she talked to a guard and convinced him to take her to an outdoor market to buy fresh food and some basic supplies.

As long as she had money to give him, and she bought him something, he was willing to risk taking her out to the market. It felt good to go out and she was amazed that she was allowed to do this, but the grim reality of the prison conditions hit her hard each time she returned.

Except for the things the Browns managed to bring, she had to start over. She had tried talking to the prison authorities to see if she could get more of her things sent over from El Inca, but all she got was excuses.

*My stuff is probably gone by now anyway, or stolen, unless Peggy managed to keep it.*

The lead female guard allowed Julienne to use her personal portable stove, which had four burners and a large tank of propane, along with pots and pans. When Julienne prepared a meal, she always made enough food for the two guards and for her roommate, Norma.

She paid other inmates to wash her clothes, sweep the dirt off the wood floor and wash dishes. She knew the women needed the money. The only thing Julienne did was the shopping and some cooking.

One morning the women were all in a good mood because someone's family member had brought in a delicacy for Charra, the cook, to prepare. Norma kept trying to explain to Julienne what they were going to have for lunch. She was excited and smiling for a change.

Julienne watched the women build a fire in a pit, then take wrought iron tongs to hold a long stalk of some kind of meat. They roasted and turned it until the skin and hair began to scorch. *It smells awful!* When it was done, they took a machete and scraped the skin off into a giant pot of boiling water, along with yucca, onions, cilantro and other vegetables. When this had simmered a while, they took the mystery stalk and chopped the meat into small pieces and added it to the pot. *I think it might be ox tail. How do I not eat it without insulting them?* She kept asking questions about the mystery meat and finally understood what they said.

Pierna de caballo - horse leg. *Oh, my...horse leg stew?! No. I can't. I love horses. I won't eat them!* She made an excuse not to join them for lunch. *I feel so bad. This is a delicacy for them and they wanted to include me. But I can't eat it.* Her stomach lurched at the thought. She apologized to the cook, a large black lady who reminded Julienne of Aunt Jemima. She said something in Spanish that Julienne didn't understand, but what she did understand was Charra's angry tone. She liked being the cook and earned a little money for it. She was offended when anyone else prepared something.

## Surviving Camp Inca

A few days later, a stray cat showed up at the prison.

"Gato," one of the inmates said to Julienne. "Mira sus ojos." She pointed to the cat's eyes.

"She might have a disease," Julienne said as she picked it up. *Its fur seems okay.* She examined the cat's eyes. One pointed in a different direction and was inflamed. She carried it to her room and ignored the women's comments about not having a pet in her room. She looked through her medical book and found suggestions for eye infections.

*Humans, cats? An eye is an eye. If I can get some chamomile flowers, I think the infection will heal.* She fed the cat to get it used to staying in her room and the next time she went to market, she bought chamomile, boiled it in a little water, and let the mixture cool. She held it on the cat's eye with a cloth, treating it each day until the infection cleared up.

"You're still a weird little cat," she said. "That crazy eye wants to float in a different direction from the other one." The cat purred as she stroked its fur. One day she realized the biggest benefit of having a cat in the room. The rats had stopped creeping into the cell. *What a relief. I'm definitely not up for another rat campaign.*

When Helen came for her next visit, Julienne showed her the cat and mentioned that now the rats weren't coming into her cell at night.

"Maybe it's God's way of providing some protection for you," Helen said. "Count your blessings."

*God's protection? Yeah, right. Look around at where I am.*

Startled, Julienne woke up one night to Norma's screams.

"What?" What's wrong?" Julienne called out, scrambling over to Norma's side of the room.

"El bebé!" Norma cried out, holding her stomach.

"The baby is coming!"

"Okay, it will be okay. Tranquillo." She stood and went to the crack in the door, shouting for a guard. Norma continued to scream in pain.

"Guard!" Julienne yelled. "We need help! The baby is coming!"

She turned back to Norma to check on her. Her knees were up and Julienne could see the tip of the baby's head. *Oh my god! I don't know how to deliver a baby!"*

At that moment, the guard came and unlocked the door. Two other guards came in to assist.

"She needs to go to the hospital!"

The guards helped Norma to her feet, and then carried her to the hospital about a block away from the prison.

Julienne couldn't sleep, wondering if everything was okay. *If I hadn't been here, would they have let Norma deliver the baby alone right here in the cell?* She shuddered at the thought.

About four hours later, the cell door opened and the guards helped Norma and her new infant back into the room. Norma lay on her bed and placed the baby on a blanket on the floor next to her.

"What a cute baby," Julienne said. She picked it up and placed it on the bed next to Norma. She rolled over and faced the wall, refusing to touch the baby.

"Are you okay? I'm surprised they sent you back right away."

Norma didn't answer.

Julienne wrapped the baby in a blanket and went back to her own bed.

The infant slept for a short while, then started to cry. Julienne listened, expecting Norma to pick up the baby and nurse it. But the crying increased.

Julienne walked over to the bed and scooped up the baby, rocking it in her arms.

"Norma, wake up. You need to feed your baby."

She didn't respond.

"Norma!" Julienne reached out and shook her arm.

"No!"

"You're not going to feed your baby?"

Norma shook her head.

## Surviving Camp Inca

The baby settled down and slept for a little while without being fed. *It's probably exhausted from crying, poor thing.* As soon as the guard unlocked their door in the morning, Julienne mixed together a little of her powdered vitamins and some water. She spooned a few drops at a time onto the baby's tongue. She asked one of the other inmates to hold the baby while she got one of the guards to take her to the market to buy some powdered milk, baby rice and oatmeal and a baby bottle to feed her. She watered it all down to a thin liquid the baby could handle.

For two weeks, Norma refused to feed the baby, or give it a name. Julienne kept talking with her, telling her the baby needed its mother and how special it was to have a child. One day, Norma picked up the baby, held him and fed him. But she still refused to name him. In Ecuador there's no requirement to name the child for up to a year.

"I'll call him Christopher," Julienne said.

*I don't understand why it took her so long to bond with the baby, but I'm sure glad she did.* That night she lay in bed wondering what would become of Norma and little Christopher. *It's such a hard life here. I hope she can handle it.*

---

Sitting in the doorway of her room, Julienne was reading and heard Latin music cranking up.

"Chicha!" An inmate called to her. "Ven a la fiesta de cumpleaños."

"A birthday party?" Julienne asked.

"Si!"

"Una barbacoa de carne de cerdo."

Julienne picked up her English/Spanish dictionary. "A pork barbecue?"

"Vamos, que es bueno." She pulled Julienne over to where eight others gathered for the festivity. A few were dancing to the music.

"Jugo de chichi," she said, handing a cup to Julienne.

"Jugo? Juice?" She took a sip and said, "Tastes a little like apple juice." Thirsty, she drank most of it quickly. *Has a bit of a fermented tang to it.*

"What does it have in it?" she asked.

"Some rice, cinnamon, sugar…it's good?"

"Yes!"

Julienne joined in the dancing, something she used to do a lot of and missed. Someone refilled her cup between songs. She enjoyed having fun for a change. When she stumbled through some of the dance steps, the others laughed at her. She laughed too, until there was more stumbling and falling than there was dancing. The room began to spin and she made her way over to a chair to sit down.

"Comer," one of the women said, putting a plate of food in front of her.

One whiff of the pork made her stomach lurch. She staggered to the toilet and vomited. The women tried to get her to come back to the party, but she felt too sick. Back in her room, she crawled onto her mattress and passed out.

In the morning she woke up with a major headache. Groaning, she poked through her toiletries and found some Advil.

*What was I drinking?*

Someone came to check on her and Julienne asked, "What is jugo de chichi?"

The inmate explained how they combine the ingredients and put them in a big pot to ferment for about a month. Julienne didn't understand everything she said, but she did realize what ferment meant. "Ferment?" Julienne put her hands over her pounding head. *Moonshine! I drank how much?* She groaned. *No wonder I have the worst headache of my life. If I had drunk any more, I would have ended up in the hospital!*

The headache passed and a few days later she felt one of her migraine's coming on. *If I can catch it in the beginning, maybe it won't be too bad.* She found Freddy, the guard, and said, "I don't have any medication for my migraine. I need you to take me over to the men's side of the prison to see the doctor."

Freddy nodded at her, but didn't move.

"You have to take me now before it gets worse."

"In a minute," he said. He walked away from her and wandered around, doing nothing.

"I need to go now," Julienne pressed, "or I'm going to be really sick."

"I said I'll do it in a few minutes."

Julienne went and sat in the doorway of her cell and waited and waited. Her head throbbed and she felt nauseated. Once again she went to him and asked.

"Don't keep asking me! I'm not even going to take you at all now!" he shouted at her. "Who do you think you are telling me what to do?"

She sat down again. Her eyes blurred and her body shook. She held her hands to her head. One of the women noticed and came over to her.

"Que pasa? Está usted enfermo?'

"Yes, I'm sick." Julienne pointed to her head and rocked back and forth.

The inmate went over and knocked on the guard's window. The female guard came out and the woman pointed at Julienne. "Doctor!" Then several inmates yelled at Freddy for not taking her to the doctor for medicine.

The two guards took her to the doctor's office on the men's side and he gave Julienne a shot that caused her to pass out. When she woke up, she was still in the office. Several broken glass containers and first aid items were scattered on the floor.

"My arm is bleeding," she said.

"You had a seizure and fell, knocking things over and cut your arm on the glass," the doctor said. He gave her a packet of pills. "Start by taking twenty of them, then decreasing by one each day until they're gone. That will stop any seizures and control the migraines."

When the guards took her back to her cell, Julienne crawled onto her mattress. The next day she heard that Freddy had been transferred to another jail. *Serves him right,* she thought.

CHAPTER 18

## Latacunga Prison
## Quito Investigation

ALEJANDRO, JULIENNE'S LAWYER, came to see her. "I come with good news," he said. "Right now all the court has on your case is the original statement that was written down by Interpol."

"I don't even know what they wrote down," Julienne said. "I was never given a translator."

"And you never signed anything. So that's good."

"When do we go to court?" Julienne asked. "Is that the good news?"

"No, the good news is that they're ready to take you out to the streets of Quito to do an investigation."

"They said that before, but then I got sent here instead. Is this going to be another false promise?"

"This time it's going to happen," he promised.

"Several investigators will take you to Quito with the photos from your camera. They want you to retrace your steps, go to each of the shops and locations where your pictures were taken. Maybe someone will remember you, or Juan and Pablo. If so, that's corroborating evidence for you."

"I don't have an address of where I went."

"Your memory, combined with the photos, will help them find the locations."

"I hope so," Julienne said. "Especially the gift shop where the paintings came from."

"You'll go to Quito by bus with a guard," he said, "and the detectives, along with some military police, will meet you there."

## Surviving Camp Inca

"Why all the police? Are they afraid I'll try to escape?"

"No, they'll need them if they find Juan and Pablo and they give them some resistance."

"Like the S.W.A.T. team on a sting operation?"

"I guess you could say that." He stood to leave. "I hope it goes well."

Sofia was assigned as Julienne's guard. She was like a grandmother and would knit while she watched the inmates. Julienne only saw her in camouflage uniforms, but the day they went out, Sofia wore normal street clothes in order not to arouse any suspicions when they visited the shops. *I guess we're supposed to look like tourists,* Julienne thought.

The detectives in charge of the investigation picked them up at the bus station in Quito. The national police, dressed in black, followed at a distance in another car.

"Tell us everything you remember," one of the detectives told Julienne. They took notes, and then said, "Together, we're going to retrace all your steps."

"I think if we start at the park, I'll remember how to get to the gift shop from there," Julienne said. "A roaming photographer took that Polaroid picture of me with Juan and Pablo. If he's still working there, he might remember me."

She and the detectives asked people in the park if they knew the photographer and if he was around. One man said he thought he knew who they were talking about, but he wasn't there that day. They made their way around the park, stopping people and showing them the photos, but no one recognized Julienne or Juan and Pablo.

"Let's go to where you bought the disposable camera."

Julienne retraced her steps there and the detectives asked the two men working, "Do you recognize the men in this photo?"

"No, we don't know who they are." They glanced at each other and shrugged.

He nodded at Julienne. "Do you recognize this young lady?"

"No."

"Of course they don't recognize me," Julienne said. "They're not the same ones who were working here at the time. I don't recognize them either."

They continued walking up the cobblestone street to the gift shop.

"That's it!" Julienne said, pointing ahead.

When they stood in front of the shop, they pulled out the photos from Julienne's camera. "This is it all right."

"Oh no," Julienne said. The entrance of the shop had an overhead door that was rolled down and padlocked. The place looked abandoned.

The detectives asked at each of the neighboring stores if the gift shop was just closed for the day. Julienne watched as people avoided eye contact and tried to look busy, particularly when the detectives flashed the photo and asked if they recognized anyone. *They're nervous; they're not going to talk,* Julienne thought. She glanced around and saw that the swat team had pulled back out of sight. *People know something's up. They don't want to get involved.*

One shopkeeper decided to cooperate. "They packed up all their stuff and left."

"When was that?"

"Two days ago."

"Are they coming back?"

"I doubt it. I heard they were going to Columbia," he said, "but I don't know for sure."

"Doesn't it seem unusual that they just cleared out two days ago when this investigation was confirmed?" asked Julienne. "I don't think that's a coincidence."

The detectives ignored her comment.

"Of course they're all going to say they don't know anything," Julienne persisted. "They don't want to get in trouble with you or with Juan and Pablo. It could be dangerous for them if they talked."

Walking back to where the cars were parked, Julienne asked if they could have lunch before going back to the jail.

"Are you buying?"

"Of course," she said. *I had to pay for my bus ticket and Sofia's. Why not add the lunch tab to the cost of the day?*

Back at the jail, Julienne fought discouragement. They had failed to find even one witness who recognized her or Juan and Pablo. Trying to be positive, she told herself, *At least I got out of this place for most of the day.*

She went to her room and found Norma clearing out her things. A guard stood outside the door.

"Where are you going?"

"She's being released," the guard answered.

Without a word, Norma scooped up her baby and a bag with her personal items in it, and left.

*She never mentioned anything about it,* Julienne thought. *Her family and her boyfriend abandoned her, so where is she going?*

The next morning Julienne was rearranging some things in the cell, hoping she wouldn't get a new roommate.

A guard came to her door. "Your lawyer is on the phone."

She walked over to the phone. "Hello? Alejandro?"

"This is Fabian."

"Fabian! Oh, I'm surprised to hear from you."

"You asked me to check on some things for you when I went to see Rosa in El Inca. I did and I'll be coming to see you and explain what's happening."

"That's great. When are you coming?"

"Tomorrow."

*I hope he has some good news,* she thought. *I guess it pays to have more than one lawyer working on your case.*

Julienne had met Rosa, an American, in El Inca and also met Fabian when he went there to meet with Rosa on her case. Rosa introduced them and Julienne asked if he could help her as well. He said he would and her father had sent some money to get him started. Many of the female inmates came around to check him out at El Inca and talked about his good looks. He was tall, blonde with green eyes and always wore a stylish suit.

He came to Latacunga the next day.

"I asked at El Inca, 'Where is the gringa?' and they told me you were transferred here."

"I'm so glad you came," she said. "Is there any news on my case?"

"I checked with the court and heard about the investigation they took you on in Quito."

"Yes, but they didn't find anyone who remembered me, or Juan or Pablo. So I don't know if it helped my case."

"At least it's some progress," he said.

"So what happens next?"

"I'm trying to get a court date for you."

"I hope it's soon. I can't wait to get out of here."

"You are so beautiful," he said, letting his eyes roam over her. Julienne blushed.

"Did I embarrass you?" He smiled. He went back to discussing her case briefly and then they talked for several hours about their lives and interests. When he left, he promised to be back soon.

"I'll look forward to it," Julienne said. "It's nice to have someone to talk to in English."

*When it's someone as attractive and intelligent as you*, she thought.

When he was leaving, one of the inmates smiled and said to Julienne, "Gato." She pointed to her eyes. "Gato."

"Oh," Julienne said. "Yes, his green eyes, like a cat."

He came back to visit several times in the next few months.

"What do you plan to do when you get out?" he asked.

"Go back to California."

"Have you thought about the possibility of staying in Ecuador for a while?"

"No. Why would I do that?"

"I have a five-year-old daughter. I think she would like you."

*Oh my god, what's happening here?*

"No, I'm not staying in Ecuador. My life is in the States."

"You could stay with me," he offered.

"Here? In Ecuador?" She was shocked.

"Sure, it would be nice for both of us, no?" He searched her eyes.

*Whoa...* She stiffened. "I really like you and appreciate your visits, but I don't want what apparently you want." *This is so embarrassing.*

After he left, she asked herself, *did I lead him on by being friendly? Is this how all Latin men respond to women being friendly?*

He called soon after and told her that he had a court date set up for her.

"Ask the director there to sign the papers for you to go and arrange for a guard to take you. I'll meet you at the courthouse."

"Finally! I get my day in court."

Her hopes rose, but when the day came, the director told her she couldn't go, that it had been cancelled.

"Why? What happened?"

"There's a taxi strike in Quito and court had to be cancelled. Talk to your attorney. He'll have to reschedule."

Julienne called Fabian and he told her the streets were in chaos.

"Taxis are on strike for more pay and drivers are putting tacks and nails all over the roads to keep others from driving. It's a mess. I don't know how long it will take to get another date."

"And hopefully there won't be another strike," she complained. *Why do I bother getting my hopes up? I need to call my dad.*

She talked with her dad and told him about the cancelled court date.

"That's frustrating," he said. "Trying to get something done there is so difficult." He sighed. "I have an update on what we've tried to accomplish on this end. As you know, we gave all the information you had about Ashley and Evan to the police and to the State Department. They haven't been able to locate them or find any record of them."

"They must have given me false names," Julienne said. "I just know he said he was from a Latin background, but he had no accent. He said he was in the Army and he did have a military haircut and claimed they were from New York."

"I passed all that information on," her dad said. "There's no record of him serving in the Army."

"And I only knew Ashley for about six months. I was in her apartment a few times. I bet the lease wasn't in her name. She would fly back and forth to New York and said she helped with her family's business."

"Now I wonder what that 'business' was," her father said.

"I doubt if anything they told me was true. I had no reason at the time not to believe them."

"We had someone check out the address where she lived and, of course, they had cleared out. No forwarding address."

"They could be anywhere. Miami, New York, California, or even another country. Maybe Columbia?" Just thinking about it shattered her composure. Tears choked her voice. "Will I be able to prove my innocence if they're never found? And where are Juan and Pablo? I doubt anyone would testify against them even if they were found. They probably gave me fake names too!"

"Don't give up hope, Julie. I've hired investigators and we'll keep knocking on doors until we dig something up that will help."

"I'm trying, Dad. But it's so hard."

Day after day, Julienne sat in her room, bleary-eyed from crying, her hair a tangled mess. Even her cat with the crazy eye had wandered off and not returned. She tried to get out of her mood by thinking positive thoughts, but when she looked around at the reality of the place, the shadows of depression returned. *It's like living in a dungeon.*

Her thoughts wandered back to California and her studio apartment on Sunset Boulevard. *I loved it there.* It was a Spanish Revival, thirty-apartment complex built by a noted architect in the 1920s. The district was home to many up and coming celebrities—actors, writers, directors and producers. In the apartment above Julienne, her handsome neighbor became a Versace model. She remembered looking out her window one day and there he was on the billboard across the street.

Another neighbor said her father was the drummer for Aerosmith. Brad Pitt lived up the street, but hung out around the pool in the complex. Nick Cassavetes sat by the pool working on screenplays. Almost everyone who lived there had famous relatives.

Ashley liked to come over and hang out because of the 'who's who' crowd. The House of Blues was across the street and Julienne's group of friends hit the clubs on weekends. The Viper Room was partly owned by Johnny Depp and was a popular hangout. Regulars included Jennifer Aniston, Angeline Jolie, Leonardo DiCaprio and many others. The Roxy, The Rainbow and other clubs all were hot spots for meeting famous people.

Julienne liked hanging with Ashley because she was always available to go places at night. Many of her other friends worked nights in restaurants and clubs and couldn't go out. Julienne's day job allowed her the opportunity to spend her nights clubbing and dancing. When she first met Ashley and asked what she did for work, Ashley avoided the subject, but when pressed, claimed she did projects for her father's business when they needed her.

*I was so naïve. If hadn't come to Ecuador, I wouldn't be in this mess. I should have just gone home.*

She looked around her cell. *Crumbling cement walls, wooden planks over dirt, bugs, spiders, and at night, rats. A far cry from Sunset Boulevard.*

The tears came in a flood.

"Julienne!" one of the inmates called from her doorway. " La Fiesta de la Mama Negra!" After her announcement, she left.

*What is she talking about? What fiesta? And what does it have to do with me?*

She forced herself up and went to shower, shampoo her hair, and put on clean clothes. The inmates were excited and anticipated going to this fiesta. She asked one of the guards what it was all about.

"La Fiesta de la Mama Negra? When the Cotopaxi volcano erupted in 1742, the people petitioned the Virgin of Mercy, the patron of Cotopaxi, to spare the city. When Latacunga escaped the wrath of the volcano, an annual celebration was set in her honor."

"I get the impression that the inmates are going to be allowed to attend?"

"Of course! It's a tradition," he said. "And the Director has been chosen to be Mama Negra. It's quite an honor."

On the day of the fiesta, the director dressed the part of Mama Negra. She had her face painted black, put on bright blue eye shadow and used blood red lipstick to create huge looking lips. She wore a long, flowing red dress with dazzling sequins and a fruit turban on her head. She would be dancing on a homemade parade float, waving a huge multi-colored fan.

Since all the guards were going, the inmates went as well. They couldn't be left alone at the jail. Julienne had no choice.

People danced in the streets to Indian music and drank lots of alcohol. As parade floats passed by, candy and small wine containers were tossed into the crowds to keep the party atmosphere going. The group of inmates stood together and watched the parade. Mama Negra sprayed milk and water on the spectators for their well-being. All this to be followed by fireworks.

*This so unreal,* Julienne thought. *I'm in prison, but here I am out on the streets watching a parade and fireworks. It's weird.* The guards were there, but paid more attention to the festivities than the inmates. *I could just walk away.* She looked up and down the street. *Of course, I'd have to have a plan on where to go. And as an American, I really stand out in this crowd.*

Frustrated with her wild thoughts, she forced herself to focus on the parade. That's when she felt the spray of milk and water coming from Mama Negra on the float. In this case, the director of the jail.

*Must be a sign.* She brushed away the damp spray on her clothes. *It's supposed to be for my well-being.*

Back at the jail, she started to daydream about escaping. When she had permission to go to the market with a guard, she began to test the limit on how far they would let her go.

"Oh, look over here," she'd say, darting ahead. The guard would follow.

*I'm doing the leading. Amazing.*

She enjoyed her little game. She did discover that if she went too far ahead, or turned onto a side street, he would stop her. She would act naïve, smile, and walk back to where she belonged.

At night she thought about a phone conversation she had with her dad. This was after experiencing all the roadblocks with unethical lawyers, with the promises of help from politicians, with the limitations of the Embassy, and not having a chance to prove her innocence in court.

"I've even hired a private investigator to track down Juan and Pablo," he said. "These investigators work on an international basis and I thought they might be able to locate them, even though the court investigators couldn't. It's costing a lot of money, but so far, no results. It's like they've disappeared off the face of the earth."

"My emotions are all over the place," she said. "I try to cling to any little sign of hope."

"Don't give up," her father said. "But if you get a chance to escape and feel comfortable that you'd be safe enough to make it to Columbia, go for it. We'll arrange for transportation to get you there and a new passport to fly you back to the States."

Julienne wondered at times if the jail recorded phone calls, but she really didn't think so. *Things are so backward here; I doubt they have the funds or equipment to do that. They don't even have enough money to feed the prisoners properly.*

A week later, after six months in Latacunga, the director of the jail told Julienne, "You're being transferred."

"Where?" Julienne asked, frightened. *Did they hear her conversation about escaping?*

"El Inca."

CHAPTER 19

## Camp Inca 2nd Time Take My Baby!

BACK AT EL Inca, Julienne was relieved that Peggy had managed to keep her room open in case of Julienne's return.

"It's almost like coming home," Julienne said. "I missed having a friend to talk to." She glanced around the room. "You kept a lot of my personal things. Thanks."

"I wasn't sure how long you'd be gone. The transfer to Latacunga was such a surprise," Peggy said. "The way they pulled it off, I think someone was trying to delay the Quito investigation you were supposed to go on."

"I think so too. But I did get to go while in Latacunga. Interesting how the shop where the paintings came from had just closed two days before we got there. Locked up and empty. No one knew anything of course."

"Someone had to have warned them to leave."

"I don't know why they transferred me back here, but I'm glad."

"I heard rumors from one of the guards," Peggy said. "The director of Latacunga was afraid you were planning to escape. They thought you were a rich American and could bribe someone to help you."

"I can't say I didn't think about it," Julienne said. "I guess part of me still hopes this whole thing will get cleared up and I'll go free."

Peggy looked at her and shook her head.

"And don't you tell me to 'butch up,'" Julienne said.

"You just need to face reality."

## Surviving Camp Inca

"What reality? That I'm going to live in this hell hole for years to come? I can't accept that. I won't."

"I'm just saying don't sit around and wait for the system to work. You work the system."

Julienne decided Peggy was right. She made a decision to become more aggressive. She needed to plan her time and take advantage of accepting help from the visitors she received.

*When someone asks me what I need, I'll tell them what to get in order to make my time here more bearable. I'll decorate my room and plan activities so there's a reason to get up each day. I need something to look forward to. I'll take as many English-speaking visitors as I can.*

Helen had mentioned to her that there was a South American Explorers Club in Quito and sometimes they would ask about visiting English-speaking prisoners, especially Americans.

"The club has an office where hikers can check in and register. Usually they want to know where the hostels are. We could let them know you're interested in having English-speaking visitors," she said."

Julienne saw a photographer come into the prison that visitor's day and had an idea. She talked with him and discovered that he was allowed to take pictures, develop them, and bring them back for you to choose which ones you might want to buy. Inmates had him take family pictures on visiting days, or photos of their children or boyfriends, all for a reasonable fee.

"Could you take my picture?" she asked.

"Of course."

The following week, he brought several photos and she chose one.

"I want you to enlarge the photo and mount it on white poster board, maybe eleven by fourteen inches. Can you do that?"

"Sure."

"Leave space on the bottom half for me to write on. Oh, and bring me a marker pen."

He brought it just as she asked and she paid him. Up in her room with the marker pen, she wrote:

California girl stranded in Ecuadorian prison, El Inca.
Please bring toiletries, food, or just a smile.
In need of good conversation.
My name is Julienne."

She asked Helen if she could get someone to post it at the Explorer Club's office.

On visit days, Julienne always dressed as nicely as she could in case someone came. She was grateful she had clothes to choose from because of the generosity of the Browns and church people. Most prisoners didn't have that same opportunity.

*I'm blessed. No, I don't like that word. It's too religious. If I were blessed, I wouldn't be here. I'm lucky.*

One of her first visitors came from Europe. "Welcome to Camp Inca," Julienne said.

"When I saw your picture, I thought you didn't look like a prisoner," he said.

Julienne shared her story with him and he listened, intrigued.

"Wow, I can't believe you've had to go through all this. You look so normal."

"Looking and acting normal isn't easy in a place like this," Julienne said.

She asked him what was happening in the outside world.

"You can't get a newspaper in here?"

"There is a local one, but it's in Spanish and I have a hard time reading it. I understand a word or phrase here and there, but don't grasp the full meaning of most of it."

They discussed many things and he asked if there was anything he could do for her. She asked him to bring her some food. "Anything that doesn't need refrigeration," she said.

The next visit day he came back with a variety of packaged food and snacks.

"I'm leaving Ecuador tomorrow," he said. "I enjoyed our visit and hope you're free soon."

Other visitors came as a response to the sign posted at the Explorer's Club and each brought her some items. She shared what she had with Peggy and a few other inmates, and always gave something to the guard for allowing the items to be brought in.

She hired Maria to do her laundry. She had fifteen children that included two sets of twins. Five of them lived with her in prison; the others lived with relatives. Her teenage daughter was pregnant and now had an infant. *What a burden to have such a large family!*

Julienne tried to help her with the laundry, but Maria got angry, so Julienne backed off. *Maybe she thinks she won't get paid if I help. I wish there wasn't such a language barrier. I was just trying to be helpful.*

Maria carried the baby around in a basket. "She looks like Little Red Riding Hood," Julienne said. Maria didn't understand her. Julienne caressed the baby's soft cheek.

One time when Maria delivered the clean laundry to Julienne's room, she put the baby in the basket and left it there when she headed for her own cell.

"Maria!" Julienne called after her. "You forgot the baby!"

"Oh, no. No." She smiled and said, "Rigallo."

Their conversation grew loud and attracted the attention of a few other inmates who gathered around to see what was going on. One was able to translate.

"Rigallo?" *What is Rigallo?*
"It means gift," the translator said. "The baby is a gift to you."
No, Maria. I can't keep your baby!"
"Si, Señoríta!"
"No, no. Come here! Take the baby."
"Maria says you have no baby. You need a baby."
"Si!" Maria said, nodding her agreement.

"No, I don't need a baby. I can't take care of a baby."

"You're thirty years old and you need a baby!" the translator said. "Maria says her daughter is not old enough to take good care of it, or support it. You're older and can take the baby back to the States where he will have a good life."

Maria kept nodding, refusing to take the basket.

"She will get the paperwork to say the baby is yours."

"She wants to give me her grandson as a gift? Tell her I can't take a baby back to the States. Everyone knows I don't have a baby."

"She said it doesn't matter. In Ecuador, you don't have to fill out a birth certificate for the baby for one year. She will get the certificate saying it's your baby and you can take it back to the States when you go free."

"No, Maria." Julienne placed the baby basket on the floor in front of her. "I can't take the baby." Julienne turned and went back into her room.

Maria shouted things in Spanish that Julienne didn't understand. *I'm sure she's calling me names.*

"She says she won't do your laundry anymore," one of the inmates said.

But she needed the money, and came back a month later, asking to do it again.

---

Julienne told some of the women that she had the oils and creams to do massage therapy. Adriana, an inmate from Chile, heard about it and came to see Julienne.

"I know how to do body treatments," she said. "That's what I used to do in Chile. I can show you."

They talked about formulas, Julienne bought a blender, and they began blending various concoctions, like carrots mixed with almond oil. They experimented with variations for body scrubs and practiced on each other. When they felt they were ready for business, they advertised by covering themselves with the carrot and almond oil mix, and walked around the gauncha in their underwear, offering their body scrub service to other inmates.

The female guard came over to them and shook her head. "Gringas locas."

"With the weird looks we're getting," Julienne said to Adriana, "I think we need more practice with our formulas."

"Yeah, orange isn't everyone's color," Adriana said, grinning.

They laughed and went to clean up. As a result of their walk about, they did get several clients and charged them seventy-five cents.

One afternoon, Julienne and Adriana sat outside in the sunshine in their shorts and a tank top. A plane flew overhead and Julienne wondered where it was going. *I wish I was on it, going to an exotic beach somewhere.* She looked around her. *I'm in the Andes Mountains, in prison. No beach here.* She told Adriana about missing the beach in California.

"I've got an idea," Julienne said. "Let's pretend we're at the beach right now." She leaned back, closed her eyes and said, "How do you like my bathing suit?"

"Lovely. But if we're going to get a tan, we need to use Coca-Cola," she said.

"Coca-Cola?"

"Yes, it will give you a beautiful tan."

They went and bought two Cokes from one of the inmates with a small store, sat back down in the sun, and rubbed the cola all over themselves.

"What are you doing?" another inmate asked.

"We're at the beach," Julienne said. "Getting a tan."

"If you want a tan, use baby oil and iodine," she suggested.

"No, no," Julienne said. "Cola will give us a beautiful bronze tan."

Again, the guard walked over to them. "Gringas locas!"

They didn't get a tan, but definitely needed a shower.

Julienne would spend days trying to do positive activities, but then the reality of her situation would hit her hard and she'd spend days in her room, alone and crying. She wrote letters to her dad and Kate, trying not to be negative and gloomy. She always started her letters with, "Another day at Camp Inca…"

If someone mentioned a lawyer who helped another inmate, Julienne would check into it. But all that seemed to come out of it was more of her father's money wasted.

"Robo elegante," Peggy told her. "That's what the lawyers do. They rob you elegantly. They make promises, get your money, and do nothing."

Julienne filed paperwork through Human Rights, kept in contact with the Embassy, followed through with leads from people who came to visit, and did anything and everything she could. Her father did the same from the States. They wrote letters, talked on the phone. The only result was the dwindling of her father's bank account.

*Robo elegante!*

---

One night Julienne and Peggy were eating dinner in their room and someone knocked on their door, then pushed it open. One of the guards said, "Gringa," pushed a woman into their room, then left.

"Hi," Julienne said. "What's your name?"

"I'm Sandra and they put me in your room because I'm American and I speak English."

"Wait a minute," Peggy said. "You can't stay in our room. We don't have enough space."

"I just got arrested and they brought me here from Interpol," she said. "I'm innocent and I need to get out of here." Her voice raised an octave. "Tell me how to get out of here!"

"Julienne," Peggy said. "Come outside. I want to talk to you for a minute." When they stepped outside the room Peggy said, "I don't like her. I think she's trouble."

"Do we have a choice?" Julienne asked. "They just left her with us."

"Look, she can spend the night, but tomorrow we'll get her another room. We're already crowded."

"Okay," Julienne said. "I think she's just scared right now. She doesn't understand Spanish and she said she's innocent. I can relate to that."

"I don't believe her," Peggy said. "She can stay on your bunk with you for tonight. That's it."

The next day the director agreed to move her to another pavilion that was more secure.

"I heard the guard say they thought she might be a flight risk," Peggy said.

---

Julienne heard two children about four years old, fighting over something. She walked over to them and saw a baby kitten smaller than the palm of her hand. It was just starting to get its hair and she could hear its tiny mews. She ran in between the two children and saw that in their tug of war, they had pulled the kitten's limbs apart. Horrified, she snatched it away from them and brought it up to her room. She examined its tiny legs and saw they were badly disfigured, bent in different directions.

"You poor thing," she said as she tried to put the legs back in position. The kitten's bones were not fully developed yet and she thought she could straighten them, but she couldn't. She sat there, holding the kitten as it mewed in pain.

She heard a commotion outside her room and Peggy burst in, yelling. "Jules, did you take someone's cat?!"

"Yes." Tears streamed down her face. "Peggy, look at what they've done to this little innocent kitten."

"Oh my god! Okay, Jules, but if you don't give it back, we're going to have a war up here."

"How can we let them hurt or kill this little kitten? We can't, Peggy."

Peggy let out a big sigh. "Okay, I'll go out and see if I can make it clear that we just want to help the kitten."

The woman and Peggy argued back and forth and she threatened to beat Peggy and Julienne with a broom.

"Let her come in and see it," Julienne called out to Peggy. "Maybe she'll change her mind."

They let her inside and showed her the twisted legs on the kitten.

"It needs to die," the woman said. "It will never walk again."

"I think I can help it," Julienne said.

"Do what you want with it," the woman said in disgust. "It's yours." She stormed out of their room and left the pavilion.

"We need to find a vet," Julienne said.

"I'll make some calls, Peggy said.

"I'll call a few people too," Julienne said. "Maybe one of my visitors knows a vet." She looked at Peggy. "I know people here don't consider cats pets, but I really want to do this. Thanks for stepping up and helping."

Between the two of them making calls, they found a vet that agreed to come out to the jail. Julienne was touched that they cared enough to try to save this helpless kitten.

"I won't charge you for this," the vet said. She gave the kitten an antibiotic, left some meds for parasites, and advised them how to care for it. "Feed it this baby formula every hour with a dropper for two weeks. As he gets his strength back, feed him a few times a day."

They thanked her for coming and Julienne told Peggy she would take the responsibility for feeding it.

"We have to give him a name," Julienne said that night.

"We also have to be careful about not telling the others he's in here. Let them think that the vet took him home. We can't let him out of the room."

"Okay," Julienne said, cuddling the kitten.

"You realize he's the only male living in our pavilion," Peggy said, grinning.

"Then we have to give him a good code name. A girly name."

Peggy groaned.

"Pink or Pinker-bell."

"Pinky-tone or the Pinkster."

"We can alternate nicknames," Julienne said. "He'll have to learn them all."

Over the next few days, Julienne realized that Pink gave her a purpose, something to feel good about, saving this little helpless creature. He grew fast, and got his strength back in his front legs and paws. One night Julienne's blanket was hanging off the side of her bunk and Pink scurried up it like he had been doing it all his life.

"That's amazing," Julienne said. "Come here, Pink." She patted her lap and he curled up, purring.

"He really needs more space to run and be active," Peggy said. "The room is too small."

"But we can't let him out," Julienne said. "Someone will report him or hurt him."

"How about if we start volunteering for the night cleaning in our pavilion when everyone is locked in their room?"

"Great idea!" Julienne said.

Pink would fly across the slick floor. Julienne and Peggy ran down the hallway, sliding in their socks. Pink would take off running after them with great momentum in his front legs, then he'd try to stop when they did by dragging his hind legs and going into a tailspin. They tried not to laugh too loud, not wanting to attract attention.

Unfortunately, the day came when the prison doctor found out about him.

"I'll give you a week to send him out, or the guards will be forced to remove him. I'm concerned that you could catch a disease from sleeping with the cat."

"I'm more likely to catch something from the prisoners and their kids than from Pink," Julienne said. She gave him a hostile glare. "Pink has had all his shots and he wears a diaper most of the time."

"You've got a week," he said.

They called the vet and she found someone who would take Pink. Julienne felt sad, but knew he would have a much better home outside the jail.

"I think he knows he's leaving," Julienne said to Peggy. "He's been pacing and mewing all day."

The vet gave them updates from time to time. Then the sad news came. Pinky died. The owner said she had him checked out at the vet and they could never find anything wrong with him. He just lost his energy and moped around.

"He seemed depressed," the vet said. "I think he died of a broken heart."

Peggy's temper flared and she cursed the owner and the vet.

"I just feel sad and empty," Julienne said. "My Pinkster is gone."

---

"I'm leaving!" Peggy said. "The two for one law passed so my sentence is reduced!"

"Wow, I'm so happy for you," Julienne said.

"But now I have to get someone to be responsible for me when I leave," she said. She paced the floor in their room.

"You mean someone here in Ecuador?"

"Yeah, until I arrange for my flight back to the States." She thought for a minute and said, "Maybe Joan would do it. She's always been so good about helping inmates. I really don't know who else to ask."

Joan agreed and the day Peggy was set to leave, she and Julienne talked and bantered back and forth.

"Your day will come," Peggy said. "Don't do anything I wouldn't do."

"What? You did everything under the sun!"

"Yeah, well…" Tears came to her eyes. "You know I believe that people cross your path for a reason. We'll be friends forever, Jules."

"Don't forget about me," Julienne said. "Write to me and tell me what you're doing."

"I'll be somewhere near the ocean in California."

They clung to each other and cried when Joan came to get her.

"You'll get out of here soon," Peggy said. "Don't worry. You're right behind me."

"I hope so."

After Peggy left, Julienne tried to control her tears and sadness by attacking the room. She scrubbed the walls with bleach and then asked someone to bring her a can of pink paint to brighten up the room. She finished the project in two days. It took longer for her spirits to brighten up.

# CHAPTER 20

## Camp Inca
## Mama Lucha's Deadly Birthday Bash

A FEW DAYS after Peggy left, the director of the prison called Julienne to his office.

"Your lawyer called to notify me that you have a court date tomorrow," he said. "A guard will take you and your lawyer will meet you there."

*Finally! This could be the day I've been hoping for. I need to call my dad!*

"That's great news, Julie!"

"My only concern is the language barrier," she said. "I understand a lot more than I did, but when it comes to court and legal issues, I get lost."

"I'll contact your lawyer and tell him to arrange for a translator."

"Thanks, Dad. Just maybe I'll be seeing you soon!"

Julienne didn't sleep much that night and was up early and ready to go when the guard came for her.

When they pulled up in a taxi in front of the courthouse, Julienne looked up at the building. *It looks more like a high school.*

Inside, the guard took her up to the second floor. They entered a room with rows of chairs and Julienne was directed by a court security guard to sit down and wait. Her guard sat beside her. *This feels like traffic court in the States*, she thought. People sat all around her, waiting for their cases to be called.

When her lawyer arrived, she asked him, "Where is my translator?"

"Hold on," he said. "Be patient."

## Surviving Camp Inca

"But court starts at eleven and it's already after ten-thirty. I need a translator now, before we start." A flicker of apprehension swept through her. "My dad said he would make sure you hired a translator."

Just then Julienne's name and case number were announced. No translator showed.

"Stand," the lawyer said. They both stood, waiting while the judge reviewed the paperwork in front of him. He motioned the lawyer forward and they talked for some time. The prosecuting attorney joined them, but Julienne couldn't understand what they were saying.

"How do you plead?" the judge finally asked Julienne.

"Innocent."

Her lawyer signed some papers on Julienne's behalf, stating her plea.

"What happens now?" she asked.

"The judge will review everything before he makes a decision." He handed her a copy of the documents he'd signed on her behalf. "You'll have to pay the $200 fee for this to be officially filed with the court."

"My dad will take care of it," she said.

He hurried off before Julienne could ask him again what happened with the translator.

On the drive back to the prison, the guard told Julienne, "You'll probably go free."

*Did he get that impression because of the conversation between the lawyers and the judge? He could understand where I couldn't. I hope so.*

Back at El Inca, Julienne called her dad and gave him an update on what transpired.

"I wired money to the lawyer for a translator," he said, his tone revealing his anger.

"And now there's another $200 fee to file the papers signed today. I'm so sorry, Dad."

"It will all be worth it if the guard is right and you'll go free." He didn't sound convinced.

Julienne wondered how long it would take for the judge to make a decision. She remembered what Peggy said about how slow things moved in the court system, especially if you didn't use bribes to speed it up. Her emotions were like a roller coaster, hopeful one minute, hopeless the next.

To keep herself busy, she let the inmates know that she was continuing to do massage therapy. She set up the massage sessions in the inmate's room, not wanting to invite them to hers. She wanted to maintain some privacy and to protect herself from those who would steal from her if they had the chance.

*I'm thankful we're allowed to lock our doors during the day. Who knows what I'd have left!*

"De lista!" A guard shouted from the pavilion gate for the roll call in the morning. As he called out names, Julienne thought he sounded familiar. As each inmate heard their name, they answered from their room, "Presente."

When Julienne's name was called, she shouted, "Aqui! Here!"

He called out again. "Julienne!"

"Aqui!" she answered, raising her voice. She heard the guard unlocking the pavilion gate. He came to her doorway and yelled, "Señoríta Julienne!" It was Freddy, the guard from Latacunga who wouldn't get her migraine medicine and got transferred because of it.

*Oh, no. Now he's back here.*

"You need to come to the door when your name is called, so I can see your face!"

"Hey, I'm sorry," Julienne said. "I didn't mean anything by not coming to the door. I was just doing what the others did."

"That's it!" he said. "You get yourself out here and mop the corridor floors this morning."

"The women aren't going to let me mop the floors," she said, looking him in the eyes. "They want to do it and get paid."

"You're not going to get someone else to do this for you," he lashed out.

She shrugged her shoulders. "Okay." She went to get a mop and bucket while he waited. She started cleaning. Two women came over, took the mop away from her and started cleaning the floor.

"See?" she said to Freddy. "They won't let me do it."

"You're not going to pay your way out of this!" he shouted. He told the women to give her the mop.

Julienne took it and finished mopping the corridor. When he left, she went and thanked the women for trying to help her and paid them something. *He doesn't realize that these women need the money and want to do it. And I need to live with them.*

The director of the prison called Julienne into his office again.

"The Day of Recluse is coming up," he said. "We need you to be in the Queen Contest."

*Not again. He's got to be kidding.*

"You're a pretty girl and we need you to represent the United States."

*He's trying to bribe me with a compliment.*

"You need to do this," he said when Julienne didn't answer.

She nodded. "Okay." *Like I really have a choice.*

Over the next weeks, she participated as she had in the past, doing the fittings with the seamstress and helping in general with the planning and process.

*At least it's something to keep me occupied instead of sitting in my room worrying about my case.*

During all of this, she had a lot of contact with Lucia, who was also in the contest. They started to hang out with each other and Julienne enjoyed her company. Lucia didn't sit around thinking and worrying. She would look for opportunities and go for it. She was aggressive and knew how to manipulate to get what she wanted. Julienne liked that about her.

Lucia included Julienne when she had visitors and they would all have pleasant conversation, plus good food that her friends and family brought in from Kentucky Fried Chicken, McDonald's and other restaurants. Sometimes Asian food or sweet desserts like tres leches cake. During these visits, Julienne forgot about prison life for a few hours.

Lucia had a baby girl when she was arrested, Nicole. She lived with her birth father, but sometimes he brought Nicole to the prison and she stayed for a few days or a week. Although Lucia had long, straight dark brown hair, little Nicole had blonde hair and blue eyes. Julienne loved playing with her.

"She looks more like your daughter than mine," Lucia said.

"She's adorable, but don't you go starting a rumor!"

Julienne started spending more time with Jael, Sylvio and Crystal. Rosa now lived in the cell next to Julienne and she hung out with them as well. Rosa had four children at home. Jael was just eighteen years old and came from an all-girl family with younger sisters. Sylvio never had to be told to butch up. She was an intellectual New York lesbian and whenever Julienne received something in the mail that was cultural or a post card from England or Rome sent by visitors who came from the Explorers Club, she'd show them to Sylvio. She enjoyed conversations with her. Crystal had blonde hair and blue eyes and had been an exotic dancer.

One day Julienne received a package from her friend Joanna and she invited Rosa, Jael, Sylvio, and Crystal to her room.

"Look what I got!" she said as she opened the package. "Kraft macaroni and cheese, Twinkies, Ho Hos, Ding Dongs, Little Debbie snack cakes…"

"Wow!" Jael said. "What a treat."

"Yea! Sugar," Crystal said.

"And here's a movie." Julienne pulled a video out of the box. "*Sleepless in Seattle*. A chick flick! Hey, let's have a party and watch the movie on my VCR and eat some of these snacks." She grinned. "Let's be girly girls and do manicures."

Moments like these helped her forget she was in prison. Until she and they went back to their rooms and reality hit once again. The smells, the bugs and spiders and flies, the shouting and fighting, all brought the truth of her situation home.

Julienne continued to set up her massage sessions in inmates' rooms. A young woman approached her one day.

"I understand you give massages?"

"Yes, I do."

"Mama Lucha would like you to come to her room and give her a massage. She will pay you well."

Julienne agreed and said she would come the next day.

"She's in Maximum Security. Come there."

"Won't I need special permission to go there?"

"We'll arrange it, just come."

When she mentioned it to another inmate, she warned her, "Mama Lucha?! Be careful."

"Why?"

"She's like the queen of the underworld in Ecuador. No one messes with her or crosses her without getting hurt."

"I already said I'd do the massage."

"Just be careful. Treat her right and you'll be okay."

When Julienne met her, she seemed like a sweet, harmless little grandma with salt and pepper hair, who painted her lips with bright red lipstick. After introductions, Julienne had her lay face down on her prison bed, played some calming flute music on tape, and lit a few large candles that had the decal of Jesus or the Virgin Mary on them. *This seems a bit hypocritical considering her reputation.*

Julienne used almond oil and massaged her back while she whispered, "Tranquillo, tranquillo." Next she worked on her spine and whispered, "I'm going to count, one, two, three. When I do, take a deep breath. When I count again, breath out."

Julienne breathed in and out along with her and sensed Mama Lucha's body relaxing. The entire massage lasted an hour.

Mama Lucha became a regular client, paid well, and often gave her extra, telling her not to tell anyone. Julienne always felt respected by her.

"May I call you Luz," Julienne asked her one day. "It means light."

She smiled and said, "Si."

Sometimes she offered Julienne coffee and sweetbread that her family had brought in that morning. "My little American daughter," she'd say.

Another time she told Julienne, "If you ever need anything, you let me know."

"Thank you."

"Or if anyone bothers you, you let me know and I will take care of it." Her demeanor and facial expression changed and her dark piercing eyes narrowed. "Even if it's a guard."

Julienne nodded, but thought, *Oh my god, what would she have done to them? I know she likes me and means well, but this is scary. Lucia is right. I need to be careful.*

Julienne heard it was Mama Lucha's birthday one day and when she came to her, she said, "Happy Birthday!"

"Gracias."

"I heard you were having a big party to celebrate."

"Yes, but you can't come."

"Why not?"

"Just trust me. I don't want you there."

*I thought she liked me,* Julienne thought. *I'm probably one of the only ones in here who is friendly toward her. I don't get it.*

"In fact, I want you to stay in your room during the party."

Julienne kept silent.

"Do you understand? Entiendes?"

Her tone and narrowed dark eyes let Julienne know she meant it.

"Yes, okay."

The prison buzzed with activity that afternoon. Mama Lucha used her influence and brought in a live band, lots of food for a big barbecue, and large canisters of propane gas to cook with. Lots of visitors came from outside the prison to attend the party.

*Something's up,* Julienne thought. *This is quite a birthday bash. I wonder if she's planning to escape!*

The music started and people danced and sang and ate. Julienne stayed in her room, but could hear the celebration.

Lucia came to Julienne's pavilion the next morning.

"Did you hear what happened last night?"

"Did Mama Lucha escape? I had this feeling something was going to happen."

"That might have been the plan," Lucia said. "Apparently there was alcohol in those big propane tanks and who knows what else."

"Alcohol? Mixed with whatever gas residue was in the tanks?"

"Everyone became violently ill and several visitors were rushed to the hospital. Not everyone came back."

"You mean people died?!"

"Don't know for sure."

"So is Mama Lucha still here?"

"I heard she was transferred somewhere. Maybe Guayaquil."

Rumors flew all day, creating lots of excitement and speculation. The prison went into lockdown that night. The Word spread that the birthday bash was intended as a mass murder through poisoning.

*She invited people she wanted to kill!* Then she realized why Mama Lucha told her not to come to the party and to stay in her room. *She didn't want me to die!*

Her heart pounded and her thoughts kept her awake that night. *What if she escaped? Did she think of taking me with her? Maybe send someone to my room to get me?*

She tried to calm her thoughts, but it wasn't working. *Will I be suspected as participating in it just because I spent time with her yesterday? Or will I be interrogated to find out if I heard anything about the evil intention of the party? Will the fact that I didn't attend make me look suspicious?*

Then came the most disturbing thought of all.

*Will any of this affect my case?*

## Surviving Camp Inca

# Julienne Burleson

CHAPTER 21

# Camp Inca
# Clandestine Night Out

No one came to interrogate Julienne and a guard said the Mama Lucha was sent to Guayaquil. *What a relief!*

The day of the Queen Contest was getting closer, but Julienne's fittings and obligations were done. To pass the time one afternoon, she joined a few of the inmates in a card game and sat next to Crystal. During the game they talked about tattoos and piercings. "I had my belly button pierced when I was a teenager," Julienne said, "but I let it close up. What about you?"

"I don't have anything pierced except my ears," Crystal said.

"Hey, I've got an idea," Julienne said. "Let's pierce our belly buttons."

"Great idea! Do you have a needle?"

"Not for that," Julienne said. "I have two really small ones."

"I'll find one and meet you in your room."

When she showed Julienne the needle, she told her she went to someone who did embroidery and got it from her.

"Whoa...it's really thick. That's going to hurt," Julienne said.

"I'll do you first," Crystal said.

"Uh...how about if I do yours first?" Julienne insisted. She took a marker pen and drew dots on her belly button where the piercing would go. "You'd better lie down on the mattress so I can get this right." She started pushing the needle through with string on it.

Crystal screamed.

"Of course it hurts! Be quiet or someone might wonder what's going on in here." She took a pillow and put it over Crystal's face to muffle the screams.

When she finished, they walked down the hall to a mirror in the shower area. "Now I need a bikini," Crystal said, admiring her image. "When it heals. Okay, now it's your turn."

Back in Juleinne's room, they went through the process again. Crystal handed her a pillow for the screams of pain, then straddled her, and started pushing the needle through.

"Do it faster!" Julienne yelled into the pillow. "Get it over with."

"I'm trying," Crystal said.

A guard stepped into the doorway and said, "What the heck is going on in here? Get off her!"

Julienne lifted the pillow off her face. Crystal popped the needle through the other side and Julienne screamed.

The guard stared at them. "What the…?"

"Can't you see we're busy?" Julienne yelled. "I'm getting my belly button pierced."

The guard shook her head and left the room mumbling.

In spite of the pain she felt, Julienne burst out laughing. "Can you imagine what she thought?" Her laughing escalated into hysterics and tears came to her eyes. "Whew!" she said. "What a tension reliever." She looked down at her belly button and groaned. "It hurts so bad. I hope it doesn't get infected."

Lucia approached Julienne about the Queen Contest the next day.

"Some high diplomats and cabinet members are going to be here," Lucia said. "Smile a lot and use your feminine wiles."

"You mean flirt with them?"

"Just be yourself," she said. "I doubt you've ever had trouble getting guys." She gave a flirtatious smile. "These are the men in authority who can make things happen. They could get us some special privileges."

The day of the contest included dancing and Lucia took full advantage of it. The Director of Prisons was there with his entourage of officials and cabinet members and bodyguards. She went right for him. They danced and kissed in a secluded corner.

Tony, the director's assistant, asked Julienne to dance and she accepted.

"You're very beautiful," he said. "With your blonde hair, you look like a Barbie doll."

"Thank you," Julienne said, flattered, but a little embarrassed.

When the event was over, Lucia said to Julienne, "Tony really liked you."

"He called me Barbie," she said. "But hey, what about you? I noticed your moves on the director."

"I know what men want," she said, smiling. "He's very good looking. Don't you agree?"

"Yes, I admit that he is tall, dark, and handsome." Julienne said.

"He told me to call him Jimmy and he wants to spend more time with me," she said. "He swore he would make it happen."

Over the next few days, he sent her flowers, notes, and food. Then she got a message from him that he had arranged for her to come out one night after everyone was locked in their cell. A few days later he called her from his office and said to be ready at eight o'clock.

"We're sending someone to pick you up and a guard will come and get you from your cell."

"Can I bring my friend?"

"What friend?"

"My American friend," she said.

"Oh, you mean Barbie, the one with the long blond hair?" He chuckled. "Yes, she can come too. I'll invite someone that I know has a crush on her."

Lucia ran over to Julienne's pavilion and dashed into her room.

"We're going out tonight!"

"What do you mean, we're going out tonight? What are you talking about? Where are we going?"

"I don't know where," she said, "but we're going out."

She told Julienne about the phone call and said, "Put on some make-up and the nicest clothes you have." She left in a hurry to get back to her own pavilion and room.

Julienne was more and more excited as she flipped through her clothes. *Lucia is always thinking outside the box. Not like the other prisoners who just accept whatever comes along. She knows how to make things happen. Even if we just get out for an hour or two.*

From her limited clothes, she chose mint green jeans with a short-waist multi-colored sweater to show off her pierced belly button. At the moment, her hair was blonde, long, and natural curly. Sometimes she changed her hairstyle because it was one thing she had control over.

Right at eight o'clock, a guard came and unlocked Julienne's cell and said to follow him. Outside the prison, a luxury town car waited. Julienne watched Lucia walk over wearing a sleeveless, light brown, flowing cotton dress and laced up granny boots. Julienne smiled. *She's so petite and would look cute in anything.*

Julienne recognized two of the bodyguards who had been guards at the prison when she first came to El Inca. They had always been nice to her.

They drove to an upscale Italian restaurant in the heart of Quito. Four of them went inside to eat—the director and Lucia, Julienne and Tony. The guards waited outside by the car.

Julienne ordered eggplant parmesan with a salad. *This looks so good. What a treat.* Lucia had steak and a salad. They each drank a few glasses of red wine. Julienne was happy that the two men spoke some English and they all enjoyed each other's conversation and company.

After dinner the four of them went for a walk to see some of the sites. From there, they drove to a beautiful apartment. Julienne saw by the way

Jimmy and Lucia looked at each other and the way they touched, something more was going to happen. She started to feel awkward.

Tony came over to Julienne. "You really are beautiful." He looked at her pierced belly button, then up into her eyes. He leaned toward her to give her a kiss.

"No, no," she said. "I'm sorry, but I have a boyfriend at home waiting for me," she lied.

"But he's not here and you are gorgeous."

He tried again to kiss her, but she stepped aside. Jimmy and Lucia were heading for another room when a call came in. Jimmy had a short conversation, then hung up. "I'm sorry, but Tony and I have to go to an emergency meeting."

Julienne was relieved. Lucia put on a sad face.

"I'll have my personal guards take you wherever you'd like to go," he said. "Here." He handed Lucia some money. "Enjoy the rest of the evening."

They went outside and as they climbed into the car, Jimmy told the four guards "Take them wherever they want to go, but have them back at the prison by midnight."

The driver nodded and started the engine. "Where to?" he asked the girls.

"The airport?" Julienne asked.

Lucia laughed. She directed them to a European Club that the bodyguards had never been to. They only frequented bars and clubs that were for Ecuadorian nationals. The guards ordered drinks for them and the girls, then stood on the perimeter of the room and watched them, giving them space and leaving them alone.

The girls walked into the upbeat energetic atmosphere where people were dancing and laughing and having a great time.

"Come on!" Lucy said, heading for the crowded dance floor. "We're not going to waste our few hours of freedom."

They laughed and danced to music of the 90s and relished the whole scene. A few women danced on the bar. A young man came over to Julienne and lifted her up onto the bar to join them for a few of the dances.

Two young European men came over and asked their names and where they were from. "I'm Lucia and that's my friend, Julienne," she shouted over the music.

"We noticed you have chaperons."

"My cousin, Lucia, is an actress here in South America and the guards follow her for security," Julienne said.

The girls moved to another space on the dance floor, not wanting to answer any more questions.

"Lucia!" someone called. She turned around and saw an old friend of hers dancing near them.

"Where have you been?" He came over and gave her a hug. "We haven't seen you in ages. It's been two years!"

"I've been traveling with my cousin. She's a famous model and actress in the States."

"I noticed the bodyguards watching you. Is that why?"

"Yes, it's for her safety." Lucia introduced him to Julienne. "She doesn't speak Spanish," she said to curb any conversation.

"How long will she be here?"

"It's been a week and we're leaving tomorrow for the States."

Julienne just kept dancing. Lucia chatted with him a short while and then said to Julienne, "We better get going. He called some other friends and told them I was here and they're on their way. This could get complicated."

Lucia talked to the guards and asked if they could take them to another club just down the street. They agreed.

This club had more of an American crowd and for a moment Julienne felt like she was back in Hollywood dancing at the Viper Room. *This is so my element,* she thought. As she danced, she had flashbacks as they played familiar songs by bands and performers she knew: *No Doubt, General Public* and *Gregg Alexander's "Don't Give Up."*

## Surviving Camp Inca

*I miss my life so much. I feel like I could just walk out of the club, up Sunset Boulevard and into my apartment. My cats would be there to greet me and I could fall asleep in my little studio apartment overlooking the lights of West Hollywood.*

She reminded herself that soon she would be back into overcrowded penitentiary living. Not really living; just lost in a world of meaningless existence.

"It's time to go," one of the guards said. "We have to get you back on time."

On the way back, Lucia said, "Jules, why the sad face?"

"Going back to that dark place is depressing."

"Hey, we're not going to give in to that," she said. "Look at what fun we had tonight." They talked about the details of their evening out. Getting out of prison when everyone else was locked up, having a great meal and conversation, dancing.

"Like Cinderella," Julienne said. "Only now it comes to an end."

"No one can take tonight's memories away from us," Lucia said as they pulled up to El Inca.

"You're right," Julienne said. "I'm thankful, even if it was only for one night."

As they climbed out of the town car, they gave the four body guards a hug and thanked them for a great evening. The men turned them over to the jail guards. As they walked into the prison, the energy felt dark and moody.

"It's midnight, Cinderella," Julienne said. They both giggled.

They sensed the resentment of the jail guards as they escorted them through the metal gates. The sound of the gates clanking shut and the padlocks snapping closed echoed through the dark corridor as they returned to their cells.

*I wonder how many questions we'll get from fellow inmates tomorrow,* Julienne thought. *They'll probably be jealous and angry, depending on what we tell them. Or maybe they don't even know.*

She lay in bed, her emotions on a roller coaster ride. The rank smell of the prison brought her back to brutal reality. Five hundred women living together, fighting, drinking, smoking, doing drugs.

*But I did get to be Cinderella for a night. Lucia does know how to make things happen. I just hope it doesn't backfire on us and get us in trouble.*

After their special night out, the director continued sending gifts to Lucia, but it was becoming more difficult to arrange taking her out because of rumors and jealousy and politics.

"I've been thinking," he told Lucia one day. "I can get you transferred to Jail Four where all this politics shouldn't be a problem."

"Okay, but can I bring my friend?"

"Barbie?" He laughed. "I'll work it out."

Lucia told Julienne about it right away.

"We're being transferred to Jail Four. I hear it's like a country club jail. It's supposed to be only for deputies of government, police officers, and military police. It's a private co-ed jail for those who might get killed if placed in a regular jail."

"The director can just do that? I'm amazed."

"It's who you know that counts," Lucia said.

One week later, they were transferred to Jail Four.

CHAPTER 22

# Jail Four
# Country Club Jail

On the drive over to Jail Four, Lucia kept talking about all the freedom they would have there.

"We'll even be able to go out on our own to do grocery shopping," she said. She lowered her voice to a whisper. "We may even be able to escape from there, especially with my connection with Jimmy."

"I'm just glad to get out of Camp Inca," Julienne said.

They pulled up to an old Victorian style house and drove into the courtyard. Decorative diamond-shaped wrought iron bars covered the large downstairs and second floor windows.

"I heard that Interpol confiscated this house in a police raid and then turned it into a jail," Lucia said as they climbed out of the car.

Julienne looked around. Military police in fatigues walked around the property with machine guns. "Wow, the guards at Camp Inca didn't carry guns."

"We'll be safe here," Lucia said. "They're here to protect the prisoners."

Margarita, a pleasant woman in her mid-forties, greeted them at the front door.

"I'll give you the tour and take you to your room," she said. "The living room, kitchen, and dining room are here on the first floor. In the morning, I serve coffee and make breakfast for everyone, and serve lunch at noon." She smiled. "Some of the men call me the mother hen."

The military police quarters were in the large bedroom on the first floor. Upstairs, a huge bedroom had its own bathroom, two sets of bunk beds, a king-size bed, and a few larger bunk beds and dressers.

"This is where you will be," Margarita said.

Julienne walked over to their window and looked outside. It overlooked the street. *We can watch cars go by from up here. I saw a large Ginsu knife in the kitchen downstairs. I wonder if it would cut through these iron bars.*

As if realizing Julienne's thoughts, Margarita said, "A guard is stationed on the roof at all times."

"To the left of the stairs, going up a few more steps, is Ryan's room, one of the inmates," Margarita continued. "His wife comes and visits quite often. The rest of the men live in the building in back of the house. They have twelve small rooms and two bathrooms."

"What bed is ours?" Lucia asked.

"Which would you like?"

"How about the king-size bed?"

"That's fine, Margarita said. "You two go ahead and get settled and I'll make you some coffee."

Lucia jumped on the bed and smiled. "When is the last time you slept in a real bed?"

"This is great," Julienne agreed.

They put away their clothes and other personal items they had been allowed to bring. They smelled coffee brewing and went downstairs.

"Here you go," Margarita said, handing them coffee mugs. She sat with them at the dining room table. "Do you have any questions for me?"

"What's your story? How did you end up here?" Lucia asked.

"I was in the wrong place at the wrong time," Margarita said. "A big corruption case in a police department brought about the arrest of almost the entire department. I got swept up with the others." She made the sign of the cross and continued, "But God will take care of me. I trust Him and I'm safe here."

*Why would she think God is taking care of her? That's a bit naïve.*

Margarita looked at Lucia. "I'm aware of why you were sent here by the director. Be careful. He's married and has kids. All he wants is to sleep with you. You must know that you'll have no future with him."

"I'm well aware of that," Lucia said. She started to say something else, but dropped it.

"Another thing," Margarita said. "You girls have to be careful here. Although you're safe, you need to realize the type of prisoners placed here. Some are in for murder, some for raping young women and men, some were drug cartel-owned police, and one used water boarding to torture some teenagers to get information out of them and they died. All of them were government employees or officials, or police officers. Tough men." She looked at Lucia and then Julienne. "You're both beautiful girls. And they're men with needs. If you were to get involved with them, imagine the drama and danger that could cause." She got up from the table, taking the coffee mugs with her. "Just be careful," she warned.

Back in their room, Julienne said, "What she said makes sense. We do have to be careful."

"She's the motherly type, wants to take us under her wing," Lucia said.

In the morning, they woke to coffee brewing and breakfast cooking.

"This is incredible," Julienne said. "How did I get here? I'm an American; this is a military jail."

"I told you, stick with me, Barbie." Lucia grinned.

Downstairs, Margarita was already serving coffee to some of the men. When she served breakfast, no one was allowed to eat until she did the sign of the cross and prayed before the meal. They all respected her and complied.

Everyone introduced themselves and as each day passed, there were no problems between the men and women. On Sundays, Margarita gave special talks about all the blessings the Lord had given them that week. Again, everyone showed her respect and listened.

The director showed up when he could so that he and Lucia could be together.

## Julienne Burleson

Julienne started working out and exercising, using bar bells and playing volleyball. She went on an apple kick and ate healthy food. The men showed respect and restraint and she felt safe. She hung out on the balcony and talked with them. They were more intelligent than most prisoners and she enjoyed their conversations. She loved the freedom of going with a guard to market and sometimes out to eat.

*Some of these men are the most demented people imaginable, yet they treat me well and I feel safer with them than I did at Camp Inca. And they believe I'm innocent, that I shouldn't be in prison. This turns my thinking upside down.*

"With all the freedom we have here, it seems like it would be fairly easy to escape," Julienne said to Lucia one day.

"You'd have to have a good detailed plan. Look around outside. Military police carrying machine guns. They could use them on us if they had to."

"You think they would?"

"Who knows?" Lucia shrugged. "Hey, the guard told me he was going to be gone for a while. Let's go down and watch TV in his room." She headed down the stairs.

"I can't believe he trusts us in his room," Julienne said, following her.

Lucia turned on the TV and then started poking around the room. She opened a large cabinet and discovered his guns. "It wasn't locked!"

"What are you doing!" Julienne said.

"I just want to see what they have." She rummaged through the cabinet and pulled out one of the guns. "Come here, I'll show you how to use this." She handed the gun to Julienne and showed her how to hold it and pull the trigger.

"I really don't want to do this," Julienne said. "I don't think I could ever shoot anyone."

Lucia put that gun back and then pulled out a machine gun. "Imagine what we could do with this!" She picked it up and pointed it around the room, pretending to shoot. "We could blow everyone up!"

"You're crazy!" Julienne said. "You wouldn't do that."

"I could do it," she bragged. "If it meant getting out of here, I could do it."

"Really? You could kill people?"

She nodded.

"Even the guys in the back?"

"I don't care," she said, "if it meant I could really go free."

"Una amiga loca!" Julienne said. "Put that back."

"Look," she said. "I found the ammo, stamps for approvals and some keys."

"Put it all back!" Julienne said, standing watch at the door. "Do you realize what kind of trouble you could get us in?" Julienne's heart pounded. "I can't believe the cabinet wasn't locked!"

"You need to toughen up if you ever want to escape," Lucia said.

They heard the guard coming into the house and Lucia quickly put the machine gun back in the cabinet and sat down as if they'd been watching TV. He glanced in the room and they ignored him, keeping their eyes on the TV. He left and went to the kitchen and they scrambled back upstairs to their own room.

---

Jimmy missed one of their times to get together and called Lucia to apologize. This happened several times.

"He's getting questioned and pressured about it," Lucia told Julienne.

Soon, he stopped coming at all.

"Ryan's pretty hot, don't you think?" Lucia said.

"He's married, and he's a prisoner. Don't even think about it."

"But he's wealthy," Lucia said. "Margarita said so."

Lucia soon had an intimate relationship going with Ryan.

"Look at this," Margarita said to Julienne and Lucia one day over coffee. She held up the newspaper she was reading. "It's been all over the news."

"Jacqueline Weis is a Columbian and involved in a big case; one of the largest drug shipments in the country. About one hundred people were involved and apparently Jacqueline was one of the masterminds of the whole operation. I hear they are sending her here."

"Why here? Is she military or police?"

"No, but her husband is in the Ecuadorian Air Force so she's allowed to come here, partly for her own protection. There are people who would like to kill her."

The day Jacqueline arrived, the dynamics of the place changed. Margarita showed her the women's room.

"I'll take the king-size bed," she announced.

"That's our bed," Lucia said. "Pick another one."

"You don't seem to understand," Jacqueline said. "I'm taking that bed. I'm married and my husband will be coming to spend the night when he can."

"Well, we were here first and it's our bed," Lucia challenged her. Her tone let Jacqueline know that she would have to fight for it. And she would lose.

"We'll let you use the bed when your husband comes for a visit," Julienne said. "Until then, pick another one."

"Fine, but just to let you know, I get the shower first in the morning." With that, she started to put her clothes and other items away in one of the dressers.

Julienne glanced at Lucia. "Can you believe this?" she whispered.

"She thinks she's a big shot, a queen bee," Lucia said. "She'll find out that she's just an inmate like everyone else."

In the morning when they went down for coffee, Jacqueline was one of the last ones to come, but made her way in front of everyone else to get her coffee. They all stared at her.

"What?!" she said. "I need my coffee first thing in the morning."

"Whoa," Lucia said to Julienne. "Hold me back. She is asking for it."

"She's a diva," Julienne said.

Later in the day when the girls were watching TV, Jacqueline walked over and switched the channel.

Lucia fumed and stood to her feet.

"Don't do it," Julienne said. "She's not worth it."

When her husband came to spend the night, they let them use the king-size bed. It was a bit embarrassing with everyone sleeping in the same room. Not much privacy.

Any harmony that existed prior to Jacqueline coming turned into a nightmare. Everything became an argument.

"I actually have thoughts of wanting to go back to Camp Inca," Julienne said one day. "That's how frustrated I am with her."

Soon after, Jacqueline began sleeping with one of the guys in the back. More drama.

News came that the current government was about to be overthrown. That would include the director. He advised Lucia that it would be dangerous for her and Julienne to stay there any longer. They needed to go back to El Inca. They weren't really supposed to be in a government facility and he wouldn't be able to protect them.

Guards from El Inca were sent to pick them up.

Julienne had lost a lot of weight exercising while she was there, so her clothes didn't fit her any more. Jacqueline liked her clothes and asked if she could buy them.

"Fine, if you have the money," Julienne said. They agreed on a price.

"I have to wait for my husband to bring the money," she said. "I'll make sure you get it."

After only four months at Jail Four, Julienne and Lucia were sent back to El Inca.

## CHAPTER 23

# Camp Inca 3rd Time Sentenced!

As the guards from El Inca walked Julienne and Lucia back into prison, the guards' demeanor and comments revealed their negative attitude.

"You two think you're so special," one of them said.

"Jail Four is for officials, not the likes of you."

"Ignore them," Lucia said.

As they walked through the final gate, some of the inmates looked at them, and then turned their backs.

"This is like the walk of shame," Julienne said.

"They're jealous."

Rosa had lived next door to Julienne and Peggy. She took Julienne's room when she left for Jail Four and now welcomed Julienne back to become her roommate. Julienne looked around the room and saw that her VCR and many other things were still there.

"I used some of your things," Rosa said. "I didn't know if or when you were coming back."

"It's okay. Thank you for keeping my things safe," Julienne said. Rosa didn't have a lot and Julienne was glad to share with her.

A few weeks later, Lucia told Julienne that Jacqueline had been kicked out of Jail Four and would be coming to El Inca.

"I hate that woman," Lucia said. "I wonder what kind of trouble she'll cause. She'll soon learn the inmates here won't put up with her crap."

"I remember one time in Jail Four you punched her," Julienne said, grinning.

"She thought she could bully me. I let her know she couldn't. That's all."

"Why does she have to leave Jail Four?"

"Her husband found out she was sleeping with some of the guys and decided to file for divorce, so she has to be transferred. His position with the Ecuadorian Air Force was her only right to be there. Her case is in Guayaquil so at some point she'll be sent there. I'm sure she'll get a heavy sentence for what she did."

"How do you find out about all this stuff?" Julienne asked.

"Mostly, guards. They like to talk. Makes them feel important."

When Julienne heard Jacqueline had arrived, she started to think about the money she still owed her for the clothes. *I can't let her get away with this. She needs to pay me.* She found out what pavilion and room she was in, walked over there to the third floor, and knocked on the door.

"Jacqueline, you need to give me my money for the clothes."

"Sorry, I don't have it." Her tone was dismissive.

"I don't believe you. I want my money."

"I just told you," she said in a condescending tone, "I can't give it to you right now."

"You'd better give it to me," Julienne said, her anger rising.

"I'll give it to you when I feel like it." She slammed the door in Julienne's face.

As Julienne turned and walked down the two flights of stairs, her anger turned to rage. *Who does she think she is! She just walks over anyone she pleases. Well, I'm not going to take it anymore. She's not going to bully me!*

At the bottom of the stairs, she found a metal pole and started swinging it like a baseball bat against the handrail and metal bars on the staircase. The sound of metal crashing against metal made a lot of noise and other inmates began to crowd around her.

"Jacqueline!" she shouted up the stairway, still pounding the metal bar, "You'd better give me my money!"

"Jacqueline! You get down here right now!" Her anger exploded into rage.

One of the guards came over and said, "Que pasa! What's wrong?"

"Leave me alone," Julienne said. She paced back and forth.

"No, no, don't do this," she said. "You don't want to get in trouble. You have such a good record. Don't do this." She tried to calm her down.

"Leave me alone!" Julienne shouted at her. "This is between me and Jacqueline."

"Jacqueline!" she screamed.

Jacqueline opened her door, walked out of her pavilion and down the stairs. "What's wrong?"

"You know what I want," Julienne said. "You give me my money right now or I'll kick your ass!" She waved the pole around in the air, threatening her. "I'll do it right here in front of everybody! I don't care. Just give it to me now!"

"But I already told you, I don't have it."

"You're lying! You arrogant little twerp! I'll beat you with this pole! No excuses. Give it to me right now!"

"Okay, okay," Jacqueline said. She hurried back to her room and got the money. She cautiously came down the stairs, glancing at the guard and the inmates standing around. She handed the money over to Julienne. The inmates stood in silence, staring.

One whispered, "I've never seen Julienne act like this before. She's gone crazy."

"I'm not taking your crap anymore!" she shouted at Jacqueline. She grasped the money, threw down the metal pole, and stormed to her own pavilion and room. "I'm through with people walking all over me," she muttered to herself. "No more nice girl."

"Are you okay?" Rosa asked. "This isn't like you. What happened?"

"I'm okay now. I have my money." She told Rosa the details of what happened at Jail Four and what an arrogant bully Jacqueline had been.

When Lucy heard about the incident, she said, "You go, girl!" She gave her a high five. "And I missed the whole thing!"

As the days and weeks passed, Julienne tried to keep herself busy, trying not to get discouraged about the lack of anything happening on her case. She decided to exercise again because she had felt so much better when she kept physically active at Jail Four.

She picked up the Walkman her father had sent and used ear phones to listen to music while she did her own step class. She listened to Cyndi Lauper singing *Girls Just Want To Have Fun* from the 80s. It brought back happy memories of hanging out with her cousin, Jodi, jumping and dancing around to the 80's music when they were young teenagers. She went to the gauncha and began on a wide set of stairs that rose up against a wall, like a set of cement bleachers. Behind that wall was the laundry area. She moved up and down the steps with the beat of the music. After a while, she turned around and realized two other inmates were following behind her.

"What are you doing?"

"Just following what you're doing," one said.

"Do you mind?" another asked.

"No, I guess not."

Over the next few days, others joined in. Julienne called over her shoulder, "Okay, come on! Keep it up!" She did an hour class.

"Hey, we want to hear the music too," they said. Someone brought a player and they listened to the tapes on it. The tapes of 80's music that Joanna had sent her. As they got the hang of it, she added floor exercises.

One of Julienne's visitors asked what they could bring her and she asked for a yoga mat. The others brought their towels so they wouldn't have to lie on the cement floor. Some couldn't handle it and dropped out. For the ones who stayed, she added walking time around the outer edge of the basketball court.

One of the American inmates said, "This reminds me of the movie, *Midnight Express*, when Billy Hayes is in prison doing walking exercise in a circle. At one point he says, 'I'm going against the grain, I'm not turning into one of them,' and he turns and starts walking in the opposite direction. The inmates get confused and freak out because he's doing it different."

Julienne had the VCR from her dad and managed to have found the movie. Several of them watched it together. Although it was a depressing movie, the walking scene was funny. And he got out of prison in the end.

The next day, after walking around the court several times, Julienne turned and announced, "Let's be rebels and pull a *Midnight Express*." She turned abruptly and marched in the opposite direction. The Spanish girls who hadn't seen the movie wondered what she was doing. The American girls chuckled.

"I'm following Billy Hayes," Julienne said as she walked. "I'm getting out of here. I'm not staying."

In between activities, she wrote letters to her parents and Joanna. She'd always encourage Julienne, telling her, "You're a fighter. You're strong. You're going to be okay."

Julienne did some massages, and hung out with Lucia or Rosa, Jael and Sylvio. In spite of all that, she still fought discouragement when alone. She couldn't seem to crawl out of the void. *I want to move forward with my life. How long will I have to stay here, living in misery?*

A few weeks later, the director of the prison sent someone to go and get Julienne.

"Julienne!" A passadora called from below her pavilion.

She stepped outside her room and called down, "What?"

"Director Carlos wants to talk to you."

A guard took her through the two gates to the director's office just inside the main gate. *I hope I'm not in trouble.*

When she stepped inside his office, she noticed the serious expression on his face.

"Bad news," he said, as he picked up a document on his desk and handed it to her.

"What is this? It's in Spanish. I don't understand."

He pointed at the number. "Diez años."

"Ten years?" She saw her name on the official document. Panic rioted within her. "Me? I'm sentenced to ten years?" A flood of tears washed down her face. "No!" she shouted, shaking her head back and forth.

"This can't be!" She let out a terrifying scream. "This can't be happening! I'm innocent! I'm supposed to go free!"

"Calm down, please calm down," he said. "I'm so sorry."

Two guards entered the office and stood near the doorway. One of them approached her in a soothing voice, "Tranquillo, Julienne."

"No! Leave me alone!" She stood to her feet and paced around the office. "You want me to be calm?" She tossed the document back on the director's desk. "You just told me I have to live in this hell hole for ten years!" She pulled at her hair and let out an earsplitting scream.

The guards glanced at each other, not knowing what to do.

"Screw you! Screw El Inca! Screw Ecuador! Where's your justice?! You have none!" Compulsive sobs shook her.

Ranting and raving, she ran out of the office and leaned against a wall. She let her body slide to the ground. She couldn't control the hysterics.

The director told one of the guards to get Lucia; he told the other one to get a bottle of tequila. When the guard returned, Director Carlos took the bottle from him, opened it, and handed it to Julienne. She took a sip. She felt shattered.

"Julienne!" Lucia came running over to her. "I'm sorry," she said. "You don't deserve this."

When she saw Lucia, Julienne broke into hysterical sobs again.

"I thought the prosecutor was on my side," she choked out. "He knows I'm innocent." She took a long swig of the tequila. "The lawyers acted like I had nothing to worry about." She took another drink. "And the guards kept telling me I was going free." This time she took several swallows of the tequila.

"Jerks! Liars! Assholes!" she shouted. She glugged down the rest of the bottle and lay down on the cement floor, sobbing. Lucia rubbed her back and smoothed her hair. "I'm so sorry, I'm so sorry," she repeated.

Because of the screaming, people from the other official offices in the area began to gather.

"Keep away from her!" Lucia yelled at them. "Get away! You didn't do anything to help her. Everyone is always lying to us. Just leave us alone!" She looked over at the guards and the director. "You too!" she shouted.

"Let them stay there as long as they want," the director said to the guards.

"Until lockdown at seven."

Lucia stayed with her and they watched the sun go down.

"I swear to you," Julienne said to Lucia, "I will get out of here. Soon. Whatever it takes."

At seven o'clock, the guards took them back to their rooms. The sound of the padlock clicking shut on the outside of her door sent Julienne into another spasm of frenzied sobs.

CHAPTER 24

## Camp Inca Escape Plan

THE NEXT MORNING Julienne called her dad to tell him about the sentence. He wept when he heard the news.

"I'll talk to the lawyer and see if there's any chance of an appeal," he said. "But, Jules, if you can find a way to get out of there, take it. As long as it's safe, if you're sure you won't get caught."

"I've certainly thought about it," she said. "Someone told me that if I escaped and made it to the American Embassy, Ecuador couldn't remove me because it's considered American soil."

"I don't know if that's true," he said. "Be cautious and careful about checking out details before you do anything. You don't want to make the situation worse."

"I suppose they could just wait for me to leave the Embassy, since I can't live there forever, and then snatch me and take me back into custody."

"Jules...you're in a vulnerable state of mind right now. You're not invincible. Don't take risks that are too dangerous."

"I won't. And I don't want to be a fugitive for the rest of my life."

"Remember, there's no extradition between the States and Ecuador. Once you're out of their country and in the States, you're free."

"Maybe I could make it to Columbia and get a new passport there," she said.

"Don't rush into any plan," he said. "You're a smart girl. Be careful. And let's not give up."

After she talked with her dad, Julienne called her friend, Joanna, in California and gave her the bad news.

"I don't know what to say…That's devastating. I still have a hard time wrapping my mind around the whole situation. It's surreal."

"Just make sure in your travels you don't do anyone a favor and bring something back to the States for them."

"Never," Joanna said. "I wish there was something more I could do. You know I told your dad what I knew about Ashley. Or whatever her real name is."

"Just keep writing," Julienne said. "There isn't much to look forward to here, but I do enjoy receiving mail."

"I will."

Julienne cried again when they hung up. Her eyes were still puffy from all the tears she had shed. *How many more are left?*

When she talked with Lucia the next day, Julienne said, "At least Carlos believes I'm innocent. One of the few."

"He's a good man. He used to be a colonel in the military. I'm glad he's the director here and not Carolina."

"Yeah, she used to call me into her office and ask me questions about you," Julienne said. "She didn't like you at all. I think she was trying to get something out of me that she could use against you."

"She was jealous," Lucia said. "At one time I dated a lawyer that she had dated." She grinned. "She hates me."

As they stood out in the courtyard talking, Director Carlos came over to them. He glanced around. "There's a strike brewing; I just wanted to warn you. You better prepare for it. There's some serious stuff going on."

"Thanks for the warning," Julienne said. Just in case the strike led to power and water rationing, Julienne checked her water supply in the buckets in her room. One was almost empty and she paid one of the women to help her fill it up. She knew that once the water was shut off, there would be long lines with five hundred prisoners waiting for their buckets to be filled when the fire trucks showed up with water. She'd been through this many times already. Sometimes water would only be available for two hours; other times not at all.

Within days chaos broke out not only in the jail, but in the country. Government officials froze bank accounts, after they had withdrawn their own funds. Angry citizens rioted and that sparked clashes between security forces and demonstrators. Guards threatened to strike because they weren't getting paid. No visitors were allowed in the jail. Power and water rationing came next. If it didn't last too long, Julienne was at least prepared for that. With the power out, the women who had them, used candles and flashlights. Not too many had flashlights because whenever there was a raid, the guards would confiscate them. Julienne lit six candles and stood them up with candle wax that she dripped on a board. *At least it won't be pitch black in my room at night.*

The news continued to trickle down through the jail. A group of indigenous people came down from the mountains and threatened to burn down the communication towers if they didn't get their money. The jail broke out in an uproar and Carlos tried to calm everyone down.

He told Julienne and Lucia they should go to their rooms to be safe. Then the news came that a group of highland Indians had stormed the Presidential Palace during a protest and the current government might be overthrown. The guards walked out on strike. The inmates rioted and locked the gates from the inside so no one could come in, including the guards.

"I don't want to be a hostage," Carlos said. He took off running to the locked gate, scaled the high wall, and jumped to the other side.

"Wow!" Julienne said. "Did you see that?"

"I told you he was a military colonel," Lucia said. "Obviously in great shape."

Military police were sent in to restore order and with Carlos gone, Carolina was brought to El Inca and became the new director of the jail, as she had been once before. With the change in government officials, Julienne feared any chance of appealing her sentence had been lost.

She stayed away from most of the inmates. She didn't want to talk to them about her sentence. She sat in her room and listened to music. When she had to go out for something, she wore sunglasses to cover her tears and puffy eyes.

The following week when visits were allowed again, Gene and Helen Brown came to see Julienne. They talked about the turmoil in the country and about Julienne's sentence. Joan told her to read her Bible and look for answers and comfort there. After they left, she flipped through the Bible, reading a little here and there, but didn't find what she was looking for. *What AM I looking for?* She didn't really know.

She put the Bible away and lay in bed, day after day, daydreaming about escape plans. *I'll run them by Lucia. She has an eight-year sentence and I'm sure she wants to get out of here as much as I do.*

"What about the Embassy being American soil?" she asked Lucia. "Is that true?"

"What? You expect them to fly you out of there in a helicopter or something? As soon as you left, the police could take you into custody."

"Well, I guess that wouldn't work. What about the way Ramie escaped? Assuming it wasn't just a straight bribe. I'd need a gun though."

"And what? You could shoot someone? Like a guard?"

"No, I doubt I could do that." Julienne sighed. "Others have escaped, why can't we?"

Whenever they got together they discussed their ideas.

"I've got a plan," Lucia said one day. "But it will take four of us."

"Who do you trust?" Julienne asked.

"I was thinking about Sylvio and Michelle."

Michelle was an attractive black girl, arrested about the same time as Julienne. They had gotten to know each other through their participation in the Queen Contest. She spoke some English and hung out with the European inmates.

Sylvio grew up in New York with an Ecuadorian father and American mother. She acted as a mule and flew back and forth between Ecuador and New York, getting drugs from the Columbians. Julienne remembered when she first came to El Inca. It was on a visit day.

No one knew her and when it was time for visitors to leave, one of the guards came over and said," Sorry, but you have to leave now." With her short masculine haircut and the style of her jeans and tee shirt, he thought she was a male visitor. Sylvio said, "Okay," and walked out to the front gate. A guard there recognized her and asked, "Where do you think you're going?" "The guard told me to leave," she said. Some of the inmates nicknamed her Studmuffin.

"I like her," Julienne said to Lucia. "She gets along well with everybody."

"Okay, then. Let's have a meeting with them," Lucia said.

The four of them met and Lucia laid out the plan. "I found out that there's a shower in the Red Zone that doesn't ever get used because it's not working," she said. "It's right up against an outside wall and there's an open field on the other side of it. We'll dig a hole in the wall inside that shower, chipping away as much as we can each day."

She looked at Sylvio and Michelle. "That will be our job. The guards won't be suspicious if we're in the Red Zone. We'll take turns chipping away and when we're finished each day, we'll put an old bed frame and whatever other storage stuff we can find, up against the hole in the wall. No one goes in there so it won't be conspicuous."

"What's the plan when the hole is big enough for us to crawl through?" Julienne asked.

"We have time to get some rope and some sheets to tie together and shimmy down. Once we're across the field, we each get a taxi. That's safer than arranging for someone to pick us up." She looked around at each one and said, "We have to go about our routines and not talk, hint or arouse suspicion that something's up."

Everyone nodded in agreement.

"Julienne, you'll be our lookout. We can't have you in the Red Zone; you'd stand out too much."

"Okay, what do I do?"

"You often exercise and walk around the courtyard in the morning. Keep doing that and if you see a guard walking into the area where we are, or anything that seems out of place, start walking fast in circles as if it's part of your exercise. That will be our signal to scatter."

"Okay," Julienne said. "I'll start tracking the changing of the guards this week, including the ones on the roof who watch the courtyard. I'll time everything and write it down."

"We need to have the hole finished by one of the visit days. A Wednesday would be best because visiting hours are over at three o'clock. When the visitors leave, the guards are always out front, not in the back where we'll be. With everyone leaving, the guards will be occupied with them and won't be as likely to notice we're gone." She smirked. "Until it's too late. We'll use a rope and sheets to repel down the wall on the outside, not too hard to do since we're all in shape. Then we run through the field and catch a cab on the other side. There are always cabs there. We'll take several, changing from one area to another until we get to the coast. There we pay a few hundred dollars to go across the strait into Columbia."

"I can apply for a new passport there," Julienne said, getting excited. "And hop a flight back to the States."

"Okay," Lucia continued. "We'll need a radio to play loud music when the guards aren't around and we're digging the hole. That will cover any suspicious noise the inmates might hear. The only problem I see is if there's an officer on the roof when we're running across the field." She glanced at Julienne. "Your tracking of their schedule is important."

Julienne nodded.

The following week they started their routine of the three going to the Red Zone to dig and Julienne hung out in the courtyard. She wore sunglasses, hoping it wouldn't be obvious that she was continually looking around.

The day came when there was just a thin layer of wall left to smash through and they made a plan to leave that Wednesday. When the day arrived and the visitors were all leaving, Julienne was about to get up from her observation post in the courtyard and go to the Red Zone to meet up with the others. Suddenly, military troops marched through the gates. Julienne controlled her panic and stood still. Four rows of them in full military garb marched right past her. She leaned casually against the courtyard wall and pretended she wasn't paying attention to them.

Lucia and the others scattered into different rooms in the Red Zone when they heard the troops coming.

"Go to your rooms!" they shouted at all the inmates. "Go to your rooms now!"

The women called to one another, asking what was going on.

"This is a Red Zone lockdown! Go to your cell!" a guard yelled.

They started tearing the place apart. As they searched the cells and other areas, the inmates yelled back and forth from cell to cell, trying to find out what this was all about.

As Julienne left the courtyard and was walking back to her room, several inmates stopped her and asked if she knew what was happening.

"I don't know," she said. *I hope my face doesn't look guilty.* She walked back to her pavilion and stayed in her room even though the lockdown was only for the Red Zone.

Inmates yelled to each other from pavilion to pavilion.

"They found a hole in wall," one yelled out. "Someone was going to escape!"

Julienne kept silent.

At nine o'clock that night, a guard came to Julienne's room. "The director wants to see you."

*Oh, no. What did they find out?*

As Julienne approached Director Carolina's office, Lucia was on her way out. She whispered to Julienne, "They questioned Sylvio and Michelle before me and I think Michelle talked."

Julienne recognized one of the officers who questioned her. He had been one of Jimmy's personal bodyguards who had been out on the town with them that night. He was the driver and now had moved up in the ranks. He spoke some English and was sent there to interrogate them.

"Julienne, did you dig that hole?"

"No, I didn't. I can honestly tell you that I didn't dig that hole."

"We already questioned the others involved."

"Listen. If I dug that hole, I would have dug it faster, and I would be free right now."

One of the officers chuckled. Another warned her, "Don't be a smart alec!"

"Okay, well it's obvious you're going to send me somewhere. Will that somewhere be warm? Or cold? I need to know how to pack."

A guard took her back to her room to gather a few personal things. The inmates in her pavilion came by and started asking questions.

"Where are you going?" one asked.

"I don't know," Julienne said.

"What happened?"

"I don't know. They're transferring me somewhere."

"Do they think you had something to do with that Red Zone business?"

"Apparently they do."

"Did Lucia do it?"

"No," Julienne said.

The guard took her to the front gate area and two hours later she, Lucia, Sylvio, and Michelle were each assigned a guard and loaded onto a school bus.

Destination unknown.

## CHAPTER 25

# Guayaquil Prison
# Attempted Escape – Inmate Shot

"No talking!" one of the guards said as the women were seated in different sections of the bus. Julienne was taken to the back.

Latin music blared through the speakers and after they had been on the road for a short time, the driver pulled out a bottle of pure grain alcohol. The more he drank, the faster he drove. The bus began weaving back and forth on the dark and winding Andes mountain road, just avoiding perilous cliffs and swerving around a mud slide.

*Oh my god,* Julienne thought. *If he keeps this up, we're going to crash!* She clung to the seat in front of her.

"Watch out!" she shouted at the driver at one point. Her heart pounded as he simply turned up the music and continued drinking. "I'm getting sick back here," she said to the guard. He was the one from Jail Four and was assigned to her for the transfer. He let her move up front.

Michelle glared at Julienne as she moved past her to the front of the bus.

*If she isn't the one who confessed, maybe she thinks I am,* Julienne thought. She sat in a seat across the aisle from Lucia.

"You don't look so good."

"I'll do better up here than sitting in the back of the bus," Julienne said. "This driver is crazy."

"Crazy and drunk," Lucia said.

"How do you think the guards found out about the escape plan?" Julienne asked.

"Someone in the Red Zone must have reported us. Since none of us live in that pavilion, they must have wondered why we were over there every day. When my name came up, they probably got suspicious."

"The director knows we're friends," Julienne said, "so she figured I wouldn't say anything. That might be why they brought me in last for questioning."

"Michelle couldn't keep her mouth shut," Lucia said. "That's what I think. Without someone confessing, they had no real proof it was us."

Sylvio tried to move closer to them to get in on the conversation, but her guard stopped her.

The driver pulled into a bus station where Michelle was taken off.

"Where are they taking her?"

"I'm not sure," Lucia said. "I heard the guard tell the driver they were putting her on another bus to Esmeraldas. That's close to the Columbia straits."

"I wonder if you and I will be sent to the same place." Julienne said.

"No. They'll want to separate us."

At the next stop, Sylvio was dropped off in Portoviejo near the coast south of Quito.

"Where am I going?" Julienne asked the guard.

"Guayaquil," he said.

"No!" Julienne said. "Peggy told me that was the worst prison in the world for women. I heard some women who went there never came back. You can be forgotten there. Lost in the system." Panic set in. "What if my dad doesn't know where I am and I can't call him from there?"

"You'll be okay," Lucia said. "Just know that the jail isn't going to bother to notify anyone of your transfer. Contact the American Embassy in Guayaquil yourself and let them know you're there. You'll be able to call your dad, just like you have been doing. Don't worry. You've learned how to survive."

They hugged and cried when it was Lucia's turn to be dropped off in Vinces.

Still a long drive south to Guayaquil, Julienne closed her eyes and managed to doze off.

At daybreak, the bus arrived at Guayaquil's prison complex. The first gate was chain link fence with an unarmed guard. Beyond the gate, stood the foreboding prison. A high cement wall divided the men's complex from the women's. The bus pulled into the dirt and gravel parking area.

Julienne gathered the few items she had been allowed to bring with her—asthma medication, some clothes, a few toiletries, and a pillow. She had given most of her things away prior to the planned escape from El Inca, figuring she wouldn't need them.

Her guard asked her, "Is there anyone you want to write a note to and let them know where you are? I'll be glad to deliver it for you."

Julienne quickly dashed off a short note to Rosa to let her know she arrived at Guayaquil.

"Thank-you," she said as she handed it to the guard. "And thanks for being nice to me when I was at Jail Four."

Another guard from the prison led her to the solid entrance gate to the women's prison. He pounded on the gate and a female guard on the other side peered through a small window, nodded, and opened the gate.

Julienne looked around. To the left was a field overrun with tall grass and weeds, surrounded by a broken, crumbling sidewalk. At the end of that walkway was a basketball court. To the right of the prison entrance stood the administration building, and beyond that was maximum security. The building complex was a one-story, horseshoe-shaped building with a courtyard in the middle. Rooms were back to back, some on the inside of the u-shaped building, some on the outside.

As Julienne walked over to the administration building, a young inmate ran up to her and introduced herself.

"I'm Martha," she said. Her face and arms were covered with scars. "I heard you were coming," she said in Spanish. "I'll protect you."

*I'll need special protection here?*

"I'll always be there for you," she said.

"Thanks," Julienne said. *With her scars, it looks like she could have used some protection herself.*

Luz Dotti, a Columbian girl that Julienne met at El Inca, came over and said, "Hi, we're going to be compañeros, cellmates. After you check in, I'll take you to my room." She nodded at Martha and said, "Martha helps with cleaning and laundry. If you ever need anything done, just ask her."

"Okay, I will," Julienne said.

When Julienne left the administration office, Luz was waiting and they went to her room.

"This is larger than the cells in El Inca," Julienne said. There was one bunk bed, but room for two without crowding. Two fans blew and cooled the hot and humid air.

"You have a screen door," Julienne commented. "Wish we had those in El Inca."

"It helps keep some of the flies and mosquitos out," Luz said. "They're really bad here."

The regular door had a window in it. The ceilings were high and Julienne noticed a small barred opening at the top of the back wall.

"That gives some air circulation to and from the room behind us on the other side of the building," Luz said. "The bottom bunk is yours. Just put your stuff down and come with me. The girls are making arepas stuffed with eggs for breakfast."

They walked to the end of the building where the kitchen, showers, and toilets were. As they walked, Julienne saw that some inmates had turned the front part of their room into a store. Their doors were cut in half and the top half swung open so you could see what was for sale, but you couldn't enter. You had to order from the doorway. One cell next to the kitchen had been turned into a little store. A refrigerator held some water and a few other items that inmates paid to keep there. Luz introduced her to some of the women and they pulled up a chair to sit and eat breakfast.

"It smells good," Julienne said.

The women said a prayer before they ate.

*This is different from any group I've met before. Maybe I'll be safe with them.*

When she walked past some of their rooms she'd noticed that many had pictures of Jesus and the crucifix on their wall.

For the rest of the day they hung out together and played cards and talked about their children and families back in Columbia. Julienne noticed guards roaming the complex. She heard some yelling and fighting going on, but the Columbian girls she was with ignored it. At six o'clock, the guards locked the gate to their area and the atmosphere changed.

Out came the drugs and alcohol. Someone offered marijuana to Julienne.

"No thanks," she said, hoping she wasn't causing a problem by turning it down.

They turned up their Latin music and started drinking and dancing.

"Come, join us!" they said to Julienne.

She accepted one drink and joined them in a few dances, until she realized the party was turning into something more. They began dancing in a sensual way, touching and kissing and changing partners.

Julienne quickly stepped away, excused herself, and went back to her room. Lying in her bunk bed, she wondered, *is this going to become a problem for me if I don't participate?* She shuddered. *I just can't be part of something like that. I miss having affection, but that's not me.*

The next day was Wednesday, visit day. She watched as a number of the same women she had seen sensual dancing with each other the night before, had men come in from the outside. They went to their rooms for sex. Some had women.

*This happened in El Inca too, but why does it feel different here?* It made her uneasy. The other thing that made her nervous was that their rooms were not locked at night like they were in El Inca. She mentioned it to Luz.

"Don't worry about it," Luz said. "Your things are safe in this section. These girls have money and can buy whatever they want. They don't need to steal from you or anyone else."

"Do they let you go with a guard outside to the market?"

"No, no one goes outside. But there's this one guy, Staline, who comes in and will get whatever you need. You pay a fee for his service. The guards trust him. He does it on the men's side too. It's his job.

"There's also a hole in the wall between us and the men's prison. Certain inmates are allowed in that area on the men's side. They charge a fee and will do favors, arrange to get things for you, or pass notes between the men and the women."

"The guards allow this?"

"They check what passes through, so there are some limits. Although, some guards can be bribed."

Julienne wandered around the courtyard and walked over to check out the hole in the wall. No one was standing there at the moment, so she peered through it. She noticed some movement in the passage, some kind of small purple bugs scurrying around. She looked closer, then jumped back. *Scorpions! Oh my gosh, if they're in the wall here are they in our cell walls too?*

As she stood there, she heard shouting over the wall. The women's building was a single story, but the men's building had two stories with a flat rooftop. From there the men could see into one end of the women's courtyard.

"I miss you!" a male prisoner shouted to one of the women. "I'll see you this weekend!"

The woman called back, "Si, amor!"

Another inmate came up behind the woman and shoved her.

"Bruja!" she shouted and pushed her again. The incident turned into a fist fight with other inmates gathering around to egg them on. The man watched from the roof, yelling obscenities. When the brawl ended, one of the women got a broom and started swinging it around in the air, screaming at the man on the roof, calling him names. Julienne only understood a little of what they said. Later Luz explained to her that the two women discovered that they each had been seeing the same man.

"Sometimes a married man will pay a guard and tell him not to allow his wife from our side to visit on certain weekends because he has a girlfriend or prostitute coming in from the outside."

The next day Julienne got permission to use the phone to call her dad.

"Did you know they transferred me again?" she asked him.

"Not right away. When I couldn't reach you at El Inca I contacted the State Department and they contacted the Embassy. They made some calls and let me know where you are. I'm so glad you called. I don't know if I can get through on the phone where you are. You'll have to call me. I keep putting more money on the calling card, so use it."

"Thanks, Dad." She filled him in on the details of the transfer and her fears about this new location. "I'm a few hundred miles from Quito, so I don't expect many, if any, visitors."

"The American Embassy in Guayaquil said they would have someone go see you," he said. "They'll bring you some more money that I sent. And the Browns will go when they can."

"I've heard so many horrible stories of this place," she said. "I'm really scared."

"I'm sorry, baby. I wish there was more that I could do. Just be careful. Remember, this will all be over at some point. Don't give up hope. I love you."

Over the next few weeks, Julienne experienced the new hell she was living in. She dealt with rats, scorpions, swarming mosquitos, the filth and mud, daily hostility and violent clashes between inmates, and children suffering from malnutrition.

*I wish I could take pictures of all this so people would believe me when I say it's like living in hell. You really do have to see it to believe it.*

She walked the perimeter of the field of tall grass and made her way to the basketball court to check it out. The broken cement had weeds growing through the cracks. *It looks pretty much abandoned.* Thankful that no one was around at the moment, she sat on the ground cross-legged and looked up at the sky, trying to calm her mind. She could still hear the noise and yelling coming from the prison on the other side. She closed her eyes and took a deep breath.

*What is that awful stench? It smells different than Camp Inca. Not like a dead rat, not urine. It smells like a dead body. It smells like death.* Tears made their way down her face. *Do I smell that way?*

The weather was hot and humid and she swatted at mosquitoes that buzzed around her. A slight breeze rustled the tall grass and she heard bees and insects buzzing. She noticed two flowers blooming in the overgrown field. *Beauty right in the middle of the weeds. Something living in the midst of death.* She wiped her tears with the back of her hand and stood up. *I've got to look for bits of beauty wherever I can find it, or I'll go crazy in here.*

As she walked back, she thought about what Peggy had drilled into her about some inmates never coming back from Guayaquil. It reminded her of the ending lyrics in *Hotel California*, a song by the Eagles that she liked.

> *We are programmed to receive.*
> *You can check-out any time you like,*
> *But you can never leave!*

The next day made those words feel like reality. The military police marched into the prison wearing full tactical gear.

"What's going on?" Julienne asked Luz.

"I heard there was an escape," she said. "They're going to search her cell and interrogate those who lived around her."

Rumors flew, some came from the guards. An Ecuadorian inmate had escaped. By the end of the day it was reported that she had been found and the military police shot her on sight. The following day it was on the news and a reporter said that the girl wasn't trying to run away once the police spotted her, but still they shot and killed her.

The words of the Eagles' song, *But you can never leave,* sent tremors through Julienne. *So much for planning an escape from here! Or living to tell about it.*

# CHAPTER 26

# Guayaquil
# Slithering Snake and Dengue Fever

THAT NIGHT LUZ was off drinking with one of the Columbian girls. Julienne was sound asleep on her bottom bunk when she heard Luz stumble in. She climbed in bed with Julienne and curled up next to her.

*She's drunk*, Julienne thought. *She doesn't realize she's in the wrong bunk.*

She had started dozing off when she felt Luz touching her body in a sensual way.

"Hey! What do you think you're doing?" Julienne flipped over her and tumbled off the bed to the floor. "You crossed the line!" Julienne shouted, standing up. "Don't you ever do that to me again. I'm not like that."

"I'm sorry," Luz said. She slurred her words. "I'm really sorry."

"Listen," Julienne said, "I like you, but not in that way. If you want to go in that direction, it's up to you, but not with me. Not ever."

Luz climbed up on her own bunk and Julienne on hers.

*If Luz tells the others about this, how are they going to react?* Julienne wondered. *Most of them are bi-sexual or lesbians. Are they that way because they're here? Or would they be the same on the outside?* She was awake most of the night struggling with her thoughts and feeling violated.

The next day she wandered off on her own and tried to avoid them. She did go to the director's office and asked if there were any other rooms available. There were none.

When she went back to their area, the Columbian girls called out, "Here comes the gringa mojigata."

Julienne considered trying to explain how she felt, but decided against it. She knew these girls were tough and arrogant, looking down on the others in prison. They knew they were the ones with the money and power. *It's best that I ignore their comments. I just wish they would allow me the courtesy of* my *choice of lifestyle without putting me down for it.* She walked away and went back to her room.

*I do appreciate that they took me in as part of their group. Probably because I'm American. But I've also seen them get into fights over relationships. Often with knives.* She saw the scarred evidence of that on some of their faces and arms. *Our doors aren't locked at night. What if they decide to come in and drag me out of bed and take turns beating me or something?* She didn't sleep much that night.

In the morning Luz pleaded with Julienne to stay.

"It's hard to find a good roommate," she said. "I wish you would stay."

"I think it best that I move," Julienne said. "I don't want any trouble and you heard their comments."

She went to the Administration Office again to petition for a new room. This time she told the director what happened and why she wanted to move. "I'm nervous about being where I am," she said. "I don't want any trouble."

Later that week the director offered to let her move to maximum security for a while until a room became available.

Surprised, Julienne said, "That's fine with me."

She was placed in a large room, big enough for four inmates. Curtains hung from clotheslines to divide each area for some privacy. It was a little cleaner than the other parts of the prison and she was relieved.

Just a few weeks later, another room became available and she moved again. This time she had the room to herself. Because none of the doors could be locked, she carried her money with her at all times.

About a week later, she was asked if a new inmate, an African girl, Monee, could share her room. Julienne talked with her and she seemed pretty normal, so she agreed to take her even though the room was small.

Monee immediately set up a shrine and laid down a special carpet in order to kneel and pray certain times of the day.

"What religion are you?" Julienne asked.

"I'm a Muslim."

The rug stayed in place all the time and Julienne had trouble not stepping on it. When she did, Monee yelled and swore at her. One time Julienne got up in the middle of the night to go to the bathroom and couldn't avoid stepping on the rug. There simply wasn't enough space in the room. When she got back, Monee screamed at her and cussed her out.

"This is my room," Julienne said. "I took you in. If you want to pray, that's fine. I respect your religion. But I'm going to walk wherever I need to walk. Especially in the middle of the night."

Monee continued her rant and Julienne lost it. She grabbed Monee's things, and tossed them out the screen door.

"I'm going to put a hex on you!" Monee shouted. "You'll be sorry!"

"Fine, put a hex on me. I don't care. Just get out of my room!"

*She reminds me of Jacqueline,* Julienne thought as she lay in her bunk. *I'm not going to let people like that walk all over me.*

Monee stayed outside with her things until morning when she went to the administration office to be assigned to another room.

A short time later, Julienne was approached by Mama Lucha's daughter.

"We just heard you were here," she said. "My mother is back here in maximum security, and she'd like you to come give her a massage."

"I'll have to get permission to go over there," Julienne said. "I'll ask the director."

She talked to the director about doing the massage, explaining that she had done this back in El Inca.

"Mama Lucha?" the director asked. She was quiet for a moment, hesitated, but said "Okay."

Julienne asked Staline to get her some almond oil, and a few days later, she went over to Maximum Security. After the massage, she told Mama Lucha what happened with the Columbian girls.

"I know you don't belong with them," she said. "You're different." She paid Julienne and said, "Come back in a few days."

Julienne continued with the massages and got up the courage to ask her, "If you had managed to escape back at El Inca, would you have taken me with you?"

Mama Lucha smiled, but said nothing.

*I think she meant yes?* Neither one of them brought it up again. Mama Lucha left Guayaquil about two months later.

---

"Julienne! You're here!"

She was out in the courtyard and glanced around. It was Goya, a Columbian girl who called out Julienne's visits in El Inca at one point. Goya was there when her parents came for a visit.

"Now I'll have someone to work for," Goya said, "and I can call your visits."

Goya was a skinny drug addict with short dark hair, and wore blue-and-white striped balloon pants, with a bright yellow shirt and a sash tied around her waist. *She looks like a gypsy,* Julienne thought. *I remember back at El Inca she always wore bright colors and didn't care if they matched or not.*

Goya was serving a twelve-year sentence and had a tough reputation in several prisons. She hung with two other inmates who were the same. When they were around, the atmosphere changed. If someone challenged them, they would fight because they had the attitude that it was their right to say, do, and take what they wanted. Julienne knew of instances where they'd stabbed other inmates in brawls. If a group was sitting around talking and they walked by, everyone got quiet. They instilled fear wherever they went.

"Sure, you can call my visits," Julienne said. "But I don't expect to have many while I'm here." She acted friendly, but didn't want to get too involved with her and her friends. *I don't need their kind of trouble.*

Julienne remembered Peggy warning her when they were around. "Watch your back, watch your front, and watch your stuff." *I don't want a confrontation with them.*

When they walked away, Julienne went to find Staline. She gave him a list of some packaged foods that didn't need refrigeration. When he brought her order back the next day, she went to the kitchen in her area and found a small dented pan to use. It looked dirty, so she washed it first, then heated water and added the powdered package of cream of asparagus soup mix, slowly stirring it.

A large open barred window stood over the cement sink. She sensed something moving and glanced up. A large black snake was slithering through the bars. She let out a terrified scream and backed away.

The inmates in nearby cells came running to see what was happening. A groundskeeper working outside the window, cutting the tall elephant grass with a machete, also heard the screaming. He ran over to the window and saw the snake. He grabbed it and chopped its head off. The rest of the snake fell onto the floor inside and was still wriggling and squirming just a few feet from Julienne. She froze and kept screaming.

The other inmates stood there staring at the snake. The groundskeeper ran around the building and came inside. He held the snake down on the cement floor and started chopping it into small pieces with his machete as if he were preparing sushi.

"Oh my gosh!" Julienne gripped the edge of the stove, trembling, hoping she wouldn't faint.

He held his hand out to her with pieces of the snake, motioning for her to take it and put it in her soup. He spoke in Spanish and Julienne didn't understand what he said. But she understood his motions.

"No! No!" she said, shaking her head and gagging.

"Es suyo," he said still trying to get her to take the snake.

The women stood around, waiting. Julienne realized they were hoping to get some pieces for themselves.

He walked over to her pan of soup and was about to drop the snake sushi into it, when Julienne shouted again. "No! I don't want it in my soup. No!" She held out her hand to stop him.

He looked at her with an expression of disgust and tossed the chopped snake back on the floor and walked out. The women scrambled for the pieces. Julienne grabbed her pan and ran to her room, shaking and trying not to spill the soup. Tears slid down her cheeks. *This is insane. How can people live like this? Eat pieces of snake from a filthy cement floor? They probably think I'm the one who's crazy. The crazy American.* She shuddered. *I can't eat snake!*

Later she walked back to the kitchen to return and wash the pan she'd used.

Blood and bits and pieces from the snake were splattered everywhere. On the window ledge, the wall, the sink, and the floor. Her stomach tightened with nausea.

"You have to clean that up!" one of the women shouted.

"But it's not my snake," Julienne said. "I didn't want it."

"Usted limpiarlo!" she demanded.

*I don't want to get into a fight over this. Maybe I can pay someone to clean it for me.* She asked several different inmates, offering to pay them, but they all refused. *They want the satisfaction of seeing me do it.*

"But I don't even have cleaning materials," she said.

One inmate held her hand out for money. Julienne reached in her pocket and gave her a few sucres, thinking she was going to do the cleaning. Instead, the woman handed her a brush and a bar of lye soap. Julienne got a bucket of water and scrubbed the window ledge, the wall, the sink, and finally, the floor on her hands and knees.

While she worked, the women stood around her, telling her she was doing it all wrong.

"Just because the snake came in the window when I was standing there doesn't mean it was my snake! I'm doing the best I can." She held her tears in check.

When she finished scrubbing, she used a broom to sweep up any remaining pieces and then rinsed the floor. The women stood and watched her the whole time. *They're acting like I committed a crime,* she thought as she walked back to her room. *That kitchen is cleaner than the rest of the prison right now. This whole place is filthy with cobwebs and spiders everywhere. How long do I have to live like this?* She couldn't hold back the tears. She stayed in her room alone the next few days. *I don't know who to associate with or who to trust. It's all so frustrating.*

Called out for a visit, Julienne was surprised to see Jose Luis. Although she received some visits from him in other locations, she didn't expect to see him here.

"I came to transfer some prisoners here to the men's side," he said, "so I decided to come see you."

"Good timing," she said. "I've been feeling a little discouraged." She told him about the snake and he laughed. They talked for about an hour before he had to leave. "It's always good to see you," she said. "Thanks for coming."

After he left she thought, I can't just sit in my room and be depressed. She went for a walk around the perimeter of the field of tall grass. *I see why they call it elephant grass.* The thick, hot and humid air had turned oppressive, which brought the mosquitoes in swarms. *At least it's quiet over here.*

She heard mewing coming from the grass, not far from where she stood. She'd heard about the feral cats that lived in the field. Their population was growing and some had started roaming into the prison, scavenging for food. One inmate had been attacked, scratched, and bitten. The only advantage with the cats was that they helped to keep down the rat population.

She cautiously made her way closer to the sound. The mewing continued and she made her way into the tall grass a short distance. A tiny black and white kitten sat alone, looking forlorn.

"Aww, are you hungry?" Julienne asked. She glanced around and listened in case the mother cat was nearby, but saw nothing. She reached down and picked up the kitten. "Well, aren't you cute?" The bottoms of its legs were black. "It looks like you're wearing little boots," she said.

"And you have a black mustache." She cuddled it to her chest. "You're coming home with me."

She took it to her room and fed him some powdered milk. He curled up in her lap and fell asleep, purring. Julienne's heart melted. *He needs me to take care of him.*

As she continued to feed him, he began to grow strong and playful. She laughed at him because he bounced around, jumping and hopping more than he walked. Whenever she called him, he would bounce backwards toward her.

"Mr. Romper Stompers. That's what I'll name you."

One day a little girl named Lola sat outside Julienne's door watching the kitten and giggling whenever it hopped around.

"You want to touch him?" Julienne asked, motioning for her to touch the kitten.

Lola nodded, even though she didn't understand English.

"Let's go find your mother and make sure it's okay with her."

Lola's mother, Elena, was glad someone played with her and gave her attention.

"Tres años, " she told Julienne.

"She's three years old?"

Elena nodded. They became friends and sometimes ate together. Julienne had Lola teach her the alphabet in Spanish, while Julienne taught her the same in English. When Julienne sang the ABC song to her, she giggled and tried to follow along.

Julienne showed her how to slurp up noodles and when she did it, Julienne said to her, "Uh oh, spaghetti O's."

Lola clapped her hands, laughing. "Hazlo otra vez!"

"Do it again?" Lola nodded. When Julienne said it again, Lola let out a belly laugh.

*What a joy Lola is. She brings some light into this dark place. So many of the children are cranky and crying all the time. Maybe because of the lack of decent food. They get no real nutrition and there's not much for them to do.*

She taught her how to say "Romper Stompers" and Lola loved playing with the kitten. As he grew, he started to disappear for periods of time and run with some of the wild cats. Every once in a while he came back to find Julienne and would rub up against her leg, wanting some attention. Once he showed up with cuts and scars from fighting with other cats. She decided it was time to not allow him in her room anymore. At times he would show up and meow and meow at the door, but eventually stopped coming around. She didn't want to take a chance on him biting anyone, especially little Lola.

Some days the temperature reached 120 degrees with high humidity and Julienne's asthma grew worse. She went to the prison doctor and he said he would get her a refill of her medication.

"How long will that take?" she asked him. "I'm really not feeling well."

"I'll write up the order and send someone right away. We should have it in an hour."

"Is the pharmacy close by?"

"It's located on the men's side of the prison," he said. "One of the inmates had been a pharmacist before being sentenced, so he's managing the pharmacy."

*A prisoner runs the pharmacy and has access to drugs? Wow.*

In spite of the medication, she started to run a low grade fever and had a headache that wouldn't subside. She felt exhausted. Her fever continued to rise and she went back to the doctor. Blood tests revealed that she had contracted dengue fever.

"Shouldn't I go to the hospital?" she asked, worried. "Dengue fever is pretty serious isn't it?"

"The antibiotics and bed rest should take care of it," he said. "We'll keep an eye on your fever to make sure it doesn't spike any higher."

Back in her room, she couldn't stand the heat. She'd awake soaked with sweat, aching all over. Martha, the inmate who did her laundry, came with clean sheets and clothes and made sure she had water to drink. Julienne paid her to give a note to Staline to buy an oscillating fan for her room.

One inmate suggested that Julienne use a product called Sea Breeze. It was like rubbing alcohol, but minty. She bought some through Staline and it did seem to help keep mosquitos away when she rubbed it all over. *At least it smells good.*

Gene and Helen Brown called the prison to let Julienne know that they were coming for a visit. They asked what they could bring her besides food.

"Books to read," Julienne said. "Anything in English." She thought for a minute and added, "a mosquito net that I can put over my bed, and some repellant."

"I know they're pretty bad down there," Helen said, "especially with the oppressive heat and humidity lately."

"Yes, and I'm just getting over dengue fever. I don't want to get it again. I feel a little guilty asking you for all these things," she said.

"We still have some money from your father to get you things like this," Helen said. "The food is from the women at church and a few clothes."

"Thank you, I didn't have time to pack much when they sent me here."

Julienne was feeling better when they came and was so glad to see them.

"Thank you for driving so far," she said. "I feel so isolated here."

"Remember, you're never really alone," Helen said. "Among the books we brought you is a Good News Bible, in case you couldn't take your other one with you. It's written in everyday language and easy to read and understand."

"Jesus is the Prince of Peace," Gene said. "Allow him to bring that peace that passes understanding into your heart."

Julienne didn't respond.

"Have you gone to the small library here yet?" Helen asked her.

"Not yet. I think they have mostly Spanish books."

"That might help you to learn more Spanish vocabulary," Helen said. "They may have some English books too. Prisoners bring their own books and exchange them for more. You might find a few English ones."

"I'll check it out," Julienne said.

They stayed for two hours and Julienne enjoyed the conversation and their company.

"We'll be praying for you," they said when they left.

Julienne sat out in the compound for a while watching other visits.

"¡**Ay**!" one inmate called out. She and her boyfriend got into an argument that turned physical and he punched her, knocking her to the ground. Julienne stood to her feet ready to shout at the guy and give him a piece of her mind, a few choice words. But she quickly remembered you don't do that in prison. *The whole situation could turn on me if I got involved. The woman would tell me not to mess in her business. Or accuse me of being interested in her man. And from then on, I'd have to watch my back around her.* She watched the man shout in anger and shove the woman back to the ground when she tried to get up. Then he stomped out. A few inmates glanced that way, but then went about their own business. Julienne went to her room.

The next day she went to check out the library. She found an English murder mystery series of cat novels by Lillian Jackson Braun. She picked up *The Cat Who Could Read Backwards* and *The Cat Who Went Underground*. As she flipped through the pages, she thought, *I miss my cats from home, Dexter and Sidney. They were such good company.* She gathered the books to take to her room to read. When she finished she decided to write a book report on each one. *I need to keep my mind sharp and it will help me from getting bored. I'll have Staline get me some notebooks.*

She started to get a few visits from missionaries in the area. One was Ana, a missionary friend of Helen and Gene Brown. When she asked if she could bring Julienne something, she asked for English books.

A representative from the Embassy came to visit Julienne as well as two other American inmates. He brought Julienne some money her father had sent.

She called her dad every week and wrote him letters. She tried to think of something positive to write, but sometimes it was difficult. She knew she was fortunate to have parents who cared and supported her. So many inmates had no one. They had to do menial work just to earn things like toilet paper or powdered milk for their children. *I'm so grateful for what I have, even though it's far from what I'm used to.*

One day a howling tropical storm dropped sheets of rain that pelted against the prison. When it was over, Julienne went outside to the courtyard. She noticed some tiny kittens in a muddy rain puddle. Some boys ran over to them and each picked one up.

*They're going to rescue them. Maybe I can help.*

The first boy got a smirk on his face, and then hurled the kitten against the prison wall.

"No!" Julienne shouted, running toward them.

The second boy did the same. Blood splatters dotted the cement wall.

"Oh my gosh, stop it!" Julienne shouted, running between the boys. "Stop that right now!" She reached down and picked up a kitten they hadn't gotten to yet.

"Señora loca!" they spat out at her and walked away laughing.

The tiny kitten was soaked and shivering. "Well this crazy lady is going to help you," she said to the trembling kitten. In her room she dried it off and saw that its eyes weren't open yet. "You're not much bigger than a salt shaker," she said, holding it close. *I hope it lives.*

Over the next days and weeks she fed him powdered milk. It never meowed, but would sit on her lap and lick her hand.

When she had a visit from a missionary, she asked for canned sardines.

"You want sardines?"

"For the kitten," she explained.

The cans had tomato sauce on the sardines, so she rinsed it off before feeding it to the kitten. As he got a little bigger, he started to walk, but with spastic movements. When he lay looking at Julienne he seemed to be looking right through her.

"I'm going to name you Chandler," she said. "You look like you're channeling or meditating." *Poor thing is handicapped.*

Another Ecuadorian inmate, Emily, took an interest in Chandler and she would sit and pet him. When her children came to visit with her husband, they played with Chandler.

"Your kids are so good and gentle with him," Julienne said.

When Emily had her next visit from her husband, she asked Julienne if she would mind watching her children for a little while so that she and her husband could have some quiet time together in her room.

"Of course," Julienne said. She had noticed that they seemed to have a good relationship, unlike most others. She saw so many inmates just shove their kids outside their cell and then slam their door shut so they could have sex while the kids had to fend for themselves. Emily and her husband didn't do that. They would set up a little picnic in the courtyard and include the children in their visit. Julienne was glad to watch the children for them.

A short time later, Emily was getting released and came to Julienne.

"My children really like Chandler," she said. "If you want us to take him, we will. That way, whenever you leave, you won't have to worry about him. We'll give him a good home."

Julienne agreed that it would be best for the cat. But she missed the comfort of having a cat curled up next to her, especially when she had another bout with dengue fever.

CHAPTER 27

## Guayaquil
## 60 Minutes Interview

THE DIRECTOR CALLED Julienne into the office one day. "We could use your help."

"With what?"

"Some missionaries donated some pharmaceutical drugs to the prison for the inmates and they all have to be sorted and labeled and placed in inventory. The information is in English, but we need to make a log in Spanish."

"But my Spanish isn't that good," Julienne said.

"You can use a dictionary to translate from English to Spanish. We're assigning Heather to work with you on this. She's American, and she's bilingual."

*They trust us with drugs? Amazing. At least it's something to do.*

"Where will we be doing this?"

"In the chapel," she said. "Once you're done, the drugs will be placed in the farmacia on the men's side."

Julienne and Heather met at the chapel the next day.

"I'm familiar with a lot of the drug names," Heather said. "We have to unpack these boxes and label each of the individual packets inside. They're like sample packets. The label on the outside of the box states in English what's inside."

"And we translate that and create the individual labels in Spanish?"

"That's it," she said, opening the first box.

Julienne got the blank labels out and the English/Spanish dictionary.

"This box has antibiotics," Heather said. She ripped open another one. "Oh, Xanax," she said. "Here, take a few of these for yourself."

"What are they for?"

"For anxiety and depression," she said, taking some packets for herself.

"I can't believe we're not being monitored," Julienne said, looking around.

"Listen, don't feel guilty," Heather said. "It's not like we're taking them to sell. It's just for personal use when we need them. It's not easy to get stuff from the farmacia." She looked in another box. "Here's some Ativan for anxiety and to help you sleep." Another box held Vitamin B shots and syringes.

"I could definitely use some of those," Julienne said. "I just got over my second bout with dengue fever. Maybe it would keep me from getting it again. I heard that Vitamin B injections were good for mosquito bites, like a prevention."

"I'll give you a shot," she said. She prepared a needle and syringe and said, "You want it in the butt?" She grinned.

"Do you know what you're doing?"

"I'm not a nurse, but I think I can handle this. Bend over."

"Ouch!" Julienne yelled as Heather stabbed the needle into her butt cheek.

She snickered. "Like I said, I'm not a nurse; I'll get better with practice."

They spent weeks unpacking, labeling, and making a log of every item, except for a few things they kept for themselves. Julienne took some of the Vitamin B injections, some antibiotics, and a few Xanax. Heather took more.

When they finished the project, Julienne said, "At least it gave us something to do."

"And a personal stash," Heather said.

"Visit!" Goya called to Julienne.

*I'm not expecting anyone. I wonder who it is.*

"Joan!" Julienne said. "What a surprise. I didn't know you were coming."

"I wanted to make sure you're all right. I heard you had a bout with dengue fever."

"I did, but I'm doing okay now. Helen brought me a mosquito net for my bed. That definitely helps. I'm surprised you came such a long distance just to visit me. I really appreciate it."

"Actually, our missionary group is here on a mission trip, partnering with Samaritan's Purse and Doctors Without Borders. We went into the jungle to help indigenous people. We brought them small ovens and taught them how to make bread and brought medicine for hepatitis and amoebas, both such common issues here."

She looked at Julienne more closely. "Are you sure you're feeling okay? You look like you've lost weight."

"I don't have much of an appetite," she said. "It's so hot and humid, I don't feel like eating. Plus the lack of decent food and the stress of being here."

"You should boil the water you drink and make sure you thoroughly wash any fruit. I brought some medicine to help detox your body of any amoebas."

"Thanks," Julienne said.

"I also have some allergy medication and inhalers. I know you've needed those on a regular basis, so now you have another supply. This is all from Samaritan's Purse."

"Wow, that's amazing," Julienne said. "Thank them for me."

"Is there anything else you need?"

"Well, I'm asking everyone for English books to read. It sure helps to pass the time."

"I can help with that," she said. "I'll bring you some tomorrow before I drive back to Quito. I wanted to see for myself if you have found peace in your heart," Joan said. "That's something that only God can give you."

"Having peace in here is pretty difficult," she said, glancing around.

"God loves you, Julienne. The peace he wants to give you is here." She pointed to her heart. "He can help you overcome any obstacles. But the choice is yours."

"I guess I'm just not there yet," she said.

"Okay," Joan said. "So fill me in on what's been going on."

On one of her weekly calls with her dad, he mentioned that he had been contacted by *60 Minutes*.

"The TV program? What did they want?"

"They're planning to do a segment on a few Americans in Ecuadorian prisons," he said. "You can be part of it."

"I don't know if I want to do that," she said. "What's their real purpose?"

"We'll talk more about it when I come."

"You're coming for a visit!"

"Yes, I'm not sure of the date yet, but I'm coming. I think Kate should stay home. I've been told that it can be dangerous in the city there."

"I think that's a good idea," she said. "I'll talk to Staline and ask him which hotel in the area would be a safe place."

"Is he the one you wrote about? The one who can buy things on the outside for the inmates?"

"Yes, that's him."

They talked a while and Julienne was glad to have something to look forward to. *A visit with my dad!*

She talked to Staline about it. "I'll be glad to escort him around and make sure he's safe."

When her dad came, Julienne clung to him and let the tears flow.

"I'm so glad you came. I find myself giving up hope at times, thinking I'll never get out of here, that what I see around me is all there is, or ever will be."

"Maybe you're looking for hope in the wrong place," he said.

She dried her tears and looked at him.

"Have you thought about God and reading your Bible to find hope?"

"No."

"Well, you should."

*My dad's telling me to read my Bible? That's something new.*

"I've been talking with Joan," he said. "I asked her why she was being so nice to me and to you, helping us out. She told me it wasn't her, it was God and that he cared about me and about you."

"She's a good person."

"It's more than that. I began to realize that I was powerless to get you out of here. My money and influence weren't enough. Do you know that Kate and I even talked with someone about hiring a rebel group to come and break you out of prison?"

"You did?"

"Yes. It was going to be very expensive, but we moved forward with talks about it. When we asked them if they could guarantee your safety, they said there were no guarantees. We ultimately decided against it. If anything were to happen to you…" His voice choked up.

"Oh, Dad, I can't believe you would do that for me."

"When you told me recently about that girl being shot by the police, I realized again that we made the right decision not to do it."

"I have fantasized so many times about escaping," she said. "All different scenarios went through my mind and I'd daydream about these crazy plots. Little did I know that you were actually thinking about breaking me out!"

"Thank God we came to our senses," he said. "I have to give Joan some credit for that. I never told her or anyone about the clandestine breakout plan, but she wrote letters to me and sensed my frustration and discouragement. She suggested that Kate and I consider going to church and letting God speak to us. So we did. We've been going for several weeks now. We've met with the pastor and have rededicated our lives to God."

Julienne watched him as he spoke. *He's definitely more at peace than I've ever seen him.*

"I wanted to share that with you, Jules. Somehow God will get us all through this and bring some good out of it."

*Good? How about getting me out of here? That would be good.*

Feeling a little uncomfortable, she changed the subject and asked if Staline was watching out for him.

"He sure is." He smiled. "He's acting like my personal bodyguard."

"You need someone like him," she said. "People in the streets can be ruthless and will kill for a dollar."

"I'll be fine," he said. "Now, show me around this place, at least as much as you can."

As he observed the condition of the prison, he said, "It's worse here than at El Inca, and I thought that was really bad."

"It's even more violent here," Julienne said. "I don't get close to anyone or talk to many inmates. Violent flare ups are common. I mind my own business so I don't get caught up in their chaos. But it sure is lonely."

Her dad stayed for a week and they spoke again about the request to have Julienne be one of the participants in the *60 Minutes* segment on Americans in Ecuadorian prisons.

"How did my name come up to be considered as part of the program?"

"Apparently, Sandra Chase recommended you," he said. "I think Sandra's daughter had some contacts and a Congresswoman has been trying to help Sandra. How well do you know her?"

"She came to El Inca and I got to know her a little there. She spent her first night in a cell with me and Peggy. After that we hung out once in a while and ate together a few times."

"I think it might be good for you to be part of the program."

"I don't want to be on TV," she objected.

"There's a chance someone might be able to go free because of this. If they expose the conditions here and show the slow and unfair justice system, maybe one of you will be picked to go free by the Ecuadorian government. To make themselves look good."

"You think that's a possibility?"

"The person who contacted me said that. I think you should do it. What have you got to lose?"

"Okay, I'll do it."

"Great! I'll let them know. Someone will be contacting you."

The rest of the week flew by and when her father left, Julienne tried to hang on to the hope that being on TV might make a difference."

Julienne received a call from a representative of *60 Minutes*, filling her in on their plans.

"We're going to film Sandra Chase in Quito at El Inca, and then we'll come to Guayaquil to do your story, and another inmate's, Jim Williams. The film crew will be there for a few days, filming the prison conditions and then Mike Wallace will do the interviews."

Michael Griffith, their entertainment attorney, came in advance to have Julienne sign a contract and the release papers. As she was signing, he said, "Do you know that this prison has been ranked as the worst prison in the world?"

"What? Really?"

"For women, Guayaquil is the worst prison; for men, it's a prison in Caracas, Venezuela."

"What is that based on?"

"Danger, violence, notorious prisoners. They don't separate inmates based on their level of crime. A simple drug user is right alongside murderers and drug lords. It doesn't matter if you have a two-year or twenty-five-year sentence."

"It's scary," Julienne said.

"We're naming the segment, *Innocence Abroad,*" he said.

"Thank you for coming. It's nice to talk to a lawyer who speaks fluent English. The list of attorneys that my father got from the embassy was so old that some had died, none of them spoke English and none handled criminal cases."

"Mike Wallace will probably want to mention that," he said, making a note.

"My dad paid a deposit to several lawyers for their services and they kept the money, but never called back."

"I'm sorry you've gone through such a hard time," he said. "Maybe when the program airs, it will be of some help."

The film crew arrived and spent an entire day with Julienne on the women's side. She showed them her room and then walked around the rest of the women's side of the prison, answering their questions about the daily routine there. They saw and filmed the rats and spiders, inmates fighting, and the children wandering around, imprisoned with their mothers. She brought them to the hole chopped in the wall between the women and men's prison, used by the inmates to pass things back and forth.

"Put your camera in there," she said. "But be careful."

The cameraman did and yelled, "Whoa!" He saw the nest of scorpions. "I don't know if America is ready to see the reality of all this. Some of it may be edited out and end up on the cutting room floor."

The day of the interviews, they brought Julienne over to the men's side of the prison. She met inmate Jim Williams and watched his interview. He was a wealthy man who imported fish from South America to Jacksonville, Florida. He had set up a fish processing plant in Ecuador and was charged with using the plant to launder drug money. He claimed he was innocent.

Congresswoman Corrine Brown was there from Florida and told Mike Wallace that drug smugglers regularly targeted American women by offering them free trips. "A lot of young women get caught up in this trap," she said.

Prior to her on-camera interview, Julienne was asked about her planned escape attempt from El Inca. *They know. That's why I ended up in Guayaquil,* she thought, *but I can't talk about it. If I admit planning an escape, could the court increase my sentence?*

"I really can't talk about that," she said.

"Tell us what your family has gone through. How do your parents feel?"

*Don't cry,* she told herself. "My dad is a strong man and has done everything he can to try to get justice for me." Her eyes watered. "My parents have been very supportive."

"This is a pretty horrific place. Have you ever thought about an escape from Guayaquil?" "No, I'd never attempt that. I don't know the area, wouldn't know where to go, and I have no contacts here. Besides, if you're attempting to escape from this prison, they shoot you."

Surprised, the interviewer simply said, "Oh?"

*He probably doesn't believe me.*

"You can check with the local media," she said. "It happened recently."

Between interviews, Julienne hung out with the crew, American Embassy representatives, and some other American inmates. When it was her turn, Mike Wallace guided her with questions as she told her story.

He concluded her interview with, "It took one-and-a-half years before she finally got to court. Local human rights advocates and church groups supported her. Even the prosecutor asked the judge for leniency. But instead of leniency, Julienne got 10 years."

After Mike Wallace and the film crew left, Julienne was taken back to her room on the women's side.

*I wonder if this exposure is going to do any good. At least the world will get a glimpse of the hell I'm living in.*

# CHAPTER 28

## Guayaquil
## Torture, Murder, Suicide

Julienne got word that a Columbian drug lord with a twenty-five-year sentence, wanted to meet her. He sent her a message that he'd arranged for her to come to the men's side the following weekend. He'd heard about the *60 Minutes* interview and wanted to meet the innocent American. The note said, "I'd like to invite you to come and have an early Thanksgiving turkey dinner in my room."

*Thanksgiving dinner?* She had some apprehension about it, but was curious. She asked two of the female inmates that she knew whether she should go.

"I don't know about this. Will I be safe?"

"We know about him," one of them said. "You should go. He'll treat you well."

"And it will give you a day out of here," the other said.

The day of the visit, a guard walked her over, but never questioned her about it. *I'm glad because I don't have a pass. This guy probably bribed the guard to bring me over.*

When she arrived at his large cell, he had a full turkey dinner waiting.

"Wow!" she said. "I wasn't expecting all this. It smells so good." She knew better than to ask how he arranged it. This was like Mama Lucha. She could make things happen and obviously, he could too. He was a good-looking man in his mid-thirties.

They sat and ate and talked for the next three hours. He asked her to share her story and she did, in detail.

"Your story is all too familiar," he said.

"It is?"

"Our cartel is notorious for setting people up this way."

Julienne stared at him.

"Did you ever wonder what would have happened to you if you weren't caught and arrested?"

"Well, my friends would have picked up their artwork in New York at the airport and I would have flown back home to California. I would never have known about the cocaine."

"No, that's not what would have happened. They would have brought you and the drugs to an undisclosed location, like a warehouse. There they would take the drugs out of the artwork and weighed it, tested it to be sure it was the right shipment they were expecting. Then they would have put a gun to your head and said, "Look, you need to do this for us again."

Julienne's eyes widened.

"Or they might have put a pretty girl like you into sex trafficking."

Shocked, Julienne could hardly breathe.

"The other possibility is that they would have pulled the trigger to get rid of you as a witness."

"How do you know all of this?" Her voice was shakier than she would have liked.

"Sweetie, I used to do things like this all the time. But, I wouldn't have gone after a girl like you to be a drug mule. I'd look for poor, down and out girls who didn't have a family. Girls desperate for money to buy drugs." He shrugged. "It all just business."

"You must be well connected," she said, trying to remain calm.

He let out a hearty laugh. "You could say that."

She looked around the large cell. He had a computer and scanner and a printer. She saw a cell phone as well. *He's probably still running his business from in here!*

She thanked him for the dinner and the guard walked her back to the women's side.

That night she thought about what he said. *I'm lucky to be alive! And not a sex slave! Maybe God was looking out for me after all. Things could have been so much worse. I could be dead!*

---

One Saturday a few of the South African girls were going to visit their boyfriends on the men's side. They invited Julienne to go with them.

"There's a Brazilian surfer who wants to meet you."

'I don't know…"

"Come on," one said. "He's blonde, blue eyes, great looking."

"A surfer?" Julienne smiled. "Well, okay."

They got their passes to visit for the day and Julienne put on her flowered sundress. They met up with the men and the small group hung out for a while talking, sharing stories. *He reminds me of a California surfer,* Julienne thought.

"You want some soup?" he asked Julienne. "One of the guys set up a small food café."

"Sure." Julienne took the soup and he bought a Latin dish. The soup was a little spicy, but she drank it down. Almost immediately, her tongue and lips started to tingle and her face felt like it was burning up.

"What's wrong?" one of the girls asked.

Another shouted in panic, "Her lips are swelling!"

"Look at her face! It's really red."

"Julienne! Can you hear me?" The girl put her hands on Julienne's cheeks. "Julienne!"

"She's turning lobster red," the surfer said. "This isn't good!"

Others gathered around to see what the commotion was.

Julienne felt like she was in a dream; their voices seemed to be coming from a distance and were distorted and incoherent. Her knees buckled and the surfer caught her before she hit the ground.

"Julienne! Can you hear me?" he asked. "Her skin is really hot," he said to one of the women."

"We have to cool her down," she said, touching Julienne's arm. "She's burning up. Get her over to the water basin!"

The surfer carried her and the group followed them. "She must be allergic to something in the soup," he said. They splashed water from the basin on her face and arms.

Julienne groaned. "Everything's distorted. I feel like I'm talking from a hole." Her words slurred a bit.

"Get her to the farmacia right away!"

The doctor checked her out and said, "Intoxication."

"But I didn't drink," Julienne moaned, barely able to speak.

"She didn't!" the surfer said. The doctor ignored him and gave her a shot. She passed out.

When she woke up, she was laying on a mattress on the floor. "Where am I?"

"In my room," the surfer said. "Are you feeling better?"

"How long have I been sleeping?"

"A few hours."

"Oh no!" She managed to sit up. "Am I late going back to the women's side?" She panicked. "We're supposed to leave before four o'clock."

"You've got some time yet," he said as he sat down next to her on the mattress. His eyes swept over her. "Nice dress," he said.

"Thanks."

She struggled to stand and he walked her over to a guard who took her back to the women's side.

In her room, Julienne wondered, *did he do something to me while I was out? Was I raped?* She changed her clothes and realized she was okay. *I'd know of something happened. Wouldn't I?*

Every weekend many women went over to the men's side to visit their husbands or boyfriends. The guards walked the women over there on Friday and brought them back on Saturday. On Mother's Day weekend, they were allowed to stay until Sunday.

"Julienne, will you watch my room for me?"

It was Martha, who had been doing her laundry. She was always nice and at times protective of Julienne, but they didn't really socialize.

"What's up?"

"I'm going to the men's side to spend the weekend with my husband. Just keep an eye on my room and make sure no one takes anything while I'm gone."

"Okay, I can do that for you."

A lot of visitors came and stayed that weekend. There were men, women, and children everywhere. Some brought in chicken, fish, and other food. It turned into a big feast with a party atmosphere. Julienne smelled homemade chicken soup and walked over to maybe buy a cup from her. When she looked into the large iron pot, she saw full heads of chickens with their beaks and eyeballs, floating in the broth, along with the claws. *Everything but the feathers! I don't think so!*

She went over to check out Martha's room. It looked like a tiny apartment. The bed was built up high enough to stand under it and she had placed a small table and chair beneath it. There was a ladder to climb up to the top and a small TV sat on a high shelf so she could watch it from her bed. Julienne glanced up at the small barred vent next to the ceiling and noticed light flickering through it.

*I better check it out and make sure it's not a fire in the wall!*

She climbed up on the bed and peered through the bars. A couple in the next room was being intimate. Julienne quietly slipped off the bed and left the room. Everyone seemed to be partying in the courtyard, so it wasn't likely anyone would bother Martha's room at the moment.

She walked around the courtyard. One of the American women invited her to join them.

They talked and laughed and some drank alcohol. When someone offered Julienne a drink, she said, "I'll just have a Coca-Cola." *If they're drinking homemade alcohol, it might make me sick.*

Someone turned up the volume on their radio and Latin music started the group dancing. Julienne put down her Coke and joined them for a few dances. She finished her Coke and got another one, but by then everything was spinning.

"Are you okay?" one of the women asked.

"I feel strange." She thought she saw a huge sailfish that someone had gutted and there were drugs inside. *Am I hallucinating?*

She heard people talking and hovering around her, but it was all in a fog. Waves of dizziness overcame her and her legs felt odd and weak. She slumped to the ground.

"What's that big fish with the drugs?" Her voice was slurred and she felt like she was talking from inside a barrel.

"What fish?" one of the women asked. "What are you talking about?"

*Did they drug me? Put something in my drink? I feel terrible.* She floated in and out of reality for several hours. When her mind began to clear, she asked those around her what happened.

"You probably drank too much," someone said.

"I saw this guy slit open a big fish and there were drugs inside of it," Julienne insisted.

"We didn't see anything like that." They snickered.

"But you were right there when it happened," Julienne maintained.

"You're imagining things."

*Someone must have put something in my drink.* She looked around and realized there were no guards anywhere in sight. *Where are they?* The partying intensified with hoots and cheers and more drinking. The smell of cigarettes and booze increased the nausea Julienne felt and she became uncomfortable with the whole scene.

As she stumbled back toward her room, she asked one of the women, "Where are the guards?"

"They just locked the place up and left," she said.

*They totally vanished?* The wild partying grew louder and more boisterous. *This is scary!* She went to her cell and barricaded herself inside with a small dresser blocking her door.

The next day Martha hadn't returned, but Julienne knew she was planning to stay on the men's side for another day. She checked Martha's room and everything seemed okay.

On Sunday, Martha still didn't return. Rumors started circulating that there had been a murder on the men's side. Bizarre stories kept trickling in. The next rumor was that two inmates had been killed.

*Oh my gosh! Where were the guards in all of this?* Then it hit her. *Maybe that's why the guards disappeared. Maybe they did the same on the men's side. Did they know something was going down?*

The guards weren't talking. Inmates from the men's side went up to their roof area and were yelling over to the women's side, telling bits and pieces of what happened.

Martha still hadn't returned. *Maybe they're on lockdown while the police investigate?*

By the end of the week, fear gripped Julienne as never before when the full story came out. Notes were sent back and forth from inmates on the men's side, giving details of what happened.

Armed men from the outside came into the prison and stormed the cell where Martha and her husband were. Apparently, her husband owed them a large sum of money from a major drug deal. They tied both of them up, demanding payment. When her husband said he had no way of paying them, they began torturing Martha in front of him. They took turns kicking and punching her. When her husband cried out that he didn't know where he could get the money he owed, they stepped up their torture. They strung her up in the cell, pulled out switchblades, and began cutting her face. Next, they stabbed her, causing her excruciating screams of pain, but they kept her alive.

"Look, if you get us the money, we'll stop," they said, according to an inmate who overheard them.

"I don't know where to go to get it," Martha's husband said. "If I had it, I'd give it to you. Just give me some time."

They lit cigarettes and burned her body all over, continuing the torment. When they didn't get what they wanted, they killed Martha's husband and left her to bleed to death.

When Julienne realized the full impact of what happened, she felt a deadweight pushing down on her. Her body was numb. Her ears buzzed, as if there had been a sudden drop in air pressure. Panic rioted within her.

*I can't believe all that could happen right inside the prison! The guards had to be in on it!* At first she tried to convince herself that the story was exaggerated. But it wasn't. The guards weren't about to talk about it. *The guards are as guilty as the killers!*

She also learned that Martha and her husband were in prison for killing their parents over some big drug deal. *This is someone I thought I knew! She was always nice to me. And now, she's dead! Tortured and killed.*

She collapsed on her bed and cried until no more tears came. A gray void descended on her. She closed her eyes, but sleep wouldn't come. Day after day, she left her cell only to use the toilet or prepare a little food. She ignored the other inmates, even the ones who had been nice to her. Her trust in people, guards or inmates, was destroyed.

*Martha was nice to me too, and look at what happened to her. At any time, someone could come to my cell and do something to me. I try to be nice, but could end up with the same fate. Even the guards are no protection.*

She sat and stared blankly at the walls of her cell for hours, not even noticing the scorpions scurrying around. Only a fearful and empty future pressed into her mind. She sank into a deep depression.

*What is the point of living in this hell hole? I'm living in a musty cement room that reeks of death.* She squeezed her eyes shut. Tears spilled through her lashes. *I feel so empty inside. Like a part of me is not there anymore.*

She spotted a glass ashtray that someone left in her room. She picked it up and flung it against the wall, smashing it. Shards of glass flew in all directions. She picked up one and sat on her bed, staring at it.

She held out her other arm and sliced the sharp glass across her wrist in two places. Blood oozed from the cuts.

CHAPTER 29

# Guayaquil
# Two for One Law

Julienne stared at the blood dripping from her wrist and something snapped inside of her.

*What am I doing!* She tossed the bloody piece of glass to the floor. *I'm not suicidal!* Smothering a sob, she covered her face with trembling hands. Blood from her wrist trickled down her arm.

"No!" she shouted. "I can't do this!" She grabbed some toilet paper, dabbed at the blood, and wrapped more paper tight around her wrist.

*I can't do this to my dad. It would kill him. My parents have done so much for me. How could I even think about such a thing?*

She took a deep breath, but continued to shake as she swept up the shards of glass on the floor. Until the cuts healed, she wore long sleeve shirts in spite of the hot weather. She struggled to crawl out of the void that engulfed her. She didn't want to stay there, wallowing in her own misery.

She talked to one of the inmates. "Does anyone ever leave this place before their sentence is up?"

"You mean get out early?"

"No, I mean is it possible to get transferred back to El Inca?"

"You should talk to Miguel Ortiz," she said. "He's on the men's side and knows all about the legal stuff."

"On the men's side?" The thought of going over there was not a pleasant one.

"He's an okay guy and I've heard of him helping other inmates out with their legal issues."

"Was he a lawyer?"

"No, but he's smart, has office equipment, and speaks English."

Julienne sent a message over to him and asked for a meeting. He sent her an official pass and a guard walked her over.

"Who did you get to sign this pass?" she asked him.

He smiled. "I have my resources. I've heard about you. The innocent American."

"Is there any way to get transferred back to El Inca?" she asked, getting right to the point.

"There's always a possibility," he said. "What is your sentence?"

"Ten years, but with the Two-for-One law, five years."

"How much time have you served so far?"

"Almost four years."

"Okay, then we should be able to work on a transfer back to Quito."

"How do I get started?"

"You'll need five diagnósticos."

"What does that mean?"

"You need to have serious reasons for a transfer, approved by five different officials. This includes your health, your studies, relations, psychology, and rehabilitation."

"I don't understand."

"For instance for the health reasons, what medical issues do you have that would possibly warrant a transfer?"

"Well, I have asthma and it's been worse here because of the humidity and poor air quality with the volcanoes and bad air trapped in the valley. I did better in the mountains of Quito. I've also had dengue fever two times and I have severe migraine headaches."

"Write down all the things you can think of," he said, "every time you've been sick and I'll help you complete a form for the doctor to sign."

"What if he won't sign it?"

"Don't you worry about signatures, I'll handle those."

She decided not to ask him to explain that one.

"Another area is mental, which requires the psychologist to sign."

"You mean things like being depressed, lonely, and fearful?"

"Yes. I imagine Martha's cruel death affected you, since you knew her personally."

She gave him a questioning look.

"I hear and know things," he said. "I wouldn't invite you here without checking you out first." He continued. "Next would be scholastics. Show that you're studious and want to improve yourself to prepare for a career when you get out. There's only a small library here, mostly in Spanish, so you're limited in what you can study."

She told him how she had been reading a lot of books and writing a book report on each one just out of boredom.

"Excellent! Keep at it and we can include books in a certain field of interest you want to study and show that those are not accessible here. We'll show that you want rehabilitation, but it's not available, and you have the discipline to work on it if the resources were offered."

"Another thing is that I had more visits at El Inca with missionary groups and others. They would bring me the basic things I needed."

"And you need to go back to the Quito court system in order to work on paperwork required on your case before your release."

"I feel better already," Julienne said, taking a deep breath. "This gives me something worthwhile to keep me busy and move forward. Thank you so much!"

Back in her cell, Julienne began making lists and working on each topic Miguel mentioned.

*I forgot to ask how long this process would take, but it has restored my hope.*

Julienne called her dad to let him know she would be working on getting all these reports together in order to get transferred back to El Inca.

"That's great, Julie! Imagine. It took an inmate to get you on track with all this, instead of one of the many lawyers we paid."

"I know, Dad. I was so discouraged and on the verge of giving up before this. After Martha was murdered, I started thinking that something like that could happen to me. I was terrified."

"We'll be praying for you and for this whole process to move ahead quickly," he said. "I'll let Joan know so she can pray too."

"Thanks, Dad." *I guess prayers won't hurt, but it's me getting this paperwork together that will get me out of here.*

She sent a note to Rosa and Lucia to let them know she was working on getting back to El Inca. She would need someone to room with when she got there, but didn't know when that would be. Lucia was still at Vinces, but Rosa was in Julienne's old room in El Inca.

She went on a reading binge and did a report on each book she read. When she finished, she brought the list and reports to the social worker.

"You read all forty-seven of these books?"

"Yes, and here's a book report on each one. I want to continue my schooling and I can't accomplish that here."

"Impressive," he said.

He handed her a report form to complete. "Fill this out and bring it back to me. I'll sign it."

Over the next two months, she completed all the required reports in each category and visited the prison medical doctor and others who were required to give their approval. She brought the papers to Miguel and he added the required official stamps and forged signatures he had in the scanner in his cell.

"These officials will never even bother to read these reports," he said. "But if they do, they'll recognize their own signature."

He wrote a cover letter on the proper letterhead requesting a transfer for Julienne to El Inca in Quito for the reasons documented in the attached papers. "You need to get these to the embassy," he said. "They will present them to the proper government officials."

Julienne called the embassy and asked for a representative to visit her. When he did, she gave him the packet of signed documents. A month later, Julienne received a message.

"You're being transferred back to El Inca."

# CHAPTER 30

## Camp Inca 4th Time Factory Fire Explosions

JULIENNE REMEMBERED HER scary bus ride through the mountains when she came to Guayaquil and asked the director if she could fly to El Inca instead. "I'll pay for my ticket," she said. "And the guard's." They turned her down and she dreaded the trip back. Sent on a public bus with a female guard, Julienne had to change buses at several terminals and had to pay for their tickets. *At least the drivers aren't drinking this time.* She looked out the window as the bus took twists and turns past mountain villages, some slum areas, some estates. The good, the bad and the ugly, each against the backdrop of beautiful mountains. *That's what I need to focus on, the positive. At least I'm going back to Camp Inca to start working toward my freedom.*

When she arrived at Camp Inca, there was a photo shoot happening and she asked the guard, "What's going on?"

"Queen Contest."

Rosa spotted her and came running over. "Come on," she said to Julienne. "Get in our picture!"

"No, look at me. I'm in my old jeans and tee shirt. You're all dressed up."

Rosa pulled her over to the photo area and Julienne relented.

"You've lost weight," Rosa said. "Are you okay?"

"I'm fine, just couldn't stomach much of the food over there and it's really hot and humid. I didn't feel like eating."

Another inmate came over and touched her cheek. "Your face! It's not cut!"

"No…"

"Your arms. No cuts or scars?"

"No…"

"We heard that you were badly beaten at Guayaquil and that your face and arms were cut. I expected to see scars. Nobody comes back from there without a few scars."

"Well, I did, but I was never beaten."

"It was just a rumor?"

Julienne saw Director Carolina walking toward them. "Give me your keys," Julienne said to Rosa. "I need to put my stuff in your room." Rosa handed her the keys and Julienne started to walk away.

"Julienne!" the director called. "Where do you think you're going? You're considered new here again so I'll decide where you'll live."

"Don't worry," Julienne said. "I've got it all arranged." She hurried away and headed for Rosa's room, ignoring Carolina.

Later, Rosa said, "If I ever said that to the director, I'd be in so much trouble.

"My new motto is, do it and ask for forgiveness later."

"Well, I hope you don't get into trouble," Rosa said.

"Hey, did the women really think I would come back with scars?"

"Most do," Rosa said. "Someone must be watching over you."

*Maybe it's all those prayers for me.*

A few days after Julienne settled in, she walked past an inmate and recognized the clothes she had on.

"Hey!" she said. "Where did you get that outfit?"

"I bought it."

"From who?"

"Crystal."

"Crystal? Well, it's mine. She stole it from me and I want it back."

"You pay me for it and I'll give it to you," the inmate said.

"No, that's not how this is going down," Julienne said. "You give it back to me by the end of today. Understand?" She stormed away.

*I'm not putting up with this! I can't believe it. I thought Crystal was my friend. I trusted her.*

At the end of the day, Julienne's outfit was returned.

That week Joan and two other women came to visit. One of the missionaries was moving back to the States and they brought Julienne plates, silverware, and other kitchen items. "Take what you need," Joan said, "and share the rest with the others."

"Thanks!"

"I also brought you a Living Bible. It's a paraphrase version that's easy to read."

"That's okay, I already have a Bible. But thanks anyway."

"I'm glad you were transferred back here," Joan said. "I need to talk to you. My husband and I are rethinking our jail ministry here. I'm not going to be coming to the prison as often as I have in the past. I'm working long hours, teaching and coaching, and the English-speaking inmates aren't interested in Bible study. I've been coming for ten years now and I know they'll miss me for the clothes and things I bring and the letters I type for them and email to their families. I want to be available to talk with them and do things for them, but my schedule really is full." She hesitated. "My heart for all of you is your spiritual life and at the moment there doesn't seem to be a big desire for that or for Bible study."

"So you won't be coming or emailing letters anymore?"

"I can do that for you. Just give them to the women who come in on Sundays for the church service. They'll get them to me."

They visited for an hour and Julienne realized she would really miss her visits and her friendship. As Joan was leaving, Julienne said, "You know what? I really would like that Living Bible you mentioned. And I'd like to do a Bible study with you."

"Are you serious? If you are, Ruth Rollins and I will come every Wednesday. But I need to be sure it's what you really want."

"It is," Julienne said.

Joan smiled. "Okay, I'll see you next Wednesday."

---

Wanting to reconnect with Lucia, Julienne asked Rosa if anyone had heard from her.

"We've written letters a few times," Julienne said, "but I haven't heard anything lately."

"I was told that she was pregnant and was transferred to Guayaquil," Rosa said.

"That must have happened right after I left there, or I would have seen her."

"Guess who else was sent there," Rosa said. "Jacqueline; and I heard they're already fighting with each other."

*I'm glad I'm not there! I'd probably be caught up right in the middle of it.*

"I heard that one of the American inmates in the Condado pavilion is about to be released," Julienne said. "I'm going to check into it. Please don't say anything to anyone. I don't want to compete or fight over it with someone else who might also be interested in living there."

"I won't," Rosa said. "I know their rooms are nicer. You'll have to get voted in by the inmates there."

"I know. It's like a prison sorority. I already heard there's a waiting list. I'll have to convince the director too."

Julienne decided to approach the inmate who was leaving soon and ask her if she could move in with her before she left. That way the room would automatically become hers since she would already be living there.

"If you can get the approval of the leaders here, it's all right with me," she said.

Julienne offered $300 to the women involved and they all agreed to her proposition. *That was easy. I bought their vote.*

Next, she had to convince Director Carolina. She knew that wouldn't be easy, so first she went to each of the diagnostics, and got their signatures.

"Why should I let you move?" the director said. "You think just because you're American you deserve special privileges?"

"Not because I'm American," Julienne said, "although we both know there are mostly foreigners living in Condado. Most of them are Americans and Columbians."

"That doesn't mean you have to be there."

"Look, let me show you the signatures from diagnostics here, and a copy of the diagnostics that got me transferred back to El Inca. I've been working hard toward my rehabilitation. I'll feel safer there."

The director glanced at the signatures of the doctor, psychologist, and others. She sighed, and then signed off on it.

Julienne moved into the room and immediately felt a little safer. The area had problems with spiders and rodents like the rest of the prison, but the women there kept their area cleaner than most.

Lucia was transferred back to El Inca for a few months, but she had baby Monique now and they didn't hang out as much as they used to. She was going to be released soon, before Julienne.

---

An announcement came from the prison officials one day that there was going to be a movie night in the courtyard for those inmates with good behavior. The word spread and Julienne and her friends made a plan to sit together. She wasn't going to invite Crystal because of the clothes incident, but decided she had to forgive and move on.

"Let's make it fun and pretend we're going to a drive-in movie," Julienne said.

"What movie are they showing?"

"I don't know, but it's something different to do."

As the equipment was being set up, the inmates gathered and were told to sit in rows on the ground, to allow room for the guards to pass through and keep an eye on things.

Rosa and Julienne saved spots for Giovanna, Jael, Studmuffin, Crystal, Nadya, Ana Maria, and a few others. They each brought a blanket to sit on and shared popcorn, candy, and drinks.

"What a beautiful night," Julienne said, looking up at the sky. "Look at the stars."

The projector started and the movie title appeared on the wall.

"The *Titanic*!" someone shouted. "I heard that's a great movie!"

It was in English, with Spanish subtitles. When Leonardo DiCaprio appeared on the screen, the women started clapping and screaming out his name.

"Leonardo!"

"Woo-hoo!"

"You're so hot!"

"Eres tan caliente!"

At the end, when the scene showed the *Titanic* sinking into the ocean, a bright glow rose up from behind the wall where the movie was playing. It seemed like it was part of the film.

"Look! It's the moon. I've never seen it so bright!"

"It's huge! Luna súper!"

"It's the supermoon. That's when it's closest to the earth."

They watched in awe as the large, brilliant moon rose above them. As the *Titanic* slowly sank into the ocean, the bright moon and stars above the courtyard expanded the visual and the inmates cried and screamed and hugged each other as they watched the ship slowly sink into the ocean.

When the film was over, they felt drained from the emotion of it, but were amazed at how the incredible moon and stars became part of the movie for them. "I felt like we were right there on the ship," Julienne said.

Lying in bed that night Julienne thought, *what a fun night. That was the closest I've come to feeling normal since I came to prison.* But she also wondered how she would feel if she had been on that sinking ship. *Would I be ready to face whatever came next?*

What came next was a loud explosion in the middle of the night. Julienne shot up out of a sound sleep. *Boom! Is it an earthquake?* A series of explosions rattled the walls of the prison. *Oh my gosh, it sounds like bombs exploding!* She ran to her barred window, expecting to see aircraft bombing and military dropping out of the sky in parachutes. The explosions continued, but she couldn't see what it was. Her third floor cell faced the street and she had a view of the volcano, but the explosions came from the other side.

She unlocked her door and ran down the hallway to the kitchen area. Other inmates came and looked out that window.

"It's a fire!" one of the women shouted.

They could see the continued explosions of fire and felt the intense heat from the towering flames. *It must be very close!* Julienne thought.

"Are they going to evacuate us?" Julienne asked.

The women started to panic and were yelling back and forth, but no guards came. The fire and blasts continued for hours, followed by billowing smoke. The shouting continued and no one went back to bed.

The next day they heard on the news that a factory where aerosol hairspray cans were manufactured, blew up not far from the prison. Someone had placed dynamite, propane tanks, and other explosives around the entire plant.

"The police and fire department got there in time to keep the explosions from being worse. If everything had exploded, it would have leveled everything within a five-mile radius," the media reported. "The factory owner was detained at the airport and is suspected of causing the damage to collect insurance."

When Julienne heard the report she realized if the explosions would have destroyed a five- mile radius, it would have devastated the prison. *It would have wiped us out!* Restless thoughts of death and dying filled her mind and kept her awake the next few nights.

# CHAPTER 31

# Camp Inca
# Life-changing Decision

THE FOLLOWING WEDNESDAY, Joan came for a visit and brought Julienne the Bible she asked for. Julienne thanked her and talked about the movie, the fire and other things, but skirted the deeper issue of her fear of dying.

When it was time for Joan to leave, she said to Julienne, "Are you still serious about wanting to do a Bible study?"

"I am."

"Well, then I'll see you next Wednesday morning and we'll get started."

---

Joan and Ruth Rollins came faithfully every Wednesday. They read the Bible, discussed what it meant, and talked about what it means to accept Jesus and his teachings and have the Holy Spirit guide your life.

"Your dad's life is changing because of his decision. He asked me one day why we were so nice to him and why we helped you. I said, 'Because we love God and we care about you. We care about Julienne. But our being nice isn't because we're good people. It's because we love Jesus and He lives in us.

"He said, 'I've put up a lot of my money, but money can't get Julienne out. I can't get her out. I feel helpless.'

"I told him to put his hope and trust in Jesus. Get back in church. Both he and Kate did that and now they have some peace."

"He told me that and I see a change in him," Julienne said. "I feel bad that he's spent so much money on me. And I'm not even guilty!"

"Really? You made no decisions along the way that got you here? You're simply a victim of circumstance?"

"Well, I didn't do the crime. I'm not a drug trafficker."

"That may be so, but it's important to think back to the steps, the little decisions that may have brought you here. God gives us free will. His Word guides us on how to live, but the choices along the way are ours and we each reap our own consequences. It's important to see and acknowledge that in order to make better decisions in the future."

"That's true. I just never thought about it that way."

"Focus on that while you read your Bible. Ask God to show you what He sees. He loves you and wants what's best for you."

As she gathered up her things to leave, Joan added, "If you have questions or need to talk before we meet next week, just give me a call."

"Thanks."

That night Julienne did some soul searching and thought back through her childhood.

After her parents separated when she was twelve, she stayed in California with her mother while her dad moved to Ohio and then to Tennessee. She didn't see her father for three years.

As a young teenager, she went to Calvary Chapel church with her mother for a while and she became a close friend of Grace Aoki. Her father owned the chain of Benihana restaurants. Julienne often stayed at Grace's house and they went to many concerts together. When they were out and hungry, they simply showed up at the Benihana restaurant in Beverly Hills to get a free meal. Julienne liked that lifestyle and decided she no longer needed to disclose her whereabouts or activities to her mother and their relationship deteriorated. *Not one of my good decisions. Now I don't even know where my mother is.*

She liked the excitement of meeting members of well-known bands at the concerts, like U2 and others. Duran Duran sang "Happy Birthday" to her on stage one time. They thought she was a few years older, and she felt no need to correct them. Lisa Marie Presley sat with the girls at one concert. One New Year's Eve they flew to New York for a few weeks and stayed in the Hanna mansion in New Jersey, and were driven around in a limousine. They danced on American Bandstand.

Her parents decided she needed to finish her last year of high school in Tennessee under her dad's supervision. She went, determined to move back to California right after she graduated. Two weeks before graduation, the school informed her that she didn't have enough credits and she needed to complete another six months. Instead, she took a GED test, passed it, and wondered why she hadn't done that earlier.

She flew back to California and her grandmother offered to let her stay at her house. She did for a while, but as soon as she got a job, she managed to get her own little apartment with a friend. That's when she became a party girl—drinking, dancing, hanging out at nightclubs, and meeting guys. There was no one to tell her what she could and couldn't do and she liked it that way. *Another bad decision*, she thought.

Through her friend, Liz, she met and became friends with two biker guys, Leo and Rudy. One night at a club, Leo flirted with a girl at the bar. Her muscled biker boyfriend came over and confronted him. Leo apologized and backed off. But when he and Rudy left, a group of bikers waited outside for them. One punched Leo, knocked him down, and kicked him in the head. When Rudy tried to jump in to help, two guys held him back. Rudy watched his friend get brutally beaten. He died on the way to the hospital.

Julienne wasn't with them when that happened, but she went with Rudy to a rocking memorial at a club where several bands played as a tribute to Leo. Afterwards Rudy asked her, "Will you come home with me and stay at our place tonight?" He had an apartment with several friends. Julienne was living with Liz. *He doesn't want to be alone tonight*, Julienne realized. She went home with him and they spent the night talking about Leo and cried together. From that point, their relationship bonded and it continued off and on for the next three years. Rudy was responsible and had a good job, but the combination of heavy drinking and partying led them into constant conflict. She finally moved out to her own apartment on Sunset Blvd in West Hollywood. She started dating a lot of guys, several of whom proposed marriage, but she reasoned that if she never got married, then she'd never get divorced. *Those relationships were definitely not good choices.*

Julienne shared all this and more with Joan as they developed a close relationship over the next several weeks, talking and studying together. Joan pointed out to Julienne some of the decisions she had made that led her to that fateful day when she was arrested.

"Your desire to live that party lifestyle is what brought you to Miami, then to Ecuador. You didn't just want to travel all over the world; you wanted to party all over the world."

"I just wanted to have fun."

"You've paid a heavy price for the enemy of your soul to deceive you into thinking that there's no consequence for a jet set lifestyle of drinking and partying and hooking up with men. But God can take all that's happened and turn it around for your and His good."

"I'm beginning to realize that God has intervened in my life and kept me safe even when I didn't see it. Like when that drug lord in Guayaquil told me I was lucky not to have been forced into trafficking or sex trade. Or lucky not to get blown away."

"You know, if you accept Jesus, there will be things in your life that don't fit in with what God's Word says. Once again, you'll have to decide, make choices. All of your own wisdom and intelligence and decisions haven't done too well for you so far. And you don't accept Jesus just to say, 'Okay, now get me out of here, get me out of trouble.' If you're serious, and want God's best for you, you've got to walk away from your old ways and do things His way. It's a process, not a quick fix."

"I'm ready for that," Julienne said. "I'm serious." Her eyes filled with tears.

Joan reached out and held Julienne's hands while she prayed for and with her.

When Julienne walked back to her cell, she felt like she had been washed on the inside. Peace replaced the turmoil within. *This is what Helen and Gene meant when they talked about peace that passes understanding.* She looked around her cell.

"Nothing has changed; yet everything has changed."

She slept well that night.

# CHAPTER 32

## Camp Inca Bakery Business

The next morning, she could hardly wait to call Joan.

"I feel like a new person."

"That's the Holy Spirit beginning his work inside you, giving you hope for your future."

After a few more weeks of study together, Joan challenged Julienne to reach out to other inmates and invite them to come to their study. "You can be a light in this dark place."

Julienne hesitated at first. *I like our times alone. If others come, I'll lose that.* She had several inmates ask her if they could come and Julienne told them no. *Some will want counseling and it will absorb too much of Joan's time.* But Joan's comment about being a light in this dark place kept invading her thoughts and she invited several English-speaking inmates to join them. One came and each week, another one or two joined until the class grew to nine, including European girls and some from South Africa. It became the highlight of Julienne's week.

In spite of her new inner peace, Julienne became restless at times about her release—particularly on days when her focus returned to the conditions around her. The inmate fights, guards taking advantage of young girls, children suffering and being mistreated, the rationing of power and water, all got to her at times. Although the Two-for-One law had been passed and she now had hopes of serving five years instead of ten, she still had another year to serve. She felt panic rising and dashed down to the phone area to call Joan and ask her to pray.

"The phones aren't working today," the guard said.

"They're out of order?"

She ran back to her cell and threw herself across her bed, and cried.

"God, how much longer am I going to be in this place? It's been over four years and I'm overwhelmed. I feel like I'm going to explode if I don't get out of this hell. I want to go home. I want to be with my family. I want a normal life." Tears of anger and frustration streamed down her face.

When the tears stopped, she saw her Bible setting on the corner of her bed and reached out for it. "Okay, Lord. Please tell me once and for all, when am I going home?"

She closed her eyes, flipped open the Bible randomly, and read the passage it fell open to. It referred to people who were in exile in foreign countries, that they would be sent home. Excited, she continued to read. "My children, I promise you this. You will not spend one day less or one day more; then I will set you free."

*What does that mean? I'm going to be set free, but when?* She read the whole chapter again and it slowly dawned on her. *Freedom would come at the appointed time. Not one day less or one day more.*

"What? That means another year!" She slammed the Bible shut. "Are you kidding me, God? One more year? Seriously?" She went into a meltdown. When the tears finally stopped, she felt drained, yet somehow relieved. "Okay, God. I have your answer. Now I have to make the best of this year. Help me."

When Joan came on Wednesday, Julienne told her about what she read and what she thought God was saying to her.

"What verses were you reading?" Joan asked.

Julienne searched her Bible, but couldn't remember or find the passage. "I was so upset that I slammed the Bible shut," she confessed. "Now I can't find it."

"You obviously feel confident about it."

"I do. Now I just need to know how to spend my time and make it positive."

Later that day the director called Julienne to her office and offered her the opportunity to run a bakery just outside the first gate. The building had housed maximum security which was now inside the gate. They had moved bakery equipment into the building from another area.

"You'll have to invest in it yourself," she said. "Buy the supplies and ingredients you'll need with your own money. Can you handle that?"

"Let me think about it," Julienne said.

"Don't take too long or I'll offer it to someone else."

Back in her room, Julienne thought, *this must be God opening a door for me. He'll help me put it together.* She sat cross-legged on her bunk and made a list of the things she would need, including an 'all access pass' in order to move freely around the jail and have the female guards open the gate for her at different times of day and night. *Yes, this could really work out.*

She called her dad and told him about the offer and the plan she was putting together.

"I'll be glad to send the funds to get it started," he said. "Your own little business; I'm proud of you."

Julienne thought of a Bible verse she had read, *Ask and it will be given to you; seek and you will find; knock and the door will be opened to you...*

Julienne went back to the director's office. "Yes, I'll do it."

"I know it will take a while to pull it together. Just keep me informed of your progress."

Julienne researched the best prices from flour and sugar vendors, then struck a bargain with them. In exchange for her commitment to buy a certain amount of product each month, they would send a baker to teach her what she needed to know to make the business successful.

They agreed and she went back to the director to get permission for them to come in and teach what she needed to learn about baking.

"How will you pay for this training?"

"It's free."

The director looked skeptical. "Nothing is free."

Julienne explained the deal she'd negotiated with them.

"And who will they be training?"

"I'm working on that. I'll give you a list of names soon."

Julienne smiled as she left the office. She could see that the director was surprised at how it was coming together. *God, you're so good. Nothing happens this fast here; except when you're in charge!*

She assembled a team of women who really needed the bakery to help support them. Since the bakery was located outside the first gate, the director wanted to eliminate the risk of attempted escape. The women had to already have been sentenced and confirmed by the courts to have only one year left to serve. They weren't likely to risk an escape attempt. Julienne brought her list of twenty women.

"Do you really need that many?"

"Yes. They'll be working different shifts, some starting really early in the morning, and we need to be sure we're covered in case someone is sick."

She left the office with the director's signature on all the permissions that Julienne had requested. For the next two weeks, classes covered how to work safely with all the equipment and how to make a variety of breads and pastries. The aroma of baking bread lifted their spirits. One of them brought in a boom box and they sang and danced around while they made pastries. They had fun and worked well together as a team.

*This is the best therapy the prison could offer,* Julienne thought. *It gives them a reason to get out of bed in the morning.*

Within the first month everything was up and running. They sold out of bread every day. Some of their inmate customers got angry when there wasn't any left, so Julienne started to limit the amount each one could buy to make it fair to the others. Sometimes she would give up her own bread or pastry just to keep the peace. As they tracked their sales going up and they started making more bakery goods. After Julienne paid back the money her dad had put into the bakery, and set aside some funds each week to reorder ingredients, the rest of the income was divided among all the workers.

The owner of a small restaurant and store across the street from the prison, heard about her success and came over to talk with Julienne.

"Would you consider making bread and pastries for us to sell for our breakfast rush?"

"How much would you need?

"About 80 to 100 croissants, toasty hot just out of the oven."

"How early is this rush?"

"We need them by 7:30 a.m."

"Give me a day or two to figure this out. I'll let you know."

The next day Julienne went to the director and told her about the proposal.

"We'll need four or five women to work in alternating shifts, starting at 4:00 a.m. in order to have the croissants ready for pick up at 7:30 a.m."

"I'll approve it, but only if you're there each morning to supervise," she said.

Julienne wanted to groan at the thought of getting up that early every morning, but didn't. She thanked her and sent a message to the owner across the street that they could start in a few days.

The first day she got up at 3:30 a.m., Julienne wondered, *what was I thinking?* She reminded herself that God had provided all of this and she stepped out into the night air. She looked up at the Andes Mountains and the stars and absorbed the peace and quiet. The women assigned to come in early showed up on time and the croissants were ready by 7:15 a.m.

Julienne asked the guard on duty to open the main front gate so she could yell across the street for the owner to come get his order. Some mornings the owner didn't hear her and the guard reluctantly allowed Julienne to walk across the street with the large basket of pastry. She waited a few minutes while the owner paid her, bought a Coke for the guard, and walked back to the prison with her empty basket.

"Thank you," she said to the guard as she handed him the Coke. She realized it was a risk for him to allow her to do that. She loved those few minutes of freedom. She took a deep breath of air that was sweeter than the prison air. She looked forward to the day when she could walk through that gate and never return. Until then, she determined to be faithful.

After one of the Bible studies, Julienne invited Joan to come to her room to see some family photos her dad had sent. She had posted them on her wall and they gave her incentive to hold on to her faith and hope of freedom.

"This one is of my little nephew, Wyatt," she said. "He's less than a year old. I look forward to meeting him." She pointed at another photo. "And this is Wyatt's mother, my step sister who is pregnant again." She teared up as she described each photo and family members. "This is a picture of my parents' lake house and boat dock in Tennessee. They said I could stay there when I go home."

"I think Tennessee would be a good choice for you," Joan said. "If you go back to California, you'll be going back to that old lifestyle. You need to be with family."

"I've been thinking about that a lot," Julienne said, "and getting married one day."

"All in good time," Joan said.

---

When not working at the bakery or going to Bible study, Julienne began working on the paperwork needed for her release. *I know how slow things work here so I'd better get started early.*

She talked with the director to ask about the process.

"You're trying to get out early under the Two-for-One law?"

"Yes, I understand that would apply to me."

"It depends on your Parts," she said. "Any bad conduct reports could extend your stay."

"I don't have any that I know of," she said. "Could you check for me?"

She pulled her file, opened it, and pushed it across the desk. Julienne picked it up.

"I have two Parts!" Although it was in Spanish, she understood enough at this point to know clearly what it said.

Part #1— hiding a cat in her room. *That's when Peggy and I rescued little Pinky Tone!* Part #2—getting caught drinking with an inmate. *A guard was the one who gave it to us!*

She tried not to panic.

## CHAPTER 33

## Camp Inca
## Volcano Eruption

*What can I do about this? There has to be a way to get the bad conduct reports expunged from my record.*

She called her dad and told him about it. "What do you think I should do? Do I need to ask a lawyer?"

"I don't have much faith in lawyers anymore," he said. "But if you have someone you can meet with, go ahead. Don't worry about the money. I'll take care of it."

"I don't know, let me think about it."

"We are so looking forward to having you home," he said. "The time is winding down."

"I know it is. It's too slow for me, but I'm glad I can stay busy with the bakery and the Bible study or the time would drag even more that it does."

"I love you, and I'm so glad you've built a relationship with Joan. She's a good woman."

"She comes in often, just to spend time with me. In fact, one of the guards told me the other day, 'Your mother is here.' Shocked me for a second!" She laughed. "She really is like a mother to me. I'm so grateful."

Julienne talked to a few women and they told her about Sergio, a new paralegal who came to the prison and had helped some inmates. He had use of an office there.

"He can get things done," one of them said.

Julienne made an appointment with him and he reviewed her file.

"Who do I need to talk to about these Parts?"

"On the first one, the doctor," he said. "On the second one, the psychologist."

She thanked him and got up to leave.

"Any time you need help, let me know," he said. "You're very pretty."

"Thanks," she said and left the office in a hurry. *Latin men!*

*Interesting. The doctor has to deal with the Part about the cat? Maybe they consider it a health issue.*

She did some investigating and found out that the doctor's stethoscope was damaged, but the prison had no funds at the moment to replace it. She arranged to buy a new one and went to his office to donate it to him.

He beamed when he opened the package. "Thank you," he said. "This is one of quality."

They chatted for a few minutes, and then she asked him to sign the paper to expunge Part 1. "I thought I was doing a good thing when I rescued the cat," she said.

He signed the papers.

She heard the psychologist was pregnant and looking forward to having her first child. Julienne bought her some baby clothes and took them to her office.

"These are for your baby," Julienne said. "You must be excited about having your first."

Surprised, the psychologist thanked her and smiled as she picked up each tiny outfit. "That's very thoughtful of you."

"There's more," Julienne said. "I told my dad about you and he wants to contribute something toward whatever you need for the baby." She handed her an envelope with $300 inside. She signed the papers for Part 2.

*I am so blessed to be able to do this*, Julienne thought. She realized that inmates in a similar situation who had no financial resources would simply have to serve a longer time.

She completed other forms needed and with the proper signatures and stamps on each, sent them off to the court. When she called the court offices a week later to be sure they were properly done and in the right hands, they informed her that they couldn't find any of the paperwork she was talking about.

"What? How is that possible?" Julienne said, panic rising in her voice.

"It's not here," the clerk said. "I don't know what happened."

"Now what do I do?"

"You'll have to do it over."

*Don't freak out,* she told herself. *Just do it over and find another way to send the papers.*

She thought about calling the embassy, but knew they had to be careful not to get directly involved with her case. She made an appointment with Sergio again.

"Julienne!" It's so nice to see you," he said as she entered his office.

She sat down and told him what had happened.

"Don't worry, chica," he said. "I'll help you." He offered to redo the papers and get the signatures needed. "They will understand and sign the papers again if they realize the court lost them."

He stood and walked around the desk, and sat on the edge of it. "Your eyes are so beautiful," he said.

"Thank you." *This is awkward.*

He leaned forward and tried to kiss her.

"No… no," she said, and stood to her feet. *Don't offend him and blow this,* she told herself. "You're a very handsome man, Sergio," she said, "but we can't do this."

His mouth twitched with amusement. Embarrassed, she hurried out of the office.

"Hey, Julienne!" one of the inmates called to her. "Did you have a good time with Sergio?" She smirked.

"What? No! Of course not!" She kept walking.

"Es muy guapo," she called after Julienne. *I know he's handsome, but that doesn't mean I'm messing around with him.*

The next day Julienne thought of an idea that just might work. The following morning when she brought bread and pastries across the street to the little restaurant, she asked the owner if he could arrange to hold some papers for Joan or Lucia to pick up so that they could take them to the court for her. He agreed. For a fee.

Once Sergio got the paperwork together, she picked it up from his office, paid him, and said she had to get back to the bakery.

A few days later, the store owner marched across the street to pick up the early morning basket of goods. She wrapped the breads in a thin towel and placed them in an over-sized basket. She placed her paperwork beneath the towel, wrapped in another towel, along with instructions of who to pass the paperwork on to. He nodded and smiled at her and left with the basket.

This time the papers made it to the proper court office

One day the director called Julienne into her office. "I know the bakery has done well, but we have to make some changes."

"Is there a problem?

"We're turning that building into a rehab center for drug addicts."

"We have to shut down the bakery?"

"Yes. It's a decision that has already been made by the officials."

"The women are going to be so disappointed," she said. "We all put so much work into it and it's been successful."

"I'm sorry, but we have no choice in the matter."

"How much time do we have?"

"One month."

Julienne walked back to the bakery, but didn't have the heart to tell the women the bad news.

"Are you okay?" one of them asked. "You don't look very happy today."

"I'm fine," Julienne said. "Just some things I need to deal with."

Back in her room, Julienne fought her discouragement. *Things were going so well. All that work and now it's over. How do I tell the women? The bakery is an important part of their lives.* She reached for her Bible and opened it. Tucked inside was a note from a missionary who helped Joan with their Bible study group.

"Dear Julienne, I'm praying for you and am blessed by our times together on Wednesdays. Here is a verse for you from the book of Isaiah. "Do not fear, for I am with you; do not be dismayed, for I am your God. I will strengthen you and help you; I will uphold you with my righteous right hand."

She slipped to her knees. "Thank you, Lord. I will not fear. Strengthen me. Show me how to handle this."

As she thought through the whole situation, she suddenly remembered the old bakery space that was no longer used. It was small, under a stairwell just below her pavilion. *We would have to scale back, but I think it could work.* Excited, she went to check out the space, and then hurried to the director's office.

"What about the old bakery space?" Julienne said. "We could make that work!"

The director looked at her and shook her head. "No. I don't think it's a good idea."

"Why not?"

"It's too small." She dismissed Julienne and went back to her work.

Julienne walked over and measured the space. *It really is small. Like a walk-in closet.* It still had an oven with five baking slats. *We'd have to cut down to half of what we're making now, but something is better than nothing.* She went back to the director's office.

"Now what?"

"I have a plan," Julienne said. "There's still an oven in that old space. We'd have to cut way back on what we're producing now, but I know it could work."

"I already gave you my answer," the director said.

"Please hear me out. This bakery has been so good for these women. It gives them a reason to get up in the morning, something to look forward to. And they're all getting along, working well together. As director don't you want positive results to continue?"

"You are going to pester me about this aren't you?"
Julienne smiled. The director let out a long breath.
"Let me think about it and I'll get back to you."
"Thank you!"
A few days later, the move was approved.

*Now I have to tell the women. The hardest part will be cutting back from twenty to five. I need to think about who needs this the most.*

When she made the announcement about the bakery, the women responded in anger. They were angry at the prison officials and upset with Julienne when she told them who would and wouldn't continue to work at the new location.

"I'm so sorry," she said.

Once the bakery was up and running in the smaller location, Julienne recognized that it was actually better for her. The large bakery had been a big responsibility and took up most of her time. Now she could focus more on her studies with Joan and on all that still had to be completed before her release. *God, you're so good. You give me what I can handle and no more.*

One night Julienne awoke at 2:00 a.m. to the loud banging of metal rods against the bars of the pavilion.

"Requisa!" an inmate shouted. Others joined in the warning.

*Raid!* She jumped out of bed and scrambled to make sure anything she considered important was hidden.

Suddenly, four military police burst into her cell, grabbed her by the arms, and started running with her down the stairs. The pavilion echoed with shouting from the other inmates.

*Are they hauling me off again to another prison in the middle of the night?* A shot of fear flooded her body. *Please, God, not again! Not now!*

At the bottom of the stairs, they ordered her to open the bakery door. Terrified, she shook as she took the key from her wristband and unlocked the door. They followed her inside and pushed her over to the oven. One officer ordered her to detach the propane tank. When she did, they took it from her and lifted it into the air, shaking it and smelling it.

"What are you doing?!" she shouted. "That's gas you're shaking around."

A female prison guard walked in and said to the military men, "That's enough! There's nothing there." She waved them out like they were little children.

"Lock up," she told Julienne.

"What was that all about?" Julienne asked, still trembling.

"They were searching for alcohol."

"What? In a gas tank? That's crazy!"

"We got a tip and found some alcohol in tanks earlier today that were brought in for one of the kiosks. So now we have to check everyone who uses a propane tank."

She took Julienne back to her cell.

Badly shaken, Julienne hardly slept the rest of the night. She remembered when Mama Lucha had several propane tanks brought inside with alcohol in them for her birthday bash. Apparently, someone else had copied the idea and thought they could get away with it

*With a short time left to freedom, I don't need any trouble.*

News of volcanic activity from Tungurahua, spread through the prison. Tungurahua, the largest of eight active volcanos in Ecuador, spewing explosive gas, ash, and rock fragments had led to the evacuation of more than 25,000 inhabitants of Baños and its surroundings.

"That's scary," Julienne said to one of the inmates. "Any chance that it will affect us here?"

"I don't think so," she said.

Weeks later, when the risk of lava and toxic gases decreased, the authorities allowed the residents to return to their homes for a major cleanup of the ash spewed over their area.

When everyone settled down and stopped talking about the eruption, more news came stating that a yellow alert warning had been issued in Quito for potential eruptions of the Guagua Pichincha volcano, known to the locals as Wawa, meaning baby. Within weeks, the warning level went to orange. The inmates panicked.

"What's going on? That volcano hasn't been active for a few hundred years."

"How serious is this? We're just five miles from the volcano. Will we be evacuated?"

"I heard that the ash could contaminate drinking water supplies," another said.

Fearful, Julienne filled her pails of water and covered them. She also stored extra dried food. *I doubt the authorities would evacuate us. Where would they put us?*

One morning after roll call, Julienne crawled back into bed. She was sound asleep when someone pounded on her door.

"Julienne!"

Julienne groaned. "Leave me alone. Let me sleep."

The knocking on the door continued. "Wake up!"

"What!"

"Get up! Look out your window."

Julienne rubbed her eyes and went over to her window. A huge plume of white and gray ash and smoke exploded in the sky. *Oh my gosh, this is it! The volcano! It looks like photos I've seen of the mushroom cloud of Hiroshima.* As she stood looking out the window, she felt overwhelmed. *This is amazing.* She stared at the gigantic mushroom cloud and thought, *I am so small, just a tiny spec in the design of life compared to that. Yet, God cares about me.*

"Do you have a camera?" The question interrupted her thoughts.

"Yes, I've got Joan's camera here. I'll take photos."

She snapped some pictures through her barred window.

The spectacular column of ash and steam ultimately ascended twenty miles high and released 5,000 tons of ash on Quito, flooding the city with gray dust. Municipal shelters housed some residents and school classes were suspended. The airport and bus stations closed.

The courtyard at the prison filled with a few inches of ash every day, which the inmates had to clean up. They wore paper masks, trying not to inhale the dust. Laundry had to be hung to dry inside. No visits were allowed.

Julienne's asthma grew worse, even though she wore a mask and kept her door closed and her window covered and taped shut. She felt claustrophobic in her sealed room and didn't sleep much. *The air is so toxic. I wonder if it can cause lung cancer.*

One day it rained and the combination of heavy water mixed with thick ash collapsed a portion of the third floor roof of the middle building. Fortunately, no one was there. The airport opened after two weeks and slowly Quito and the prison returned to normal before the holidays.

All Souls' Day came first, when locals visited the tombs of dead friends and relatives, placing flowers, wreaths, photographs, stuffed animals and other trinkets at the gravesite. At the prison, observance of the holiday turned into a weekend party with dancing, special food, and lots of Colada Morada, a purple sweet drink. Julienne knew how their celebrations got out of hand and decided to stay away from it all, spending most of the weekend in her room.

A few weeks later came Thanksgiving, a holiday not celebrated in Ecuador. Non-American inmates called it Dia de Pavo, Day of the Turkey, when selfish Americans stuffed themselves with turkey and lots of other food.

Julienne remembered how Peggy used to call the embassy and ask them to bring turkeys to the prison for the Americans for Thanksgiving. Julienne made the call and asked the embassy if they were going to do that this year. They said it wasn't in their budget. Julienne mentioned it to Joan.

"Don't worry," Joan said. "I know the ambassador's wife. I'll talk with her."

She reported back to Julienne and the Bible study group that the ambassador's wife promised to bring them a turkey dinner with all the trimmings and would even come and visit and eat with them. They served ten inmates and had a great time.

Julienne called her parents to wish them a Happy Thanksgiving and told them about the dinner they were having.

"This is my last Thanksgiving here!" she said. "Next year I'll be home with you!"

After dinner, Julienne read some of the mail she had received, some old, some new. One letter was from Peggy in California. "Hey you! Wuz up, Chickee?" Julienne laughed. *That's so Peggy.* "Greetings from the U.S.A. – the real life in case you forgot. Ha! Ha! Girl, hope all is well and you are getting through this detention in hell stage of your life." She went on to tell about her job and that her first cat since their 'Pinky.' This one rescued from the street. "I wish you the best. Just get through this and come back here where you belong!"

Another was from Michelle, a Spanish school teacher and human rights activist, who made Julienne her class project after she heard about her from the State Department. She had her students send letters, candy and sometimes tee-shirts.

A post card from her friend, Joanna, brought a smile to her face. "Hi! I'm having a great time traveling. Have been in Amsterdam, Brussels and am writing this from a café in Praha…" *We talked so often about traveling the world together,* Julienne thought. *I'm glad she's getting to do it.*

She read a note from her dad in February. "Hey baby, Got your email from Joan. We were thinking tonight how great it would be if you were here and we could all go out and celebrate your birthday. Very soon! We are all praying very hard that this comes to an end quickly. Now that you've added your prayers, I am sure it will definitely happen. Hug the wonderful people who are helping us. Our prayers go out for them. Have a Happy, Happy, Happy Birthday! Love you much, Dad."

She tucked the notes away in a small stack received from family, friends and even strangers who stopped by to visit. She felt blessed to have had them cross her path and enjoyed going through the notes and reading them over and over again.

---

The classes with Joan were very practical, teaching how to apply what they studied. She talked with Julienne again about reaching out to others.

"Christmas is a great opportunity to do that," Joan said. "Many know the Christmas story, but it isn't really personal for them. Let's plan something special to let them know God loves them and wants to be part of their lives."

They planned a Christmas dinner and invited a group of English-speaking inmates. One missionary made a birthday cake for Jesus. Joan and others collected little gifts to bring in. Shampoo, soaps, washcloths, toilet paper, personal toiletries and other items were each giftwrapped and placed in the center of a large table covered with a white tablecloth with place settings of paper plates and cups. Church volunteers helped prepare a full turkey dinner and brought it in.

"I have something I'd like to say before we start," Joan said once everyone was seated. "I'm aware that when the prison doesn't supply you with a decent bed or blankets, or personal toiletries, or the food you need, it could be that you came today just for those things." She smiled. "And that's okay. I'm glad you're here. But I want you to know why I'm here." She glanced around at their faces.

"I'm here because I love Jesus and it's His birthday today." She nodded toward the birthday cake on the table. "And I'm here because I love you girls. Jesus put that in my heart." Tears glistened in her eyes. "So now let's pray and thank Him for this wonderful meal."

Julienne's heart swelled with love for Joan and for Jesus.

After her prayer, Joan announced, "Enjoy!"

The girls chatted while they ate, asking about the wrapped gifts in the center of the table.

"I'm going to read you the Christmas story from the Bible," Joan said. "And every time I say the word 'gift,' you can each choose one from the table and unwrap it. If you want to trade your gift with someone, you can. Once you open it, the gift is yours. You can keep it or trade it for something else."

The women really got into it, listening for the word, and then scrambling for a gift each time, until they were all gone.

"Well, it looks like there are no more gifts," Joan said. "But the story's not over. So just wait."

"Jesus is the most important gift that God offers to us. And the good news is that it's a free gift." She looked around the table at the torn Christmas paper and their small stash of gifts. "I see that you don't mind taking free gifts. I just watched you do it! Jesus is your free gift from God. I'm not asking you to accept that or make a decision about it today. But I want you to know that He's the one who can give you peace in your heart. Even while you're inside this prison."

Julienne brushed away a tear. The women sat in silence, listening to Joan's words.

"We have Bible study here every Wednesday. Julienne is part of it. We'd like to invite each of you to attend. When you come, you'll receive a Bible to keep." She smiled as she looked around the table. "Now, let's have some birthday cake. Merry Christmas!"

"Merry Christmas!" they shouted in unison.

When it was time to leave, the women gathered their gifts and divided up the leftover food to take back to their cells. They thanked Joan for the dinner and a great time.

"I've never heard the Christmas story presented that way," one said. "I'll be here on Wednesday."

"Me too," another said.

Julienne helped Joan and others clean up. When Joan was leaving, Julienne thanked her and said, "It was amazing."

They hugged and Joan said, "Now let's remember to pray for each of them."

"I will," Julienne promised. "I know I have to reach out and be willing to share you with them. But it's not easy."

The following Wednesday almost everyone who attended Christmas dinner came to the Bible study class. Julienne handed out Bibles as they arrived. She was so excited. Joan shared Bible verses with them that touched on personal issues they had to deal with, taking care of themselves inside and out, having self-respect, and not allowing men or women to take advantage of them. This included unplanned pregnancies and prostitution with the potential result of Aids.

"Interesting," Joan said. "Satan whispers to you that it's okay to participate in certain behavior; then when you do it, he tells you how bad you are. This leads you to believe that God won't forgive you. But that's a lie. God loves you and wants what's best for you."

"What we want to learn here is the truth. Not your opinion and not my opinion. If I see something in God's Word, I have a choice to make. I can say, 'God, you know what you're talking about so I choose to believe you. Or you can say, 'God, you don't know what you're talking about' and continue on making poor decisions.

The room grew quiet.

"What I want to do in this class is challenge your thinking, your opinions. Let's search God's Word together and discover the truth. I don't want us to get 'religious' and toss around our own ideas, including mine. Let's find the truth." She smiled and said, "One more thing. There's nothing you've done that God isn't willing to forgive you for. He offers you that through His son, Jesus. Your free gift. Now you get to choose."

She closed the session in prayer and announced she was available to pray personally with anyone who wanted to. Several did.

Julienne got on her knees that night and thanked God again for Joan. *I'm learning so much!*

When New Year's Eve came around, Julienne avoided the festivities. From her room, she could hear the loud Latin music and singing and shouting. Some inmates made paper mache piñatas and placed pictures of government leaders on them, including the United States and Latin countries. Near midnight they lit them on fire, tossed them in a pile, and smashed bottles. They flaunted their sexuality, a few with boyfriends, but mostly girls with girls. The alcohol flowed, the music blared, and the crowd got rowdier. *I'm so glad this is my last New Year's Eve here. What craziness!*

She thought back to the MTV New Year's Eve bash one year when she had a chance to hang with Dave Wakeling with the *General Public Band*. Dave pulled her up on stage at one point and danced. A bunch of groupies joined them and flooded the stage. On that same trip, she saw Robert De Niro at Hard Rock Café, and danced the night away at Studio 54 and the Ritz. *I thought I had arrived. The big time life. Look where it got me.*

Back to reality, she turned on the tiny TV in her room and managed to tune in to the Time Square celebration with Dick Clark. With 'rabbit ears' the black and white picture consisted of squiggly lines, but every once in a while it would clear for a minute. She heard the countdown. "Five, four, three, two, one. "Happy New Year!"

She walked over to her cell window and looked up at the stars. In spite of the clamor and chaos of the partiers, she felt at peace. When she crawled into bed and opened her Bible, she read, *I know the plans I have for you, declares the Lord, plans to prosper you and not to harm you, plans to give you hope and a future.* Jeremiah 29:11 "Thank you, Lord, for your promises." She closed her Bible and whispered, "Happy New Year."

## CHAPTER 34

## Camp Inca Stabbing Attempt and Freedom

JULIENNE FILLED HER days with the bakery, with Bible study, and hanging out with a handful of friends who she felt wouldn't cause her any problems. She wanted to keep a low profile and avoid the daily prison gossip and fights.

At times, the days seemed to fly by, but when Julienne looked at a calendar, the days weren't passing fast enough. She wished she could fast forward her countdown to freedom. Joan's regular visits helped control her anxiety.

"Did I tell you that one of the guards refers to you as my mother?" Julienne told Joan.

"Well, you're like a daughter to me," Joan said, "so that makes me proud."

On the next visit day, a small group from the South American Explorers Club came to the prison and brought some items for several prisoners. One of the prisoners was Christine, a South African inmate. When the passadora called out her visit, there was no response. Several attempts were made, but Christine never showed up.

Julienne was concerned as were several other inmates.

"We're really worried," one of them said. "It's not like her not to answer for a visit."

Christine was a recovering drug addict and Julienne hoped she hadn't relapsed. *Something's definitely wrong. She looked forward to visits. Since she doesn't have family nearby, it's the only time she gets personal items she needs. The Explorers Club always brings gifts with them.*

Several inmates joined Julienne to search around the prison for her. No one could find her and the visitors left. The thought briefly crossed Julienne's mind that maybe she had escaped, but didn't really think she was capable of that. She continued her search and after passing through Christine's pavilion several times, she decided to go there once more.

One of the girls from that floor came over to Julienne and said, "She's in her room now."

Julienne knocked on her door. No answer. "I know you're in there, open up." Still no answer. "Come on, Christine. Everyone is worried about you. Your visitors left and now the guards will start to look for you. Open the door."

Christine opened the door and it was obvious to Julienne that she was high on something. "Take this!" Christine said. She grabbed Julienne's arm and shoved a small bag of freebase powder into her hand. "Get rid of this for me," she said. "I messed up."

"What are you doing! Julienne forced the bag back into Christine's hand. "What if a guard sees me with this?"

"I'm sorry," she said.

"Take it and go flush it right now!" Julienne pushed her out of her room and pointed toward the bathroom. She followed her to make sure she did it.

"I'm such a bad person," she sobbed. "I'm so sorry." Her eyes were dilated and she seemed on the verge of passing out.

"Come on," Julienne said, supporting her as they walked back to Christine's cell. She got her into bed and stayed with her until she fell asleep.

Back in her own room, Julienne thought, *how dare she put drugs in my hand a few months before I'm about to leave. What if the guards showed up at that moment? My release could have gone up in a puff of smoke!*

Then she realized she hadn't prayed for Christine, so she did, and her anger subsided. *I've made this all about me, when it's all about her. She feels so unloved and unworthy that she turns to drugs to cover the pain.*

"I'm sorry, Lord. Help me to show Christine your love for her."

## Surviving Camp Inca

It took several days to go through withdrawal, but Christine got past it and thanked Julienne for helping her. She even agreed to come to Bible study and Joan began counseling her. Joan's ministry to the inmates grew and she obtained a special prison pass to come in on any day she needed to. More women's lives began to change and Julienne was amazed and grateful for Joan's commitment to them.

Julienne talked with Joan constantly about leaving prison. "It's all I can think about. I dream about the day I walk out that front gate."

"Don and I are flying back to the States on July 5," Joan said. "Let's agree in faith that you'll be flying home with us."

"I've been told many times that nobody gets out of here on their exact release date, let alone early," Julienne said. "But I know God can make that miracle happen. Let's buy my airline ticket back to the States for July 5! I know I'll be out by then."

When she started to feel restless, Julienne would go on a cleaning spree and give things from her room away to other inmates. She rearranged her cell every few days.

One day the director came by her room. "What are you doing? Where do you think you're going?"

"Home," Julienne said. "I'm going home."

"This is your home."

"Not for much longer."

"You still have six months to go."

"No, I have less than two months to go," Julienne said with confidence.

The director walked out of her room shaking her head. "Whatever, chica loca!"

Julienne knew it was time to turn over the management of the bakery to someone else. She chose an Ecuadorian inmate who showed responsibility, needed the money to survive on, and still had a year to go on her sentence. She took it over and scaled down to three women so they could each split a little more money while they shared the workload.

Another inmate Julienne spent time with was Marianna. She was in for murdering her fiancé, then trying to commit suicide. She shot herself in the head, but she survived. The doctors removed one bullet, but removal of the other was life threatening, so it remained lodged in her brain. The inmates rumored that she was crazy and could snap at any time, but Julienne found her to be friendly and they enjoyed their time together. They lived in the same pavilion.

She ran a small store that sold crafts made by the inmates. It was located just outside the first gate and the guard only allowed one or two inmates at a time in the store, and moved them right along. One day, Marianna asked the guard if Julienne could stay a little longer.

"She's helping me do some work in here," she said.

He relented and gave them a little more time, but when it was close to the time to close the courtyard, he said they had to leave.

They talked while they walked arm in arm down the corridor to their pavilion. Suddenly, Marianna jerked her arm away. Julienne swung around and saw Marianna struggling with Goya, who held a broken glass bottle in one hand and a knife in the other. Anger flashed in her eyes and her short matted braids stuck out all over her head. She wore a boot on one foot and a sneaker on the other.

"I'm going to kill you!" Goya shouted at Julienne.

Marianna grabbed her by the wrists and held tight, trying to keep her from swinging her arms and cutting whoever was in her way.

"What are you doing!" Julienne screamed at Goya.

"Run!" Marianna shouted. "Run and hide!

Goya swung at Marianna with the knife and started to break free of her grip.

"Go. Now!" Marianna shouted again.

Julienne dashed down the corridor and found Sylvio and Sammy. "Goya is after me!" she yelled. "I don't know why!"

"Come with us!" They ran down the stairwell and hid her in a small covered space in the back of a little store under the stairs.

Goya broke free from Marianna and ran back and forth, yelling, "Julienne! I will find you!"

Julienne crouched in the corner. Her heart pounded.

"When I find you, I will kill you!"

The shouting and commotion brought several guards who tackled Goya and dragged her to solitary confinement.

"It's okay, you can come out now," Heidi said.

Julienne crawled out of her hiding spot and the guards asked her what happened.

"I don't know," she said. "Marianna and I were walking and talking, minding our own business and Goya attacked."

"Something must have motivated it," the guard said.

"I have no idea," Julienne said. She looked at Marianna and asked, "What did Goya say to you?"

"Just that she wanted to kill you."

"But why?"

"I don't know. She just kept saying that she wants you dead."

"That's so weird," Julienne said. "She's never been my enemy. She's done work for me in the past. I never trusted her, but never felt like she would harm me."

"She's always been just way out there, a loose cannon ready to go off," Marianna said.

Solitary confinement was on the first floor, just below their pavilion and across the passageway. For the next few hours, the inmates heard Goya screaming, "When I get out of here, I'm going to kill that girl!"

She slammed herself against the walls and kept banging a metal pipe against the bars. "Voy a matarla!" She pounded her fists on the solid metal door to the cell.

Julienne thought about her limited contacts with Goya, trying to figure out why Goya was so angry that she wanted to kill her. *We've never had a confrontation and I always paid her for calling visits or doing some other things for me. I even gave her food at times. I know she's been in many fights with others. She has cuts all over her face and arms. Still, I want to know the reason for this outburst against me.*

The next morning she asked the guard, "Can I go over and talk to Goya? I want to find out why she's freaking out on me and wants to kill me."

"Are you sure you want to do that?"

"Yes," Julienne said. "Can I take someone with me to translate? I want to be sure we understand each other."

When Julienne and the inmate who was translating approached the solitary confinement cell, Goya came over to the bars, looking wild.

"Why are you trying to kill me?" Julienne asked. "What did I ever do to you?"

"I heard you were leaving," she said. "It's not fair that you're going free before me. I've been here way longer than you have. And it's not fair."

The translator jumped in and asked questions of her own. "But it doesn't make sense. What did this gringa ever do to you?"

"Nothing. She didn't do anything."

"So what's the problem?"

"She's a spoiled American. Everything comes easy to her. It's not fair!" Her voice grew louder and angrier. "I do everything to try to get out of here, and now she's going free?" She wrapped her fingers around the bars and shouted at the top of her lungs. "She's never going to leave! Only over my dead body! Can you all hear me out there? Julienne's going to die before she gets to go free! I'll make sure of that! You can count on it!"

"Don't worry," the guard said to Julienne. "We'll keep her in maximum security until you leave."

Julienne had a long talk with Marianna that night.

"Thank you for protecting me," she said. "You've been a good friend."

"That Goya is crazy!" Marianna said.

"I know you haven't come to Bible study because you struggle with English," Julienne said.

"And because I know some of those girls don't want me there."

"Do you consider yourself a Christian?"

"I know a lot of people would have trouble with that because I killed my fiancé." She hung her head. "I killed him in a rage and regretted it right away. How could I live with myself after what I did? That's why I tried to kill myself."

"The important thing is that you've asked God to forgive you and He has. Now you have to forgive yourself."

"I know…" she said, her voice choked with emotion. "I'm going to miss you when you leave."

---

"I feel like I'm coming out of my skin," Julienne said to Joan. "This is my last week here, but I still don't know what day. I can't sleep. I can't eat."

"Now you're making me nervous," Joan said. "We need to focus on what still might need to be done."

"Sorry. I know you've been running around getting all kinds of things taken care of for me. I've had as little contact as possible with other inmates to avoid any more problems. I sure don't want anything to stop me from getting out on time."

"All that's really left for you to do is to go out and sign the final release papers," Joan said.

"I've had a terrible time getting a guard who is willing to take me there," Julienne said. "I thought we were going yesterday, but the director said no. I don't know why." She took a deep breath to calm down. "I feel like I'm running on fumes."

"So is it arranged for tomorrow?"

"That's the plan. I hope I don't get the run around again."

When Joan left, she took a few clothes that Julienne planned to keep. Julienne asked her to wash them and get the jail smell out of them.

The next day the director gave her a pass to go outside the prison with a guard to sign the release papers. Julienne could hardly contain herself on the way back. Once the director added her signature, Julienne could leave. But when they returned to the prison, she was told the director left early. She groaned with frustration and went back to her cell.

The next day the director didn't come in to work at all.

The day after that she finally came in, but waited until the very end of the day before she would sign the papers. She even led Julienne to believe that she might have her stay another day, but finally signed.

*She's evil!* Julienne thought. *She just wants everyone to know that she's in control.*

As the guard walked her through the first gate, Julienne ran as fast as she could to the final gate. Joan and Don were waiting in a car just outside. Julienne dashed over to them, shaking and laughing and crying.

"It's finally over!" she said, throwing her arms around Joan. "I'm so happy!" As they pulled away from the prison, Julienne shouted out the car window, "I'm freeeee!"

At Joan's house, they rejoiced over God's goodness.

"It's June 20 and I'm a free woman!" Julienne said. "God is great. I know it's because of all your prayers and others too. God got me out early. It's a true miracle."

"I need to call my Dad!" she said. "I'm free!" she shouted into the phone. Tears of joy streamed down her face. They talked for a few minutes and she could hear the emotion in her father's voice. "We're flying out of here on July 5, Dad. Can you believe it? That's exactly five years from the date I flew to Ecuador. That's what God promised me. Not a day more or a day less."

"It's getting late," Joan said to Julienne after her call ended. "Why don't you take a nice hot shower and get some sleep."

Julienne slept soundly and woke up feeling and smelling clean. She stretched in the clean, comfortable bed and saw the clothes Joan had washed and placed in the room. As she dressed, tears came to her eyes as she realized the jail smell was gone.

All that was left to do was to get her passport back.

*That shouldn't be a problem.*

## CHAPTER 35

# Joan's House – Ecuador
# Poor Decision – One Last Fling

"Today I need to get my passport back," Julienne said. "Once I've got that I can relax."

"I don't know about the relax part," Don said, smiling. "We have a lot to finish up at Alliance Academy."

"Let me know if I can help with anything," Julienne said. "I'd love to see the school. Actually, I'd love to see anything other than a prison!"

She took a taxi to the Ecuadorian Consulate to retrieve her passport, but was told she had to pay a large fee for its return.

"There's not supposed to be a charge for this," Julienne said. "That's what I was told."

The clerk shrugged his shoulders and refused to give her the passport.

"I can't believe this," she said to Joan later. "They are so corrupt."

After a short discussion, Julienne said, "I'll call someone I know at the American Embassy. Eduardo gave me his personal number. He's a courier for the embassy. Maybe he can help."

She explained the situation to Eduardo. "I have an idea," he said. "Meet me there tomorrow."

Julienne took a taxi and met Eduardo at the Consulate. "Just follow my lead," he said as they walked over to the clerk.

"I understand you are holding this young lady's passport," he said. "I'm here as a representative of the American Embassy. Her passport is actually the property of the American Embassy and I must insist you return it now."

The clerk stood there and stared at him.

"If you refuse to abide by this protocol, I will contact your embassy," he said.

"No, no," she said. "Let me get it for you."

Eduardo took the passport and handed it to Julienne.

"Thank you!" she said when they were safely outside.

"Just don't tell," he said. "I'm really not in a position of authority to do this. I wanted to help you, but I don't want to get into trouble."

"Don't worry. Wow. Thank you so much!"

The next day she found out she needed a visa exit stamp on her passport in order to leave the country. She called the Ecuadorian Consulate office again to ask where to get the stamp.

"Have you been in Ecuador more than ninety days?" the woman asked.

"Yes, but why does that matter?"

"There will be a fine, based on the date of your entrance stamp."

"What?" She started to say she'd been in prison for five years and was just released, but thought better of it. *It might make things worse.* "How long will it take to straightened this out?"

"You need to come to our office," she said.

"I'm not going back there," she said to Joan. "Let me call an official I met when I was in Jail Four. Maybe he can help."

She found his number, called him, and explained her situation. "Could you please help me with this?"

"Sure, I can handle that for you," he said. "It will just take a few hours."

"Can you get July 5 stamped on it as my exit date?"

"No problem."

By the end of the day, Julienne held her stamped passport in her hands. "And it only cost me twelve dollars!"

The following week was a busy time for everyone with Joan and Don finishing up their final work at the academy. Julienne went with them to see the school and met many of their friends.

Another day she visited the Browns. "You saved my life," Julienne said. "I don't think I would have survived in the beginning if it hadn't been for both of you."

"We're so glad you're out and free," Helen said. "What a glorious day."

A friend of the Browns involved with the Peace Corps, took Julienne up to a volcanic resort with natural hot springs. "It's so serene and beautiful here," Julienne said. "I'm starting to feel normal again."

One day Julienne decided she needed to go out on her own and she called a taxi to go into town. She had only been gone for a short while, when she started to feel uneasy, like she was being followed. She took a cab back to Joan's house.

"You're back early," Joan said.

"It's so strange to go out without a guard at my side," she said. "I felt really nervous."

Phone calls for Julienne came in daily.

One man who had visited her in prison a few times and had brought her books, wanted to throw a party for her. She hardly knew him and with Joan's advice, she said no, she couldn't do that. He was persistent and called again.

"You can stop by our house for a short visit with Julienne," Joan told him.

"He came to the prison to visit another inmate and would sometimes talk to me," Julienne said. "I really don't know much about him."

He came to the house with his two sons who were in their twenties. They told Julienne they were thinking about moving to the States, to New York. *Do they want to stay in touch with me?* she wondered. "We brought gifts for you to take home, souvenirs." They brought in bottles of alcohol from their car. When they left, Julienne picked up one of the bottles.

"They have twist tops on them and they're leaking!"

"And they want you to take them to the States?" Joan said. "Imagine the questions at the airport!"

A flash of fear crossed Julienne's face. "That's scary. We don't even know for sure what's in them."

They poured the liquid out and tossed the containers in the trash.

Another woman, Bianca, kept calling.

"When can I get together with Julienne?" She was adamant.

"Who is this woman?" Joan asked Julienne. "She's aggressive."

"Again, just someone visiting another inmate and when she found out I was an American and spoke English, she'd visit with me. She did recommend a lawyer to me once, but that didn't work out."

The next time Bianca called, she offered to have a party for Julienne, at Joan's house if necessary.

"Look," Joan said, "I'm responsible for Julienne until she goes back to the States. We're busy, but if you want to see her, you can come to church on Sunday and see her there."

"That was a good answer," Julienne said, smiling. "Let's see if she shows up."

She did come, along with her husband and family. They visited briefly after the service and then Joan said, "I'm sorry, but we have to leave now. We have plans."

"I'll come visit you in the States," she told Julienne. "We'll go to Disney or something."

Afterwards, Julienne asked Joan, "We have plans?"

"Not specifically," Joan said. She warned Julienne that they had to be careful. "A lot of people might just want to use you for something and you've been through enough without taking that chance again."

When Lucia called, Julienne was excited. "It would be so good to see her again," Julienne said. "She wants to take me out to dinner."

"I don't know," Joan said. "I don't feel good about it."

"We're just going to TGF Fridays. They just opened up here."

"I don't think you should go out with her," Joan said again.

"But she's my best friend."

"Yes, but you're not prisoners anymore. She's out living her life and you're about to go back to the States to live yours. So your relationship will change."

"But I have to see her," Julienne pressed. "I feel like I owe her that much."

"Well, you're an adult and can make your own decisions," Joan said. "It just makes me uncomfortable."

Joan gave her a ride to the mall where the restaurant was located. "Remember, we're getting together with my pastor and his wife tomorrow. You should try to be home by 10:00 p.m. tonight."

They entered the mall together and Julienne said, "I'll feel safe here."

Lucia saw them and hurried over, giving both of them a hug. Joan talked with them for a few minutes and then left.

At the restaurant, when the waitress came over to take their order, Lucia said, "Let's order margaritas!"

Julienne hesitated.

"Come on, you know you want one."

Julienne grinned. "I do like margaritas."

"Loosen up! You're free now. A margarita is no big deal. Let's celebrate!"

They ordered drinks and dinner and talked and laughed, enjoying each other's company.

"Two more margaritas!" Lucia called to the waitress.

Two good-looking men came over from another table and introduced themselves. "We're soccer players from Argentina, would you mind if we join you?"

"We'd love it," Lucia said. She flashed a smile at Julienne.

"Another round of drinks!" they called out to the waitress.

After a short visit, Lucia motioned for Julienne to follow her to the restroom.

"They think we're going to hang with them all night," Lucia said. "Let's just slip out. I'll call a taxi."

They took a taxi to a nightclub where some of Lucia's friends met up with them. The band was playing and the dance floor was crowded. They all did a few tequila shots and the noise and music rose to a new level. Julienne started to feel the effects of the alcohol and went to sit down. She felt sick.

*I've got to get out of here. I don't even know what time it is, but it's late.* She staggered around looking for Lucia. *Where is she?* When she couldn't find her, she panicked. *I need to call Joan to come pick me up.*

"¿Dónde está el teléfono?" she asked someone. They pointed to the manager's office and she asked to use the phone. She tried to dial Joan's number, but it didn't go through. Then she couldn't get a dial tone. *Forget it. I'll just get a taxi.* She dropped the receiver and walked outside.

She looked up and down the street and her panic rose. *Where am I? I don't recognize this street.* Disoriented, she flailed her arms, hoping a taxi would come, but none did. She went back inside the nightclub. The blaring music, the strobe lights, and the crowd of people overwhelmed her and she stood there, sobbing.

The bouncer came up to her and asked, "What's wrong? Can I help?"

"I need to go home! I don't even know where I am!" She looked around and spotted Lucia talking with someone. She rushed over to her.

"How could you just disappear and leave me?" She spat the words out. "We spent all those years in jail together and we were friends." Her voice rose. "How could you do this to me?"

"No, no!" Lucia said. "Don't say that kind of stuff." She turned to her friend and said, "Don't pay any attention to her, she's drunk. She doesn't know what she's talking about."

"Oh…now I'm crazy?" Julienne lashed out at her. "I'm telling the truth!" she said to the man Lucia was with. "We were in jail together." She started to cry. "I just want to go home."

"I'll take her home," he said to Lucia. She agreed and gave him Joan's address. "I'll stay here," she said.

Julienne climbed into his pickup truck and mumbled, "Please God, get me home. I'm sorry…" Tears flooded her cheeks.

When they arrived at Joan's house, he helped Julienne out of the truck and left as soon as Joan and Don came outside.

"I'm so sorry," Julienne said. "What time is it?"

"Three o'clock," Joan said. "We've been really worried. Let's just get you inside and into bed." Her voice had an angry edge. "And we won't be going to the pastor's in the morning."

Even through the haze of alcohol, Julienne sensed by Joan's tone that this was not the time to talk. Julienne barely made it to the bathroom before she became violently sick. She rinsed her mouth, washed her face, and glanced in the mirror. Her eyes were bloodshot and her hair a tangled mess. She groaned and stumbled into bed. She slept until mid-afternoon, then showered and went to face Joan and Don, her head pounding.

"I feel so bad about this," Julienne said. "You were so good to me the whole time I was in jail. You visited me, supported me…" The flood of tears began. "I really messed up and I'm sorry."

"Do you realize that I signed my name to be responsible for you?" Joan asked. "If something happened to you or you disappeared, I'd be liable. I could actually be charged and go to jail myself." She took a deep breath. "Don and I paced the floor all night, waiting and wondering where you were, if you were okay." Her face clouded in anger. "The worse thing is that if something serious happened, it could affect the jail ministry."

"The words 'I'm sorry' aren't enough, but I really am sorry. I should have listened to you. I've only had my freedom for a few days and I've already abused it." Weeping, she put her arms around Joan. "Please forgive me."

"I do forgive you," Joan said. "And I hope this experience will be the last of this kind."

"It will, I promise."

Back in her room, Julienne got on her knees and prayed. "God, please forgive me. My heart is so heavy. You've protected me through so many situations, and then I go and mess up. I'm sorry. I'm never going on a bender again."

That night they went out to eat with Joan's pastor and his wife and Julienne apologized for her behavior the night before, even though they hadn't heard what happened. "I want to thank you for everything you and your church did for me while I was in jail," she said. "You have no idea what it meant to me. I'll never forget it."

Over the next few days, others called wanting to see Julienne, but she said no to all of them.

---

"Today's the day!" Julienne said. "My suitcase is packed."

"Let me check it," Joan said.

Julienne unzipped the suitcase. "These are all my earthy possessions."

"When you get home, you're going to throw away most of this, for sure the clothes. You'll want new things. Just leave most of it here."

Julienne started sorting and removing much of what she had packed.

"The only two things you're going to have on you are your passport and your airline ticket."

"Not even my purse?"

"No. We're taking no chances on anything going wrong. If you don't have a purse, no one can slip anything into it. Don't even put anything in your pockets."

"Now I'm getting nervous," Julienne said.

"There's no reason to worry. We'll check in the luggage. Since the three of us are traveling together, it won't be a problem."

At the airport, a customs official made Don open the bags. Julienne started to tremble. Joan reached for her hand and whispered, "There's nothing to be afraid of. We're fine." She squeezed her hand.

Don opened the first suitcase and the police noticed the prayer cards in stacks. "You're missionaries?"

"Yes, we are." Don smiled at him.

The police motioned for him to close the luggage and waved him on.

As they boarded the plane, Julienne felt an adrenaline rush. *Just a few more minutes and all this will be over.* Five minutes later, the engines came to life. They taxied down the runway. Julienne held her breath until the plane left the ground. She felt light-headed and happily overwhelmed as they rose into the sky.

"It's real now," Julienne said to Joan. "I'm truly free."

"God is good," Joan said.

"And he keeps his promises. I flew to Quito exactly five years ago today. His promise to me was 'not one day more.'" Her mouth curved in a big smile. She watched out the window as Ecuador disappeared from sight and they flew above the clouds.

*It's so beautiful.* She wondered what God had next for her life.

# CHAPTER 36

## Knoxville, Tennessee
## New Beginning

WHEN THEY ARRIVED at the Miami airport, they went to the women's restroom. When Julienne stood up in the stall, the toilet flushed by itself and she jumped. *I didn't even flush it!* She went to wash her hands and told Joan what happened.

"It scared the crap out of me!"

Joan laughed. "The same thing happened to me. It's the new technology. Things have changed since you've been away."

Julienne soaped up her hands, but couldn't figure out how to turn the water faucet on. "What? The toilet flushes by itself, but the water in the sink won't turn on." She stepped outside the restroom and rinsed her hands at a water fountain. They laughed until tears came. "What else are we going to discover?"

In Miami, they stayed with Joan's brother for a few days. When they arrived at his house, Julienne got down on her hands and knees on the lawn and kissed the ground.

"I'm on United States soil!" She walked around the yard and stretched out on the grass under the palm trees. *I'm free. I'm really free!* Julienne hardly left Joan's side. She felt safe with her. They went out to eat a few times and went shopping at a mall.

"I feel overwhelmed," Julienne said. "I'm free to make so many choices."

Julienne was flying to her parents' home in Tennessee; Don and Joan to their home in Tampa.

## Surviving Camp Inca

"After being in prison, there's going to be life adjustments," Joan said. "For every year you were in jail, you need a month to recuperate and adjust. Live with your dad and step-mom, go to church with them. Talk to the pastor and let him know what you've been through. Slowly make new friends who are living the lifestyle you want to live. If you go back to California to the ones you partied with, you'll go back to the same old problems. I've seen that happen. I don't want you to become one of those statistics."

"I'm going to miss you," Julienne said. "I need you in my life."

"Any time you need to talk, just call me."

Flying alone to Tennessee, Julienne experienced a wide range of emotions. *I've always been so independent, now I feel like a kid alone on a plane. Insecure.* When she thought about being with her parents, she was happy and excited, but anxiety set in. *I'm in my thirties now. I'll need to get out on my own soon. Get a job. Get an apartment. Get a car.* She took a deep breath. *Just take it a day at a time,* she told herself.

Her parents were waiting for her just outside the gate at the Nashville airport. She ran to them and they tearfully embraced.

"I hope you're hungry," her dad said. "We're taking you to the Opryland Hotel for lunch."

"This is incredible," Julienne said as they entered the hotel's atrium filled with beautiful plants and cascading waterfalls. "It's a tropical paradise."

Over lunch they talked about Julienne's options.

"Joan suggested to us that you give yourself a few weeks to adjust before looking for a job," her dad said. "You can stay with us as long as you want. Later you can stay at the lake house if you prefer. It's quite small, but comfortable. Have you thought about what you'd like to do for work?"

"Well, I think I'd enjoy doing spa treatments, like body scrubs, massages, manicures. I studied a book on reflexology and that's really interesting. I'd need some training for that and to be licensed."

"Remember, you can always build your Amway business. "I've done well with it."

"Do you still go to their meetings?"

"Yes, I'll take you to the next one."

"I remember you used to ask me what kind of business I was going to own; never what kind of job I was going to have."

"And I recall when you were eleven what you said you wanted to be," he said. "An ice skater or an astronaut." They both laughed.

At the house, Julienne set up an e-mail account to keep in touch with Joan. She e-mailed her daily, knowing she could trust sharing her thoughts and feelings with her.

"Do I have that jail smell?" Julienne asked her stepmom, Kate, one morning.

"No…"

"I still have a few clothes from prison and even though they've been washed several times, I worry about it. I don't want that smell to follow me."

"If you're concerned about it, let's go shopping for some new clothes. Just get rid of anything you brought back with you."

"Maybe that's why I think about the spa business. I want to smell good. It's hard for me to forget that prison stench."

Five days a week for two months, Pastor David from her parents' church came out for Bible study with them. Sometimes they met at their lake house, a small cabin with a loft bedroom. Julienne enjoyed the peace and quiet. It didn't take her long to decide to move in there. Julienne's confidence and stability grew spiritually and emotionally.

She applied for a job with a phone book delivery company that advertised in a local Latin newspaper. They hired her immediately when they found out she knew Spanish. *And to think of all those years I rebelled against learning the language. Now it's helped me get a job. I should have focused on it sooner.*

After a few months of working, she got her own apartment in Knoxville and applied to a local beauty school to become a licensed nail technician. When she graduated, she worked at an upscale salon.

She continued attending church on Sundays with her parents, but then discovered there was a Calvary Chapel in the area. Her fond memories of Calvary Chapel in California led her to check them out and she went to one of their Wednesday night meetings. On her first visit, she met Ann Hilt.

"I recognize you," Ann said. "I saw you on *60 Minutes*! God placed you on my heart and I've been praying for you ever since. And here you are!"

Tears came to Julienne's eyes. "Now I know I'm in the right place."

"God is amazing," Ann said.

She met Pastor Mark and Tracy Kirk and shared her prison experience with them. They prayed with her and she left feeling part of this church family already.

She continued to go to church with her parents on Sundays, but every Wednesday night she went to Calvary Chapel.

"We need to introduce you to some of our business friends and their children who are about your age," her dad said. "I want you to come with me to a meeting in Alabama. You'll love it. There might be thirty thousand people there."

Fear gripped Julienne for a moment. *Am I ready to handle being in a big crowd like that?* A few nights earlier she had awakened to the sound of helicopters flying overhead and her first conscious thought had been, *Are they coming to take me back to jail?* She had to fight those brief flashbacks of fear.

"Okay, Dad. I guess it's time for me to get out there."

When they arrived at the stadium where the meeting was held, Julienne could feel the energy from the crowd of people arriving. Everyone was dressed up. *I'm glad Kate took me clothes shopping!*

Her dad introduced her to one of his associates, who was stepping out of a limousine at the entrance. "And here's his son, Scott."

*Wow, he's really cute. What a nice suit.* She said hello and immediately thought *I'm not good enough for someone like that.*

The speakers talked of true freedom through financial independence and not being captive to finances. *Like I was captive in jail. Maybe my dad's right and this could work for me.*

Another speaker said, "Who do you know? Everybody knows someone. That's who you approach about this business." *I don't really know anyone. I've cut myself off from all my old friends, except for Joanna. The people I know are in jail!*

Her dad bought the motivational CDs during one of the breaks and said, "Start listening to these every day and they'll help you."

Julienne listened to them and began to feel that maybe there really was life after prison. The next meeting was in Knoxville and she went with her dad again. During a break, she went to the hotel lobby to find the ATM machine and get some cash. Next to it, stood another machine and she looked it over, wondering what it was.

"It's a Doppler Radar machine."

Julienne looked up and faced a good-looking man, dressed in an olive-toned suit. He carried a cashmere coat with a scarf draped over his arm. *He smells really good,* she thought.

"You punch a zip code into the machine and it gives you a weather report for that area. It's great when you're traveling." He smiled at her. "Are you traveling? Staying at the hotel?"

"No, I'm here with my father for a business meeting. I used to live in California, but live here now."

"So what do you do?"

"At the moment, I draw maps for phone book delivery."

Just then, Julienne's dad walked over and said, "Gary!"

"Hey, Bob. Good to see you."

"You too," he said, shaking his hand. "I see you've met Julienne, my daughter."

"Your daughter? I didn't know you had a daughter."

"You know each other?" Julienne asked.

"Gary's in Amway too," her dad said. "The meeting is starting. Let's go inside."

## Surviving Camp Inca

---

Julienne kept running into Gary at meetings and they enjoyed talking together.

She decided to join a gym in town and started working out on a regular basis. One day near the end of her exercise session on the elliptical machine, Julienne thought about what Joan had said to her recently.

"Pray about everything you do, every decision. Discipline yourself to do that and you'll be right where God wants you. He'll speak to you and you'll know in your heart what's right for you."

Julienne prayed, "Lord, show me what you want for me. Will I ever meet someone and fall in love and get married? Show me a sign of what's next."

She stood, looking out a large window in front of her. A bird landed on the window ledge and seemed to be staring at her through the window. His head swayed back and forth.

"Are you trying to communicate with me?" She smiled at the bird.

An inner voice came to her mind. "The next one that walks in the door is the man you're going to marry." *What? Did I just make that up in my head?* She heard the door open and turned to look. Gary walked in with his gym bag. Thinking she must be losing it, she swung back to look at the bird. It flew away.

"Hey!" he called to her. "I didn't know you worked out here."

"Yeah, I do."

"Did you just get here?"

"Ah, yes."

"Ok; well let me go put my gym bag in a locker. Save a machine for me. I'll be right back. I'll work out with you."

Julienne groaned. *Another hour!* They talked while they worked their way from machine to machine.

The next day, Betty, one of the women at work, asked her, "Do you have a boyfriend?"

"No, but I met this nice guy at the gym. We've run into each other here and there. He gave me his phone number."

"If you really like him, you should call him," she said.

"Ask him out?"

"Just ask him if he wants to work out with you after work."

"I don't know…"

"There's the phone," she said, pointing to it. "Make the call. Just do it."

Julienne picked up the phone and dialed Gary's number. *What if he says no?*

When he answered, she said, "Hi, this is Julienne. Do you remember me?"

"Yes, of course I do."

"I'm going to work out at the gym after work and was wondering if you wanted to meet me there."

"Sorry, I already have plans tonight. I can't."

"Okay, well, maybe another time."

"How about tomorrow night?" he said.

"Oh, okay. That will work."

"See you then."

She hung up and smiled at Betty.

"I told you!" she said, grinning.

After their workout at the gym, they went out for coffee at a nearby deli.

"So, tell me about yourself," Gary said. "You're from California, moved here. What else?"

*Should I tell him? I guess if I want an honest friendship, I need to. Although, he may not be interested after he hears my story.* She took a deep breath. "Actually, I so have a story." She spent two hours telling him about her Ecuador prison experience. When she saw the shocked look on his face, she thought she might never see him again. *So much for that still, small voice. Stupid bird!*

When they were leaving, he asked if he could see her again.

"Well, let me ask you something," she said. "Do you have a girlfriend?"

"Sort of."

"Sort of?" Annoyed, she asked, "What does that mean?"

"It's not going so well. We've talked about breaking up recently."

"Well, I guess we can just be friends," Julienne said. "I don't date guys who are dating other girls."

They continued their friendship, mostly talking on the phone. Julienne told him about Calvary Chapel and gave him some of their teaching CDs to listen to.

"I've been a Christian since age eighteen," he said. "I really liked the CDs you gave me. I'd like to go to church with you."

They went together and she started to look forward to church even more. Their relationship grew as they attended church and saw each other at business meetings or at the gym.

*We've been friends for five months and spend so much time together and get along so well, why hasn't he asked me on a real date?*

One time over coffee, Julienne told Gary about a guy at the gym who asked her out on a date. She described what he looked like and asked Gary if he knew him and if he thought she should go out with him.

"I know who he is, but don't know him personally," he said.

"So should I go?"

"Well, you're every man's dream, so of course he's asking you out."

"Every man's dream, but one." Embarrassed, she said, "Did I just say that?"

He laughed. "Yes, you did. I guess I deserved that."

That weekend, Julienne's cousins from Ohio called and asked her to meet them at Pigeon Forge. "We haven't seen you since we were teenagers. It'll be fun to catch up."

Right after that, Gary called. "Do you want to go out on a date?"

"A date? No, I can't. I'm going to the mountains with my cousins. Besides, I still won't date anyone who has a girlfriend."

"That relationship is long over," Gary said. "Call me when you get back."

"Okay, I will."

When she returned she got a phone call from the guy at the gym who had asked her out a few times. She'd never gone out with him, but he said he was interested in the Amway business.

"Would you come to my house and tell me about it?" he asked her.

"No, but I'll meet you at a restaurant."

"Okay," he said. "How about tonight?"

She agreed and put a presentation packet together. At the restaurant he asked if she wanted to have dinner.

"No, I'm good," she said. She explained the business plan and he smiled and kept staring at her. "So what do you think?" she asked. "Are you ready to get started? Do you have any questions?"

"Yes, will you marry me?"

"Uh…I'm going to the restroom and let you rethink that question. I'll be back in a minute."

When Julienne returned to their table, she asked, "So do you want to get started?"

"Marry me."

"Okay, this meeting's over. I'm out of here!" She gathered the presentation papers and walked out, leaving him sitting there.

When she left, she called Gary. "Where are you right now?"

"I'm at home."

"Can I stop by?"

"Sure."

They sat out on his patio and Julienne told him what happened.

"I'd better start officially dating you before you marry someone else!" he said.

That weekend he took her on a marathon date. They went on a fundraiser walk for diabetes at six in the morning, followed by a visit to a local park, and then lunch. Later, they went dancing at Market Square where they ran into Gary's aunt and uncle, coming from a show where the Four Tops were playing.

"We're heading home. Why don't you use our tickets for the last half of the show?"

They went down to the Old City and finished off the night enjoying the show.

On another date, they went to the Riverside Tavern. Gary kissed her for the first time and Julienne asked, "Do you hear fireworks?"

"No…"

"Okay, never mind."

They kissed again. "I definitely heard fireworks!" Julienne said.

"I did too!"

They turned and looked toward the stadium across from the tavern. A big fireworks display had just begun. They both laughed. After that, they were inseparable.

## CHAPTER 37

# Knoxville, Tennessee
## Proposal – Fireworks - Marriage

One day Julienne received a call from an old friend in California, Liz.

"I heard from your ex-boyfriend, Rudy. The local hospital called him about your mother. She was in a homeless shelter and had a heart attack and was rushed to the hospital. They found her identification in her belongings, along with your name and others. One was Rudy, so they reached him and then he called me because he didn't know where you were. It sounds serious. She's in intensive care." She hesitated. "She's on life support and there's talk of taking her off of it. They've been looking for a family member to sign papers."

"No!" Julienne said. "Do you have the number at the hospital? I'll call them right now."

Liz gave her the number. "If you come out and need somewhere to stay, you're welcome to use my place. I'm sorry you have to face this. You've been through so much already."

"No!" Julienne shouted into the phone after reaching the hospital. "I don't give my permission to remove life support! I'll fly out there tonight if I can get an airline ticket."

She called her dad. "I'll buy you a ticket," he said. "You need to go out there."

Then she called Gary and told him what happened. "I finally know where my mother is and now this…" She burst into tears.

"I'm sorry," Gary said. "I can't imagine how you must feel. Your dad's right. You need to fly out there right away. I'll be happy to drive you to the airport."

"My dad doesn't want me to go out there alone," she said.

"I'll go with you," he offered. "Let me call the airlines and I'll get right back to you."

Gary couldn't get a flight out that night, but booked one for the next day. Julienne flew out alone that night. She'd made arrangements to stay at her friend Joanna's for a week. Then go to Liz's place if she needed to stay longer.

At the hospital, Julienne told the receptionist, "I'm here to see Andrea Estrada. I'm her daughter." The receptionist told her where to go. The doctor was in her mother's room.

"We don't expect her to make it," he said. "The kindest thing may be to let her go. We'll leave that choice up to you." His voice was kind and comforting, but Julienne was angry.

"No one is going to remove her life support!" she said, her voice loud and wavering. The doctor left the room.

She looked down at her mother, unconscious, in a coma. Her dark hair was stringy and needed shampooing. Her face, gaunt and pale. An IV needle pierced her hand, a tube was in her mouth and down her throat, a respirator controlled her breathing, and monitoring devices tracked her heart and blood pressure. She looked worn and frail. Tears streamed down Julienne's face.

She pulled a chair up to the bedside and held her mother's limp hand. The one without the needle attached to it. Her skin felt cold.

"I haven't seen you in seven years," she said to her. "You can't leave me now."

She reached in her purse and pulled out her Bible and a devotional book, *God's Creative Power* by Charles Capps. She took a deep breath, let it out slowly, and began to read. One statement hit her. "Jesus said, 'I have told my people they can have what they say, but my people are saying what they have.'" Some prayers were specifically for healing, others for comfort or hope. She read them aloud, as much for herself as for her mother. She hoped she could hear them.

After a few hours, she could no longer stay awake and dozed off in the bedside chair. The nurses came into the room a few times to check on her mother, but nothing had changed. The whooshing sound of the respirator pumping air into her mother's lungs brought her strange comfort. *At least she's still alive.*

A nurse brought her a cup of coffee. Julienne thanked her, and then pulled a hairbrush from her purse. She brushed her mother's hair with soft, gentle strokes. When the nurse came back, Julienne left for a short while. She made a quick call to her dad to give him an update and then drove to the airport in a friend's car to pick up Gary.

Back at the hospital, Julienne noticed a clear plastic bag on the window ledge. It held her mother's rumpled clothes and scuffed, worn shoes. She cried softly. Again, she picked up the book of prayers and read. At times she put the book down and read from the Bible, looking for all the promises she could find. The doctor came in and checked on her mother. "No change." He left and went on to his next patient.

"I'm sorry," Gary said.

She picked up her Bible. "This is her life support!" she said. "And mine."

With Gary at her side, she kept up this routine for several days. Suddenly one day, her mother opened her eyes.

"Mom!"

Julienne pushed the call button and two nurses came in, checking everything. "This is a miracle," one of them said.

"Yes, it is!" Julienne said. She held her mother's hand. "I'm here," she said. "Just relax, don't try to talk." She glanced over at Gary and said, "With that tube down her throat, she can't talk anyway."

Julienne visited and talked to her mom, sharing with her what was going on in her life. At one point, Gary said, "Ask her if she wants to move to Tennessee."

"Mom, would you like to move to Tennessee and live near me?"

She nodded, yes. Julienne cried and whispered "thank you" to Gary.

Gary had to fly back to go to work, but Julienne stayed a few more weeks. Her mother's health improved. She had to get back to Knoxville and to work, so she made arrangements with the social worker there to put her mother on an airplane when she was strong enough to fly.

Gary helped her find a nice apartment in an upscale assisted living facility and within a month they had her mother settled in there. As her health improved, she became involved in some activities and she and Julienne spent many hours together, talking and laughing and sometimes crying. Gary treated her like his own mother, which made Julienne's heart bond even more to him.

One day they went out to the lake house and rode on his family's pontoon boat that was docked at a small marina near his house. He stopped it in the middle of the lake.

"I want to talk to you about something," he said.

*Oh no. He's going to break up with me. He's been acting sad about something.*

"An opportunity has opened up for me to go to Atlanta to work. You know I've been going there a few days a week to help build custom closets, but they can't get enough good help to keep up with the business they're getting. They offered me a sign-on bonus and a raise if I go there full-time."

*So where does this leave us?* She wondered.

"I want you to come with me," he said.

"Not without a ring on my finger. Is this a proposal?"

He cleared his throat. "Well, not officially, because I don't have a ring on me."

"My life is here," she said. "With my family, my job at the salon, my church family…but let's talk again when you have a ring in your hand."

She told her dad about it and he said, "I really like Gary and so does everyone else. It's about time you two make it permanent. You've been dating for over three years."

"I'm so happy for you," Kate said. "You couldn't find a better man than Gary."

Gary invited Julienne to the Riverside Tavern for dinner and reserved the same table they had on their first date. A large bouquet of flowers sat on their table.

*This is it! He's going to propose!*

They had a leisurely dinner and afterwards Gary stood up and said, "Could I have everyone's attention please?" Other diners quieted down and looked at Gary. "This is Julienne and she's the love of my life. She's the best part of my life. I love her more than I can say." He slipped down on one knee in front of Julienne and asked, "Julienne, will you marry me?"

"Yes! I love you. Of course I'll marry you!" she said. People clapped and cheered as Gary slipped a ring on her finger.

"Champagne for everyone!" he said. The diners offered a toast of congratulations.

When they left, Gary drove down the road and stopped at a park. "I have something in memory of our first kiss," he said, grinning. "I wanted to do this at the restaurant, but with the Sheriff's office right across the street, I didn't want to get thrown into jail."

"What?"

"Remember how we heard fireworks the first time we kissed?" He pulled some from the back seat of his Jeep and said, "Come on." He lit a match, then the fireworks.

"Wow! You are so romantic," she said. "I have to thank that little bird."

"What bird?"

"I'll tell you about it another time." Her face glowed and she smiled and held out her hand with the ring on her finger. "Kiss me," she said, as the fireworks exploded.

Life became a whirlwind of activity with Gary starting his new job and Julienne planning their wedding, organizing for their move, and applying for jobs in Atlanta. They decided to get married in Panama

City Beach, Florida in a beautiful oceanfront hotel and invited thirty-five guests.

"This is my dream wedding," Julienne said. "I love the beach and we'll be with family that we love." She smiled and said, "That includes both of my mothers. What a blessing."

They talked briefly about a honeymoon to some place exotic, like Hawaii or Tahiti. But when they checked the cost, they decided to stay at the hotel in Panama City Beach for five days on the beach instead.

"Maybe we can go someplace exotic on our tenth wedding anniversary," Julienne said.

"After all, getting married is the easy part. Staying married will be something to really celebrate! Besides, some family members will be staying at the beach for the weekend. We'll have a family honeymoon." She smiled. "Love it."

She asked her little nephew, Wyatt, now age five, to be in the wedding party.

"No," he said.

"No? Why not?"

His little mouth quivered and he started to cry. "Because you're going to marry Gary and move away and probably have your own kids and then you'll forget about me and Trent."

She gathered him in her arms and assured him she loved him and his little brother Trent and would be back to see them as often as she could. He brushed away his tears with the back of his hand and said, "Okay, I'll be in your wedding, but I'm not carrying the ring and I'm not carrying the flowers."

"Would you like to be my train man?"

"Yes! I like trains."

"Well, then you'll carry my train." *Wait until he realizes that it's my dress!* "He's so adorable," she said to Gary.

"You're not changing your mind about wanting children, are you? We talked about this and we agreed that neither of us wanted to have children."

"I haven't changed my mind," she said.

He grinned at her. "Well some women have a way of changing their minds. I just want to make sure you're still okay with it."

"Yes, I am."

She and Gary had many discussions about what they each wanted for their future so that their marriage would succeed. That included whether or not to have children. They wanted to make sure there would be no misunderstanding after they were married. Julienne told him she didn't plan on having children of her own. She loved the little ones in her family and that was enough. Gary was relieved because he had been married twice before and already had two adult children. Julienne knew that was why it took him a few years to propose. He had shared with her how difficult and hard the breakups were and he didn't ever want to experience that again. Julienne was confident he wouldn't have to worry about that. Their commitment to each other was sealed along with their commitment to the Lord.

October 24, 2004 arrived as a beautiful day in Panama City Beach. Julienne was waiting in a side room before the ceremony. Gary had left to buy Julienne a wedding present. Her dad kept calling her room, asking "Is Gary back yet? Where's your husband?"

"Dad, I don't know. I'm not in charge of him. I'm not married to him yet."

A short time later, the wedding coordinator from the hotel came rushing in. "I have some bad news. Your Disk Jockey isn't here and there's no music! Everyone is seated outside, waiting to start."

"Is Gary here?" Julienne asked her.

"Yes, he is."

"Then what's the problem? I'm marrying Gary, not the DJ!" She laughed. "Nothing is going to ruin my wedding day."

Her dad came to get her and said, "Let's do it."

She put her arm through his and he sang in her ear, "Dum, dum de dum…" as they began their walk to the front. Julienne grinned at him, trying not to laugh. When they stepped outside, a large flock of birds sat in the palm trees, loudly singing and chirping.

"God sent my music," she whispered to her dad.

Gary beamed as he watched his bride walk toward him.

# Epilogue

Julienne's story is not over. After her release, she dealt with nightmare memories of those five years behind prison walls. She and Gary moved to Atlanta for several years because of a job opportunity for Gary, and then moved back to Knoxville to be near family. There she went through a sad time dealing with her dad's death after six months of his struggle with cancer. To add fuel to the fire, Gary's father died three weeks later. But they were thankful for the time they got to spend with them.

She recognized that the peace she found with God while still in Camp Inca prison, helped her to work through forgiveness toward those who betrayed her and caused her the pain of incarceration in spite of her innocence. As she overcame these and other obstacles, she moved forward to fully live the life God had planned for her.

When she and Gary celebrated their 10th anniversary in Hawaii, she marveled at how many doors God had opened for her. Her successful marriage, great friends and relationships, moving into a beautiful home, her office at AlmaDiem LLC in Knoxville where she practices her reflexology business, and the opportunity to share her story and challenge others to become pro-active with their spiritual, emotional, financial, physical and relationship issues. Letting go of the negative and focusing on the positive moves you forward to success.

**What are you doing to free yourself from YOUR Camp Inca?**

- Spiritual. Find peace with God. *Julienne found hers while still in prison.*

- Emotional. Find enlightenment in your dark places. *It will make you strong.*
- Financial. Persevere! Don't give up. *Don't let your problems define you.*
- Physical. Take care of yourself. *Be the best you can be.*
- Relational Connect with others and *learn to forgive.*

*Be grateful for your life no matter where you've been or where you are. It's a vehicle to your freedom. I was in a real prison, but sometimes our spiritual, emotional, financial, physical, or relational prisons can be just as devastating. Put a plan into play; leave negatives behind, stay focused on moving forward toward your dreams, and ultimately, your freedom.*

Julienne Burleson

To contact Julienne, or to schedule her to speak to your organization, group, business, or to your church, go to her web site:

www.campinca.com
**Facebook: Surviving Camp Inca**

# Thank you!

I would like to give a special thanks to my husband, Gary, who has always been super supportive in everything I do. I love you, Gary, with all of my heart. Special thanks to my bonus mom, Kate, for always loving me as her own. Special thanks to Joan & Don Ewan for always visiting me in prison, especially in my darkest hours. Thanks to Gene and Helen Brown and all the missionaries that regularly visited me and prayed for me. I'm grateful for my Mom, Andrea, to have her in my life again. Grateful for Jodi, Elise, Greg, Wyatt, Trent, Richard, Tim, Joanna, Lucia, Monique, Rosa, Jael, Sylvia, Giovanna, Peggy, Mariana, Jose Luis and Ann. Thanks to my Atlanta friends and to my L.A. family. Thanks to Joanne Jacquart for her many hours and dedication. Thanks to Sharon & Byron's friendship and support. Thanks to the gals at Alma Diem. Thanks to Cumberland Presbyterian Church for prayers and support. Thank you, Calvary Chapel of Knoxville, for being such a great church family to me when I so needed it. Thank you, Dad, for loving me so much and always being there for me. Thank you Jesus for keeping me safe, for wrapping your love, protection, shield, and your armor around me while I was in prison, and now that I am Free.

*Be strong and of good courage. For the Lord your God is with you wherever you go.*
Joshua 1:9

Made in the USA
San Bernardino, CA
22 June 2015